WRITERS
TY TEMPLETON, JACOB SEMAHN, BRIAN CLEVINGER, CLAY McLEOD CHAPMAN, JOE CARAMAGNA & TODD DEZAGO

ARTISTS
TY TEMPLETON; NUNO PLATI; RAMON BACHS & RAUL FONTS; AND CRAIG ROUSSEAU

COLOR ARTISTS
WIL QUINTANA, NUNO PLATI, MUNTSA VICENTE & PETE PANTAZIS

LETTERERS
VC'S JOE CARAMAGNA, CLAYTON COWLES & JOE SABINO

COVER ARTIST (ISSUES #8-9)
TY TEMPLETON

EDITORS
TOM BRENNAN & ELLIE PYLE

SENIOR EDITOR
STEPHEN WACKER

Collection Editor: **Cory Levine** • Assistant Editors: **Alex Starbuck & Nelson Ribeiro**
Editors, Special Projects: **Jennifer Grünwald & Mark D. Beazley**
Senior Editor, Special Projects: **Jeff Youngquist**
SVP of Print & Digital Publishing Sales: **David Gabriel** • Head of Marvel Television: **Jeph Loeb**

Editor In Chief: **Axel Alonso** • Chief Creative Officer: **Joe Quesada**
Publisher: **Dan Buckley** • Executive Producer: **Alan Fine**

MARVEL UNIVERSE ULTIMATE SPIDER-MAN VOL. 2. Contains material originally published in magazine form as MARVEL UNIVERSE ULTIMATE SPIDER-MAN #5-8. First printing 2013. ISBN# 978-0-7851-6411-1. Published by MARVEL WORLDWIDE, INC., a subsidiary of MARVEL ENTERTAINMENT, LLC. OFFICE OF PUBLICATION: 135 West 50th Street, New York, NY 10020. **Printed in the U.S.A.** ALAN FINE, EVP - Office of the President, Marvel Worldwide, Inc. and EVP & CMO Marvel Characters B.V.; DAN BUCKLEY, Publisher & President - Print, Animation & Digital Divisions; JOE QUESADA, Chief Creative Officer; TOM BREVOORT, SVP of Publishing; DAVID BOGART, SVP of Operations & Procurement, Publishing; RUWAN JAYATILLEKE, SVP & Associate Publisher, Publishing; C.B. CEBULSKI, SVP of Creator & Content Development; DAVID GABRIEL, SVP of Print & Digital Publishing Sales; JIM O'KEEFE, VP of Operations & Logistics; DAN CARR, Executive Director of Publishing Technology; SUSAN CRESPI, Editorial Operations Manager; ALEX MORALES, Publishing Operations Manager; STAN LEE, Chairman Emeritus. For information regarding advertising in Marvel Comics or on Marvel.com, please contact Niza Disla, Director of Marvel Partnerships, at ndisla@marvel.com. For Marvel subscription inquiries, please call 800-217-9158. **Manufactured between 12/17/2012 and 1/21/2013 by SHERIDAN BOOKS, INC., CHELSEA, MI, USA.**

10 9 8 7 6 5 4 3 2 1

WHILE ATTENDING A DEMONSTRATION IN RADIOLOGY, HIGH SCHOOL STUDENT PETER PARKER WAS BITTEN BY A SPIDER THAT HAD ACCIDENTALLY BEEN EXPOSED TO RADIOACTIVE RAYS. THROUGH A MIRACLE OF SCIENCE, PETER SOON FOUND THAT HE HAD GAINED THE SPIDER'S POWERS...AND HAD, IN EFFECT, BECOME A HUMAN SPIDER! FROM THAT DAY ON, HE HAS ENDEAVORED TO BECOME THE...

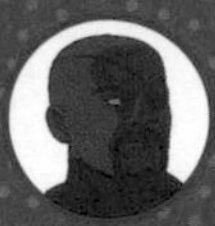

NICK FURY

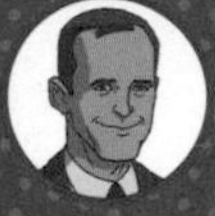

PRINCIPAL COULSON

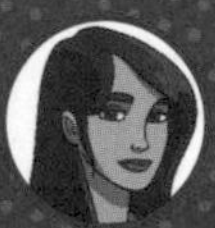

MARY JANE WATSON

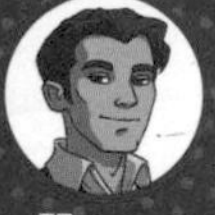

HARRY OSBORN

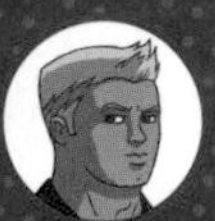

FLASH THOMPSON

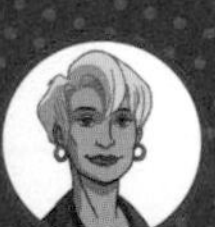

AUNT MAY

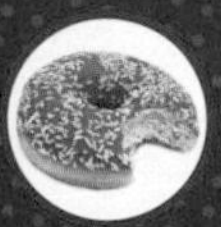

A DONUT (YUM!)

MARVEL

ULTIMATE SPIDER-MAN™

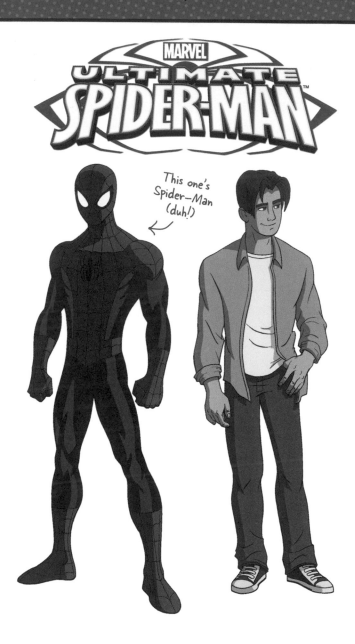

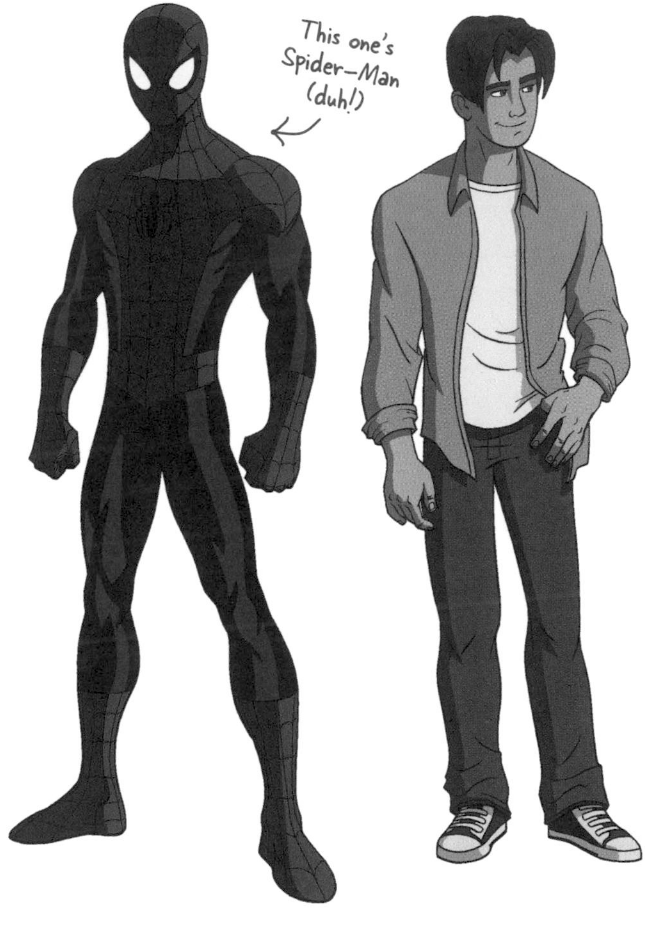
This one's Spider-Man (duh!)

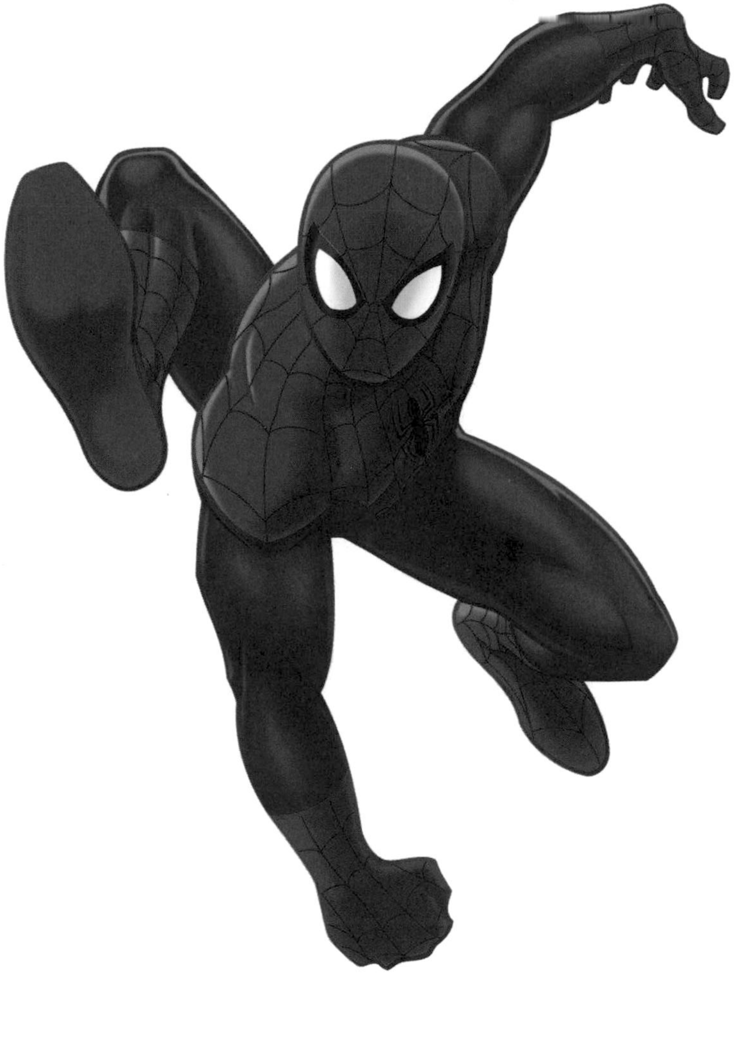

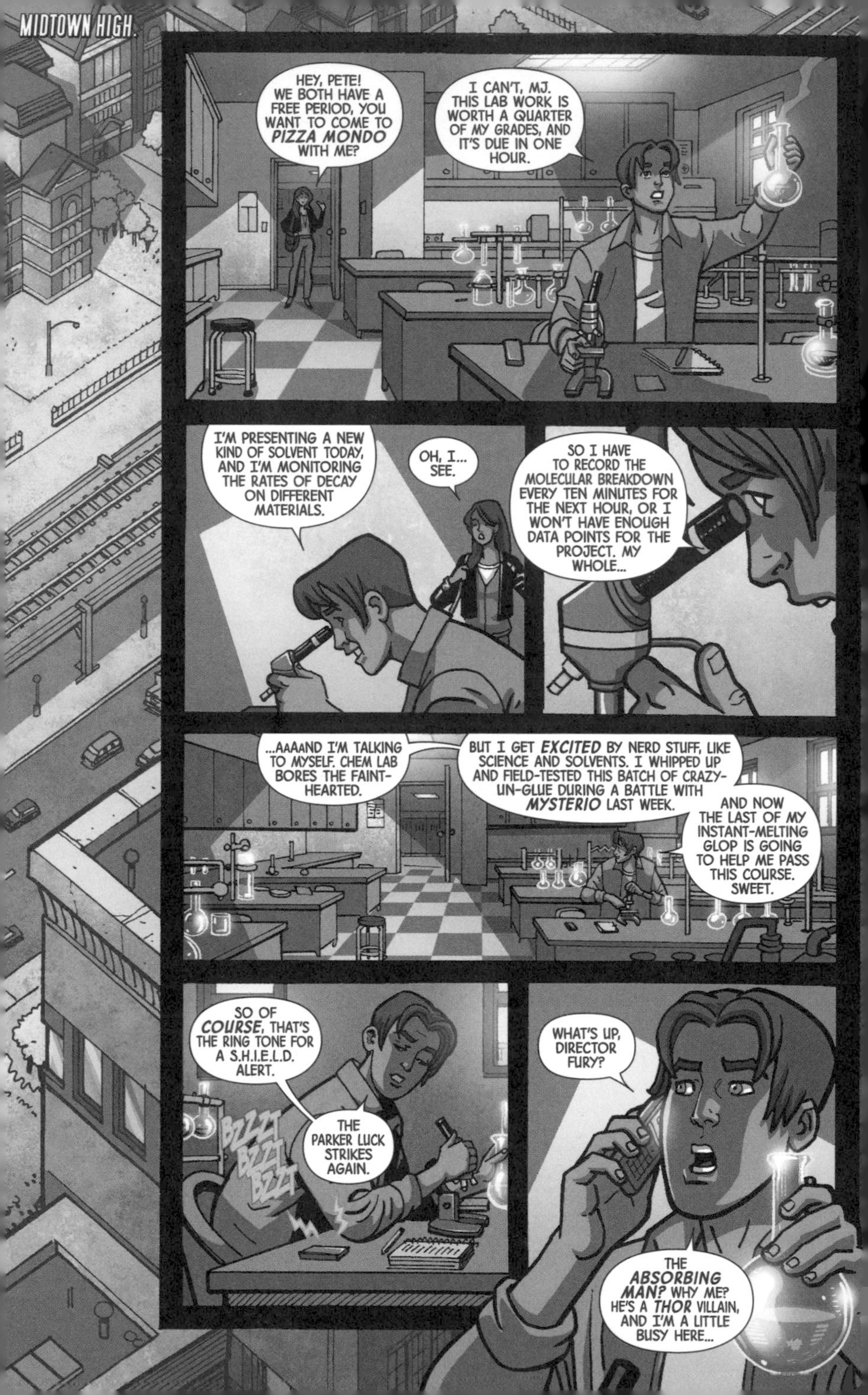
MIDTOWN HIGH.
HEY, PETE! WE BOTH HAVE A FREE PERIOD, YOU WANT TO COME TO PIZZA MONDO WITH ME?
I CAN'T, MJ. THIS LAB WORK IS WORTH A QUARTER OF MY GRADES, AND IT'S DUE IN ONE HOUR.
I'M PRESENTING A NEW KIND OF SOLVENT TODAY, AND I'M MONITORING THE RATES OF DECAY ON DIFFERENT MATERIALS.
OH, I... SEE.
SO I HAVE TO RECORD THE MOLECULAR BREAKDOWN EVERY TEN MINUTES FOR THE NEXT HOUR, OR I WON'T HAVE ENOUGH DATA POINTS FOR THE PROJECT. MY WHOLE...
...AAAAND I'M TALKING TO MYSELF. CHEM LAB BORES THE FAINT-HEARTED.
BUT I GET EXCITED BY NERD STUFF, LIKE SCIENCE AND SOLVENTS. I WHIPPED UP AND FIELD-TESTED THIS BATCH OF CRAZY-UN-GLUE DURING A BATTLE WITH MYSTERIO LAST WEEK.
AND NOW THE LAST OF MY INSTANT-MELTING GLOP IS GOING TO HELP ME PASS THIS COURSE. SWEET.
SO OF COURSE, THAT'S THE RING TONE FOR A S.H.I.E.L.D. ALERT.
BZZZT BZZZT BZZZT
THE PARKER LUCK STRIKES AGAIN.
WHAT'S UP, DIRECTOR FURY?
THE ABSORBING MAN? WHY ME? HE'S A THOR VILLAIN, AND I'M A LITTLE BUSY HERE...

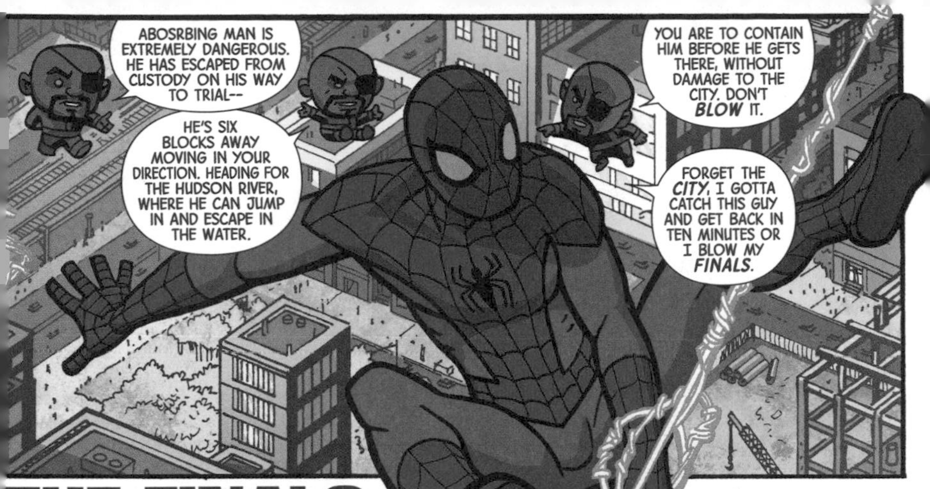
ABOSRBING MAN IS EXTREMELY DANGEROUS. HE HAS ESCAPED FROM CUSTODY ON HIS WAY TO TRIAL--
HE'S SIX BLOCKS AWAY MOVING IN YOUR DIRECTION. HEADING FOR THE HUDSON RIVER, WHERE HE CAN JUMP IN AND ESCAPE IN THE WATER.
YOU ARE TO CONTAIN HIM BEFORE HE GETS THERE, WITHOUT DAMAGE TO THE CITY. DON'T BLOW IT.
FORGET THE CITY, I GOTTA CATCH THIS GUY AND GET BACK IN TEN MINUTES OR I BLOW MY FINALS.

THE FINALS COUNTDOWN

STORY & ART BY TY TEMPLETON

COLOR BY WIL QUINTANA LETTERING BY VC's JOE CARAMAGNA

TOM BRENNAN — ASSOC. EDITOR
ELLIE PYLE — ASSISTANT EDITOR
STEPHEN WACKER — SENIOR EDITOR
ALONSO, LOEB, QUESADA, BUCKLEY & FINE — THE BOSSES

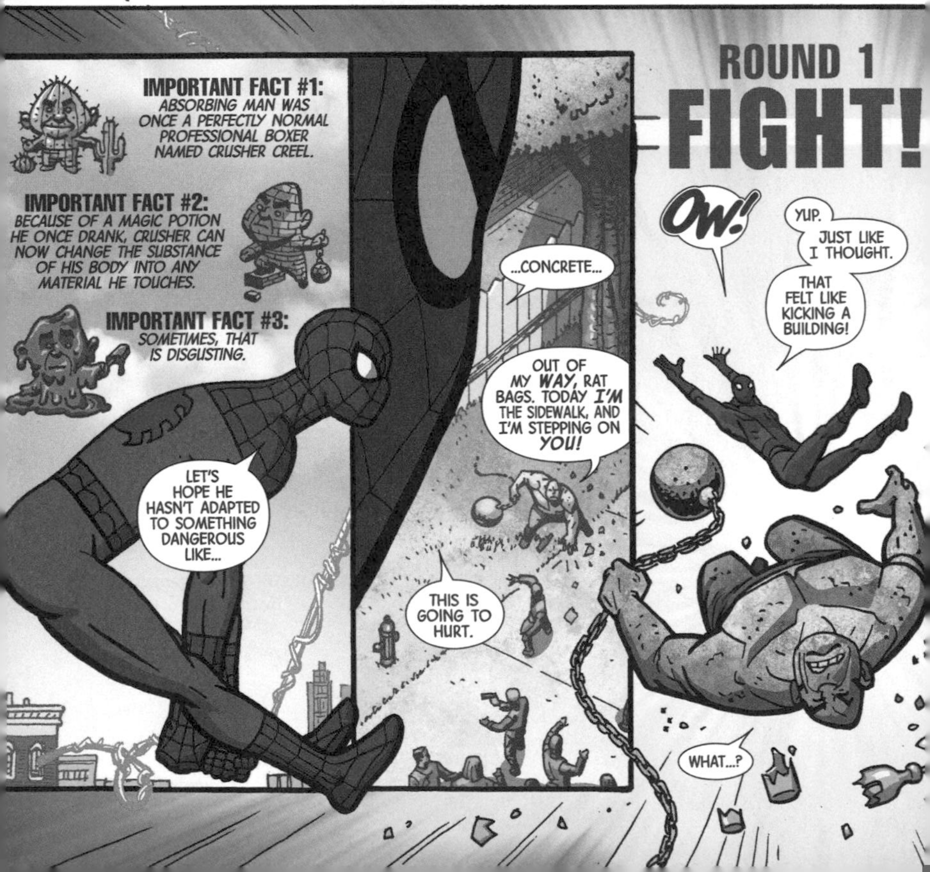
IMPORTANT FACT #1:
ABSORBING MAN WAS ONCE A PERFECTLY NORMAL PROFESSIONAL BOXER NAMED CRUSHER CREEL.
IMPORTANT FACT #2:
BECAUSE OF A MAGIC POTION HE ONCE DRANK, CRUSHER CAN NOW CHANGE THE SUBSTANCE OF HIS BODY INTO ANY MATERIAL HE TOUCHES.
IMPORTANT FACT #3:
SOMETIMES, THAT IS DISGUSTING.
LET'S HOPE HE HASN'T ADAPTED TO SOMETHING DANGEROUS LIKE...
...CONCRETE...
OUT OF MY WAY, RAT BAGS. TODAY I'M THE SIDEWALK, AND I'M STEPPING ON YOU!
THIS IS GOING TO HURT.
ROUND 1
FIGHT!
OW!
YUP. JUST LIKE I THOUGHT.
THAT FELT LIKE KICKING A BUILDING!
WHAT...?

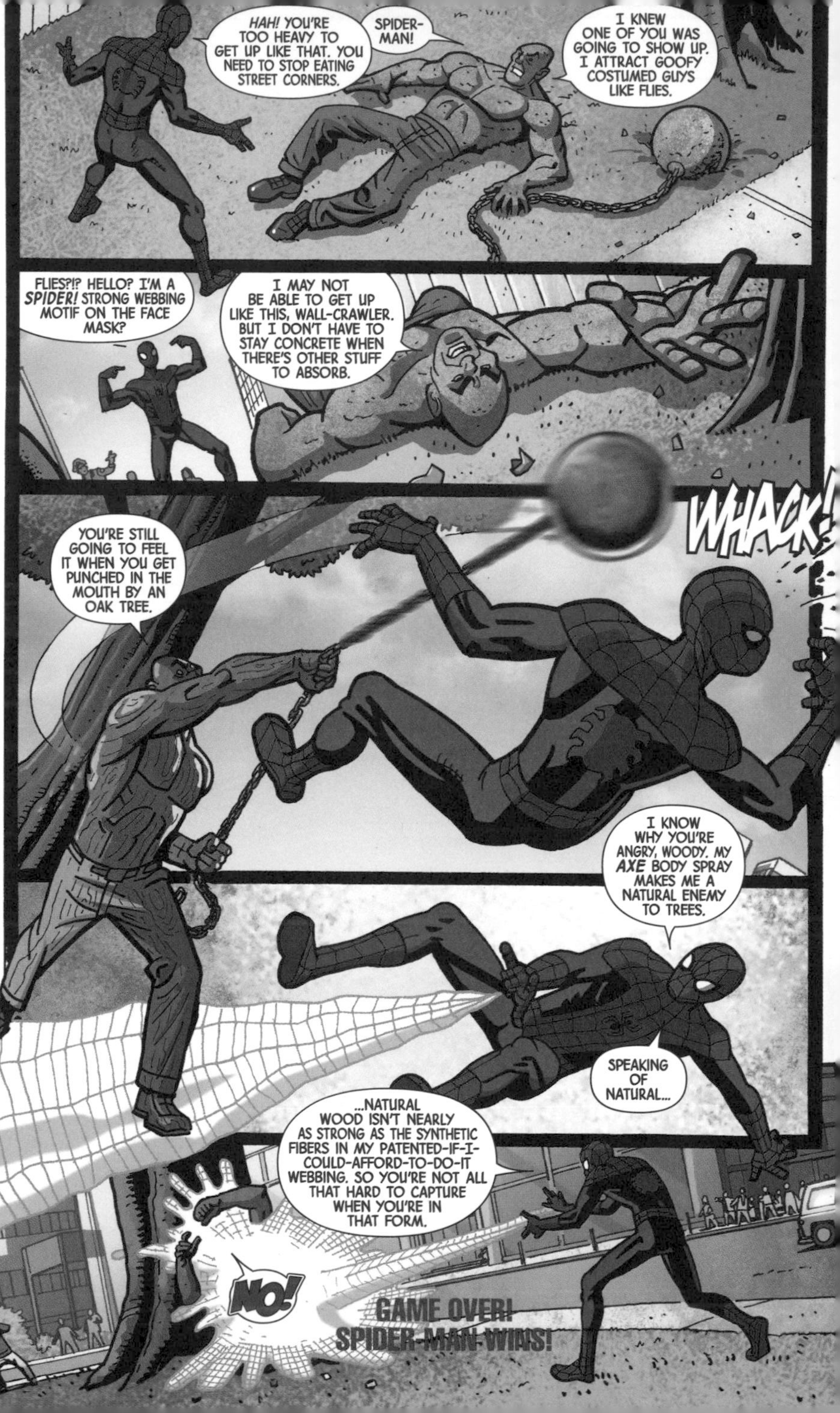
HAH! YOU'RE TOO HEAVY TO GET UP LIKE THAT. YOU NEED TO STOP EATING STREET CORNERS.
SPIDER-MAN!
I KNEW ONE OF YOU WAS GOING TO SHOW UP. I ATTRACT GOOFY COSTUMED GUYS LIKE FLIES.
FLIES?!? HELLO? I'M A SPIDER! STRONG WEBBING MOTIF ON THE FACE MASK?
I MAY NOT BE ABLE TO GET UP LIKE THIS, WALL-CRAWLER. BUT I DON'T HAVE TO STAY CONCRETE WHEN THERE'S OTHER STUFF TO ABSORB.
WHACK!
YOU'RE STILL GOING TO FEEL IT WHEN YOU GET PUNCHED IN THE MOUTH BY AN OAK TREE.
I KNOW WHY YOU'RE ANGRY, WOODY. MY AXE BODY SPRAY MAKES ME A NATURAL ENEMY TO TREES.
SPEAKING OF NATURAL...
...NATURAL WOOD ISN'T NEARLY AS STRONG AS THE SYNTHETIC FIBERS IN MY PATENTED-IF-I-COULD-AFFORD-TO-DO-IT WEBBING. SO YOU'RE NOT ALL THAT HARD TO CAPTURE WHEN YOU'RE IN THAT FORM.
NO!
GAME OVER!
SPIDER-MAN WINS!

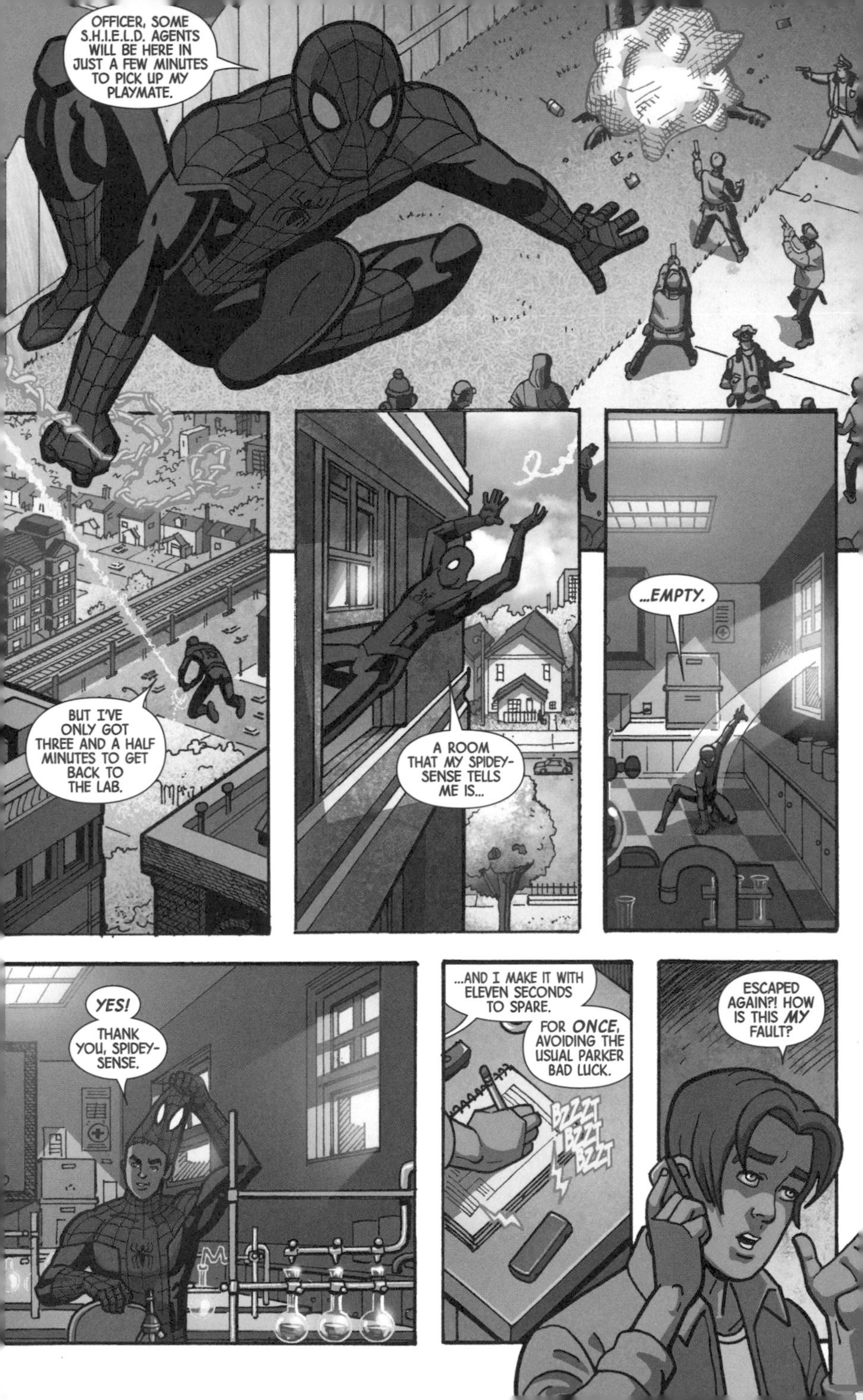
OFFICER, SOME S.H.I.E.L.D. AGENTS WILL BE HERE IN JUST A FEW MINUTES TO PICK UP MY PLAYMATE.
BUT I'VE ONLY GOT THREE AND A HALF MINUTES TO GET BACK TO THE LAB.
A ROOM THAT MY SPIDEY-SENSE TELLS ME IS...
...EMPTY.
YES!
THANK YOU, SPIDEY-SENSE.
...AND I MAKE IT WITH ELEVEN SECONDS TO SPARE.
FOR ONCE, AVOIDING THE USUAL PARKER BAD LUCK.
BZZZT BZZZT BZZZT
ESCAPED AGAIN?! HOW IS THIS MY FAULT?

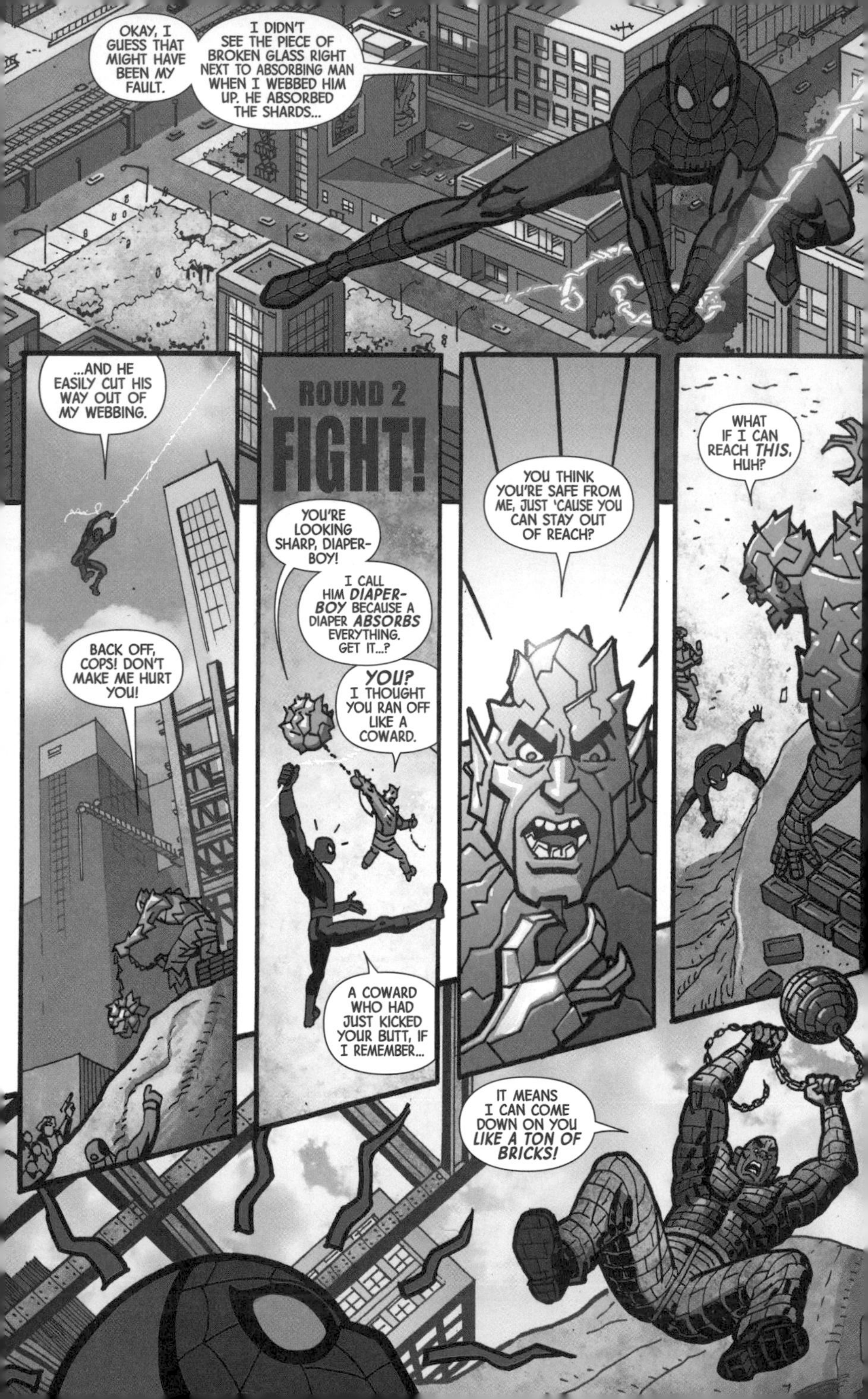
OKAY, I GUESS THAT MIGHT HAVE BEEN MY FAULT.
I DIDN'T SEE THE PIECE OF BROKEN GLASS RIGHT NEXT TO ABSORBING MAN WHEN I WEBBED HIM UP. HE ABSORBED THE SHARDS...
...AND HE EASILY CUT HIS WAY OUT OF MY WEBBING.
BACK OFF, COPS! DON'T MAKE ME HURT YOU!
ROUND 2
FIGHT!
YOU'RE LOOKING SHARP, DIAPER-BOY!
I CALL HIM *DIAPER-BOY* BECAUSE A DIAPER *ABSORBS* EVERYTHING. GET IT...?
YOU? I THOUGHT YOU RAN OFF LIKE A COWARD.
A COWARD WHO HAD JUST KICKED YOUR BUTT, IF I REMEMBER...
YOU THINK YOU'RE SAFE FROM ME, JUST 'CAUSE YOU CAN STAY OUT OF REACH?
WHAT IF I CAN REACH *THIS*, HUH?
IT MEANS I CAN COME DOWN ON YOU *LIKE A TON OF BRICKS!*

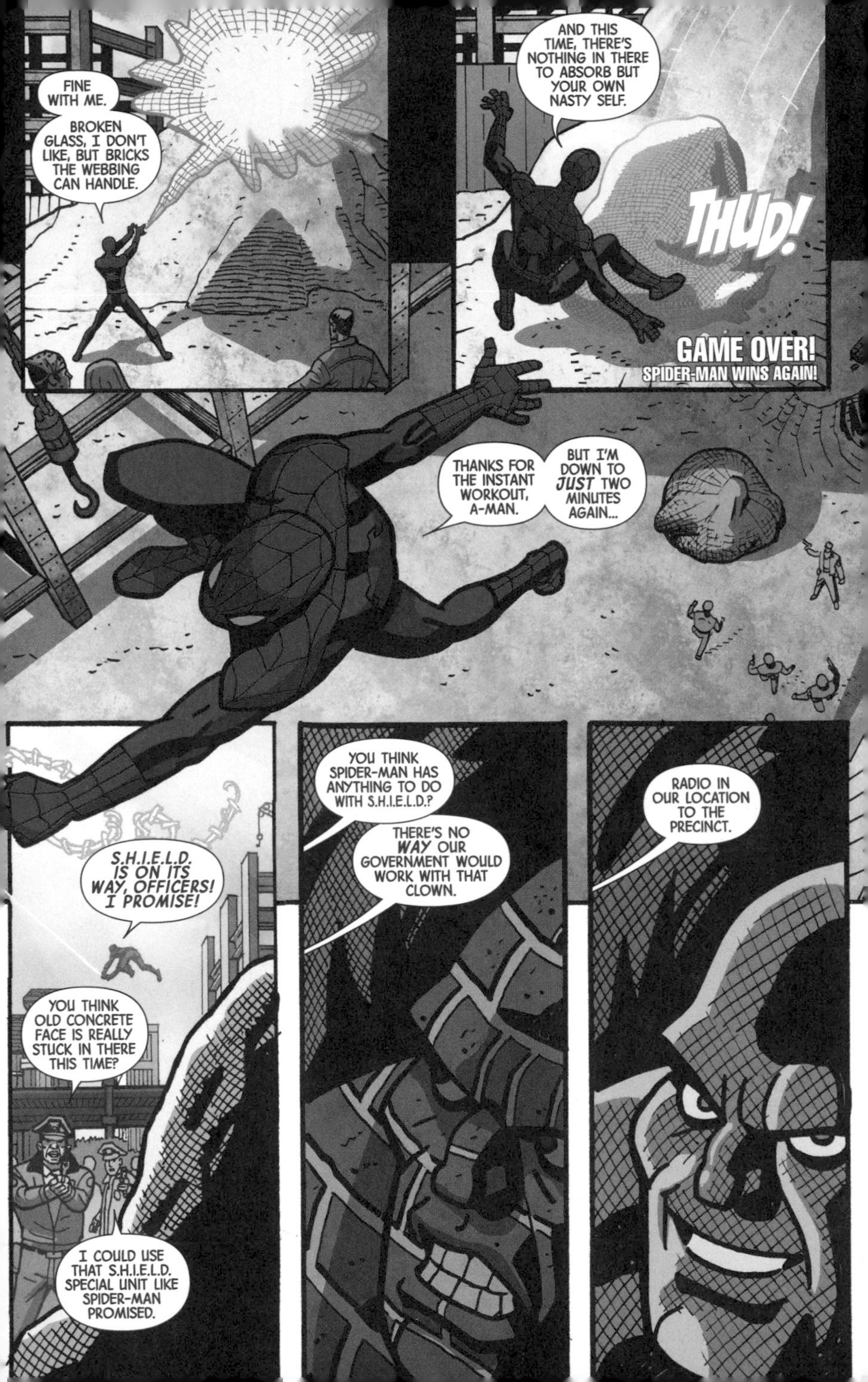
FINE WITH ME.
BROKEN GLASS, I DON'T LIKE, BUT BRICKS THE WEBBING CAN HANDLE.
AND THIS TIME, THERE'S NOTHING IN THERE TO ABSORB BUT YOUR OWN NASTY SELF.
THUD!
GAME OVER!
SPIDER-MAN WINS AGAIN!
THANKS FOR THE INSTANT WORKOUT, A-MAN.
BUT I'M DOWN TO JUST TWO MINUTES AGAIN...
S.H.I.E.L.D. IS ON ITS WAY, OFFICERS! I PROMISE!
YOU THINK OLD CONCRETE FACE IS REALLY STUCK IN THERE THIS TIME?
I COULD USE THAT S.H.I.E.L.D. SPECIAL UNIT LIKE SPIDER-MAN PROMISED.
YOU THINK SPIDER-MAN HAS ANYTHING TO DO WITH S.H.I.E.L.D.?
THERE'S NO WAY OUR GOVERNMENT WOULD WORK WITH THAT CLOWN.
RADIO IN OUR LOCATION TO THE PRECINCT.

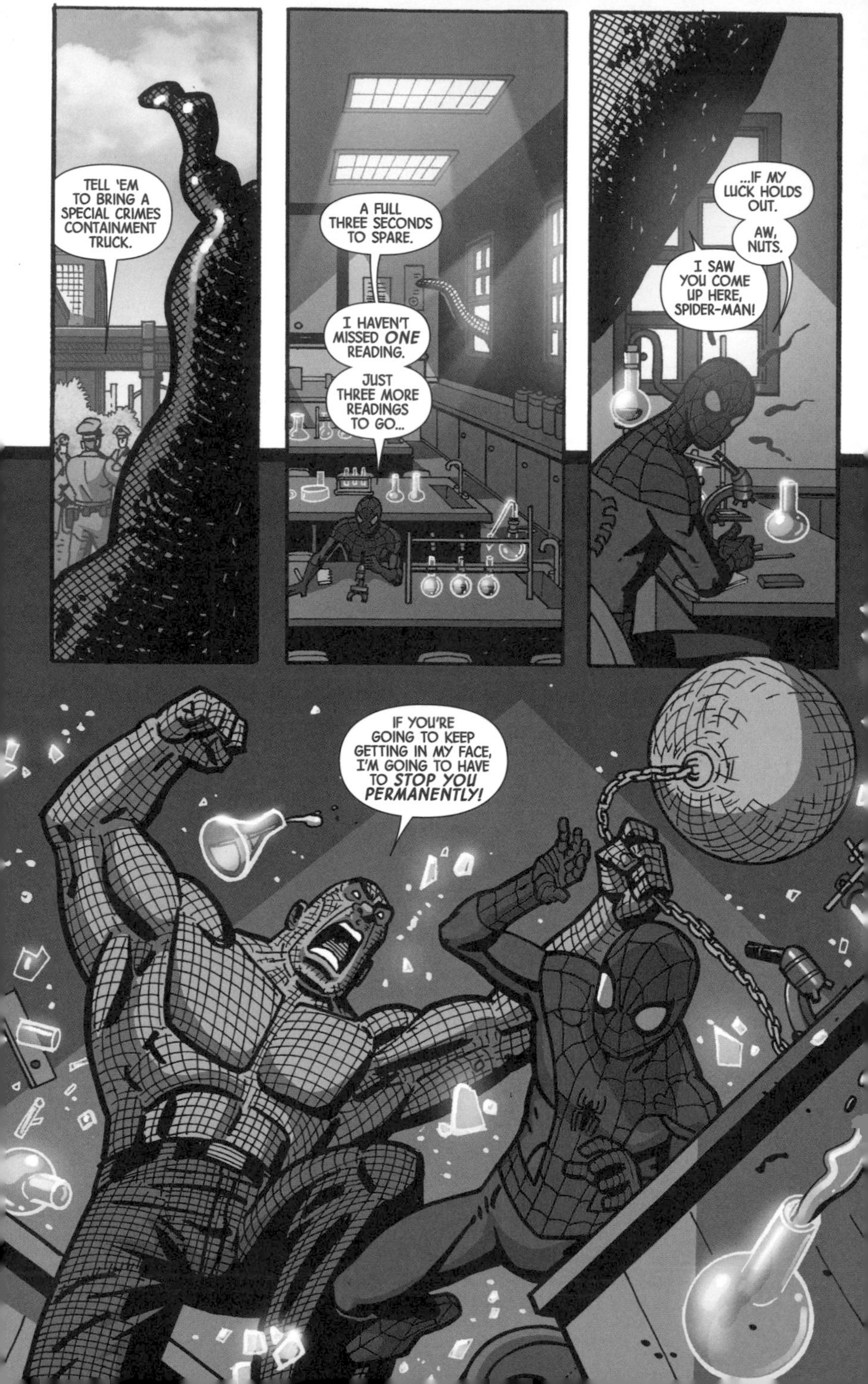
TELL 'EM TO BRING A SPECIAL CRIMES CONTAINMENT TRUCK.
A FULL THREE SECONDS TO SPARE.
I HAVEN'T MISSED ONE READING.
JUST THREE MORE READINGS TO GO...
...IF MY LUCK HOLDS OUT.
AW, NUTS.
I SAW YOU COME UP HERE, SPIDER-MAN!
IF YOU'RE GOING TO KEEP GETTING IN MY FACE, I'M GOING TO HAVE TO STOP YOU PERMANENTLY!

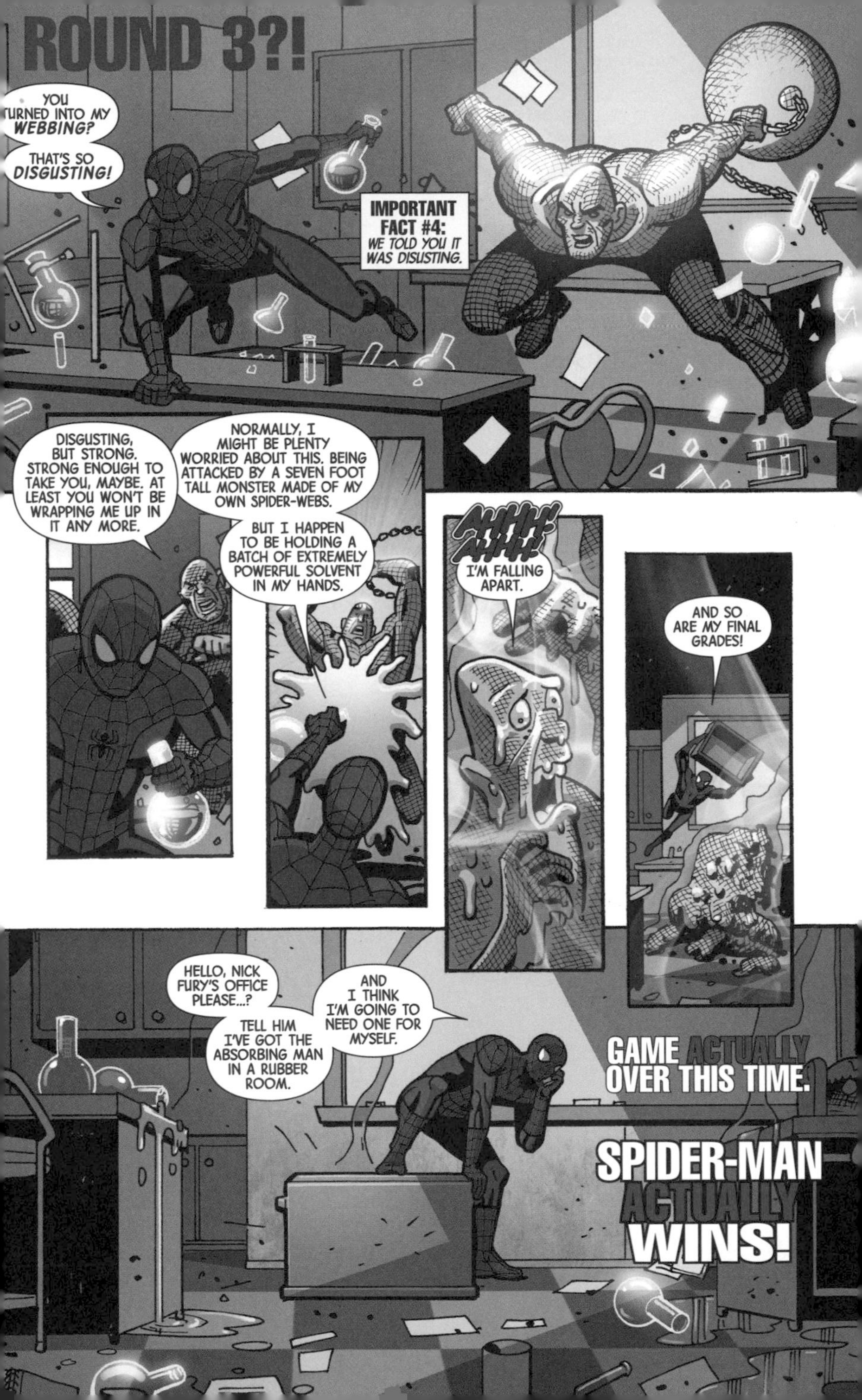
ROUND 3?!
YOU TURNED INTO MY WEBBING?
THAT'S SO DISGUSTING!
IMPORTANT FACT #4: WE TOLD YOU IT WAS DISUSTING.
DISGUSTING, BUT STRONG. STRONG ENOUGH TO TAKE YOU, MAYBE. AT LEAST YOU WON'T BE WRAPPING ME UP IN IT ANY MORE.
NORMALLY, I MIGHT BE PLENTY WORRIED ABOUT THIS. BEING ATTACKED BY A SEVEN FOOT TALL MONSTER MADE OF MY OWN SPIDER-WEBS.
BUT I HAPPEN TO BE HOLDING A BATCH OF EXTREMELY POWERFUL SOLVENT IN MY HANDS.
AHHH! AHHH!
I'M FALLING APART.
AND SO ARE MY FINAL GRADES!
HELLO, NICK FURY'S OFFICE PLEASE...?
TELL HIM I'VE GOT THE ABSORBING MAN IN A RUBBER ROOM.
AND I THINK I'M GOING TO NEED ONE FOR MYSELF.
GAME ACTUALLY OVER THIS TIME.
SPIDER-MAN ACTUALLY WINS!

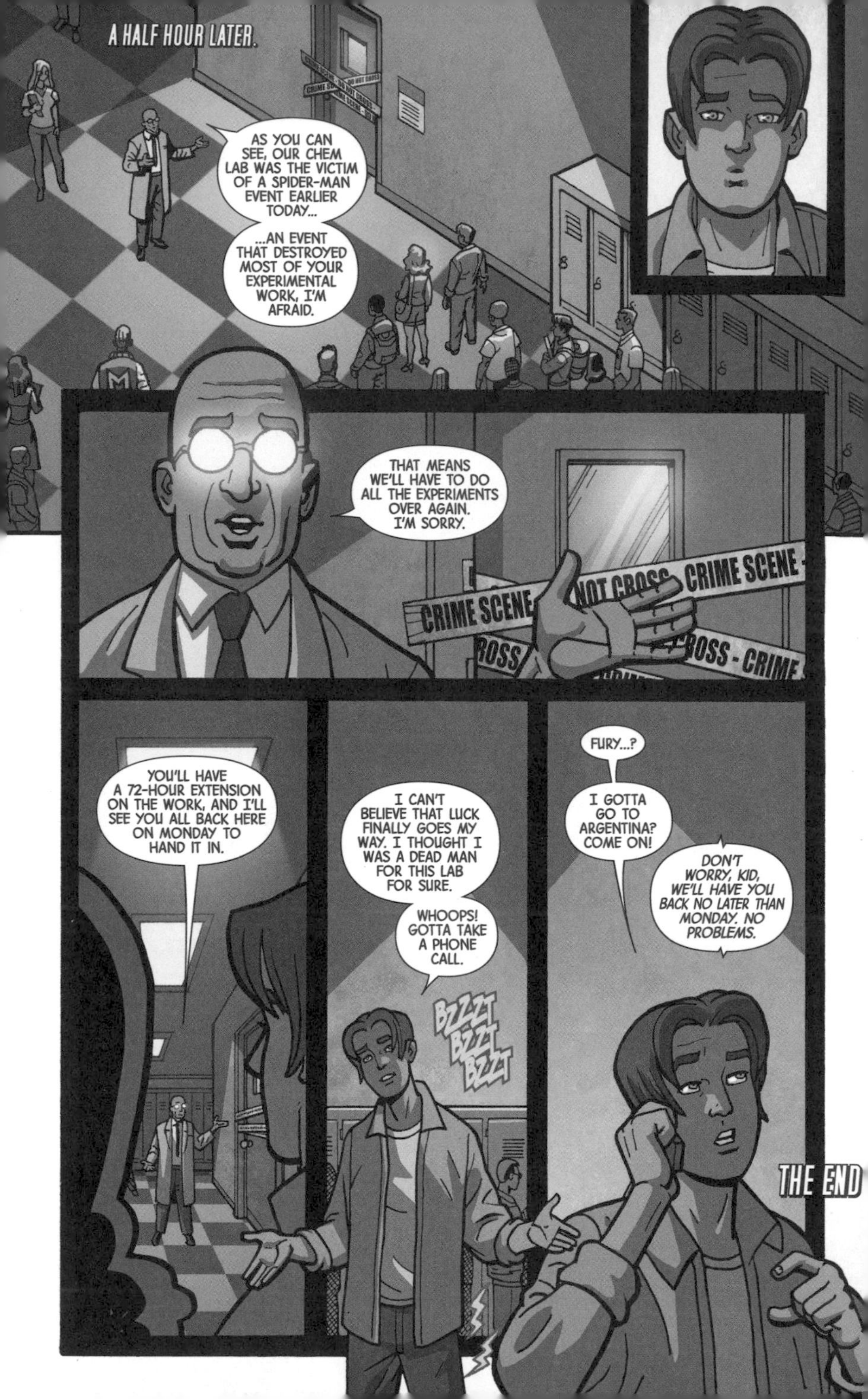
A HALF HOUR LATER.
AS YOU CAN SEE, OUR CHEM LAB WAS THE VICTIM OF A SPIDER-MAN EVENT EARLIER TODAY...
...AN EVENT THAT DESTROYED MOST OF YOUR EXPERIMENTAL WORK, I'M AFRAID.
THAT MEANS WE'LL HAVE TO DO ALL THE EXPERIMENTS OVER AGAIN. I'M SORRY.
CRIME SCENE
NOT CROSS
CRIME SCENE
ROSS - CRIME
YOU'LL HAVE A 72-HOUR EXTENSION ON THE WORK, AND I'LL SEE YOU ALL BACK HERE ON MONDAY TO HAND IT IN.
I CAN'T BELIEVE THAT LUCK FINALLY GOES MY WAY. I THOUGHT I WAS A DEAD MAN FOR THIS LAB FOR SURE.
WHOOPS! GOTTA TAKE A PHONE CALL.
BZZZT BZZT BZZT
FURY...?
I GOTTA GO TO ARGENTINA? COME ON!
DON'T WORRY, KID, WE'LL HAVE YOU BACK NO LATER THAN MONDAY. NO PROBLEMS.
THE END

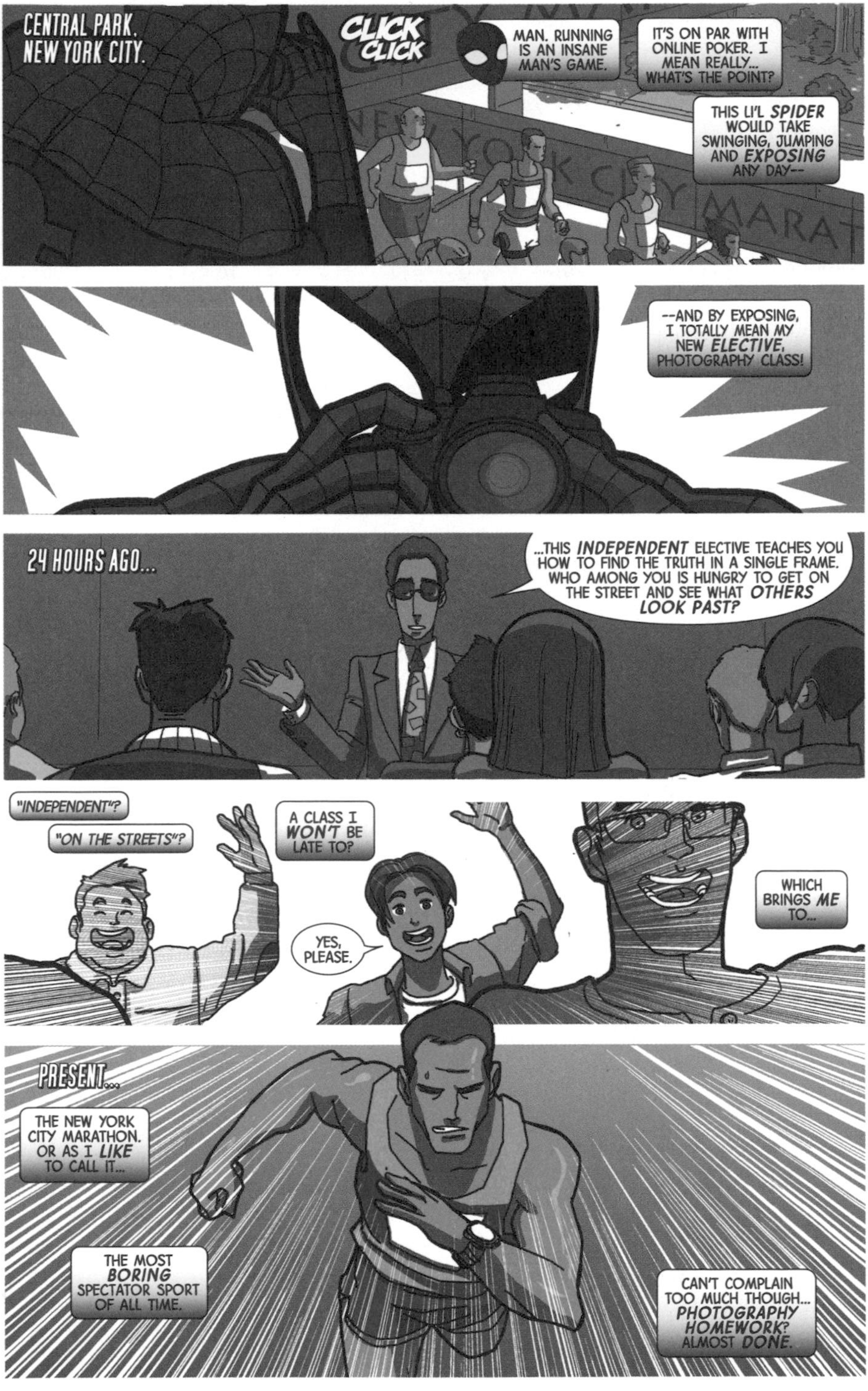

CENTRAL PARK, NEW YORK CITY.
CLICK CLICK
MAN. RUNNING IS AN INSANE MAN'S GAME.
IT'S ON PAR WITH ONLINE POKER. I MEAN REALLY... WHAT'S THE POINT?
THIS LI'L SPIDER WOULD TAKE SWINGING, JUMPING AND EXPOSING ANY DAY--
--AND BY EXPOSING, I TOTALLY MEAN MY NEW ELECTIVE, PHOTOGRAPHY CLASS!
24 HOURS AGO...
...THIS INDEPENDENT ELECTIVE TEACHES YOU HOW TO FIND THE TRUTH IN A SINGLE FRAME. WHO AMONG YOU IS HUNGRY TO GET ON THE STREET AND SEE WHAT OTHERS LOOK PAST?
"INDEPENDENT"?
"ON THE STREETS"?
A CLASS I WON'T BE LATE TO?
YES, PLEASE.
WHICH BRINGS ME TO...
PRESENT...
THE NEW YORK CITY MARATHON. OR AS I LIKE TO CALL IT...
THE MOST BORING SPECTATOR SPORT OF ALL TIME.
CAN'T COMPLAIN TOO MUCH THOUGH... PHOTOGRAPHY HOMEWORK? ALMOST DONE.

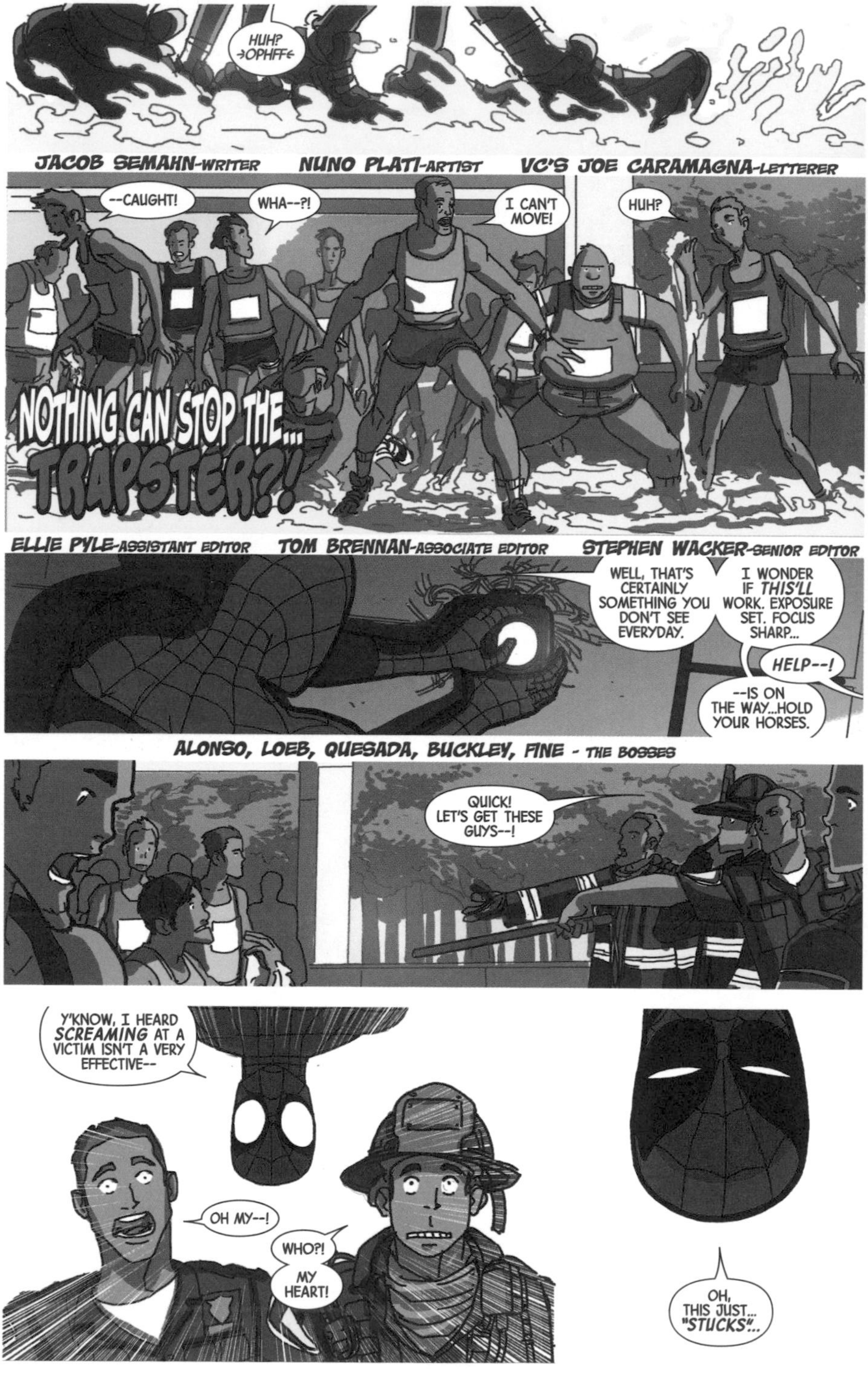
HUH? →OPHFF←
JACOB SEMAHN-WRITER NUNO PLATI-ARTIST VC'S JOE CARAMAGNA-LETTERER
--CAUGHT!
WHA--?!
I CAN'T MOVE!
HUH?
NOTHING CAN STOP THE... TRAPSTER?!
ELLIE PYLE-ASSISTANT EDITOR TOM BRENNAN-ASSOCIATE EDITOR STEPHEN WACKER-SENIOR EDITOR
WELL, THAT'S CERTAINLY SOMETHING YOU DON'T SEE EVERYDAY.
I WONDER IF THIS'LL WORK. EXPOSURE SET. FOCUS SHARP...
HELP--!
--IS ON THE WAY...HOLD YOUR HORSES.
ALONSO, LOEB, QUESADA, BUCKLEY, FINE - THE BOSSES
QUICK! LET'S GET THESE GUYS--!
Y'KNOW, I HEARD SCREAMING AT A VICTIM ISN'T A VERY EFFECTIVE--
OH MY--!
WHO?!
MY HEART!
OH, THIS JUST... "STUCKS"...

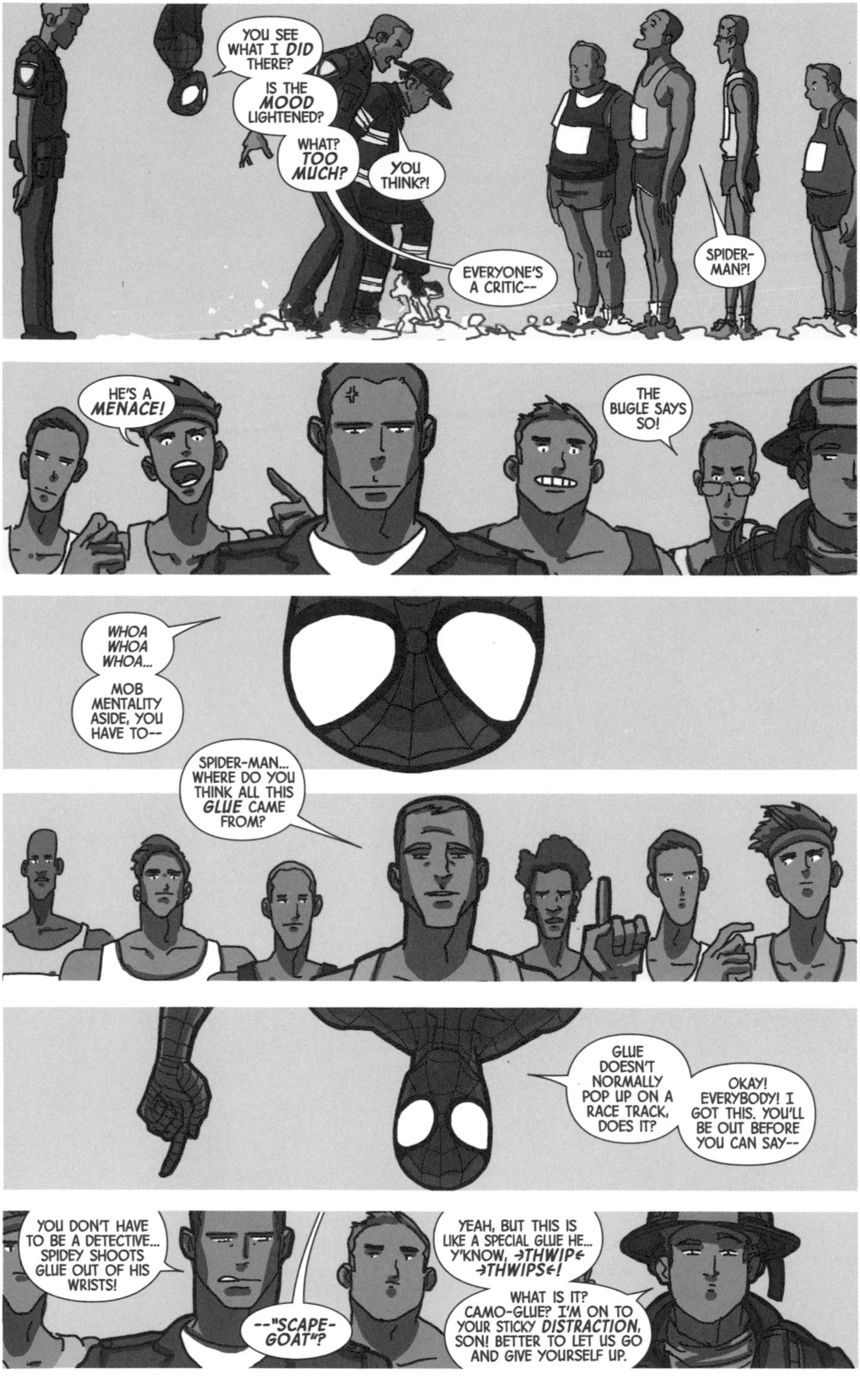
YOU SEE WHAT I DID THERE?
IS THE MOOD LIGHTENED?
WHAT? TOO MUCH?
YOU THINK?!
EVERYONE'S A CRITIC--
SPIDER-MAN?!
HE'S A MENACE!
THE BUGLE SAYS SO!
WHOA WHOA WHOA...
MOB MENTALITY ASIDE, YOU HAVE TO--
SPIDER-MAN... WHERE DO YOU THINK ALL THIS GLUE CAME FROM?
GLUE DOESN'T NORMALLY POP UP ON A RACE TRACK, DOES IT?
OKAY! EVERYBODY! I GOT THIS. YOU'LL BE OUT BEFORE YOU CAN SAY--
--"SCAPE-GOAT"?
YOU DON'T HAVE TO BE A DETECTIVE... SPIDEY SHOOTS GLUE OUT OF HIS WRISTS!
YEAH, BUT THIS IS LIKE A SPECIAL GLUE HE... Y'KNOW, →THWIP← →THWIPS←!
WHAT IS IT? CAMO-GLUE? I'M ON TO YOUR STICKY DISTRACTION, SON! BETTER TO LET US GO AND GIVE YOURSELF UP.

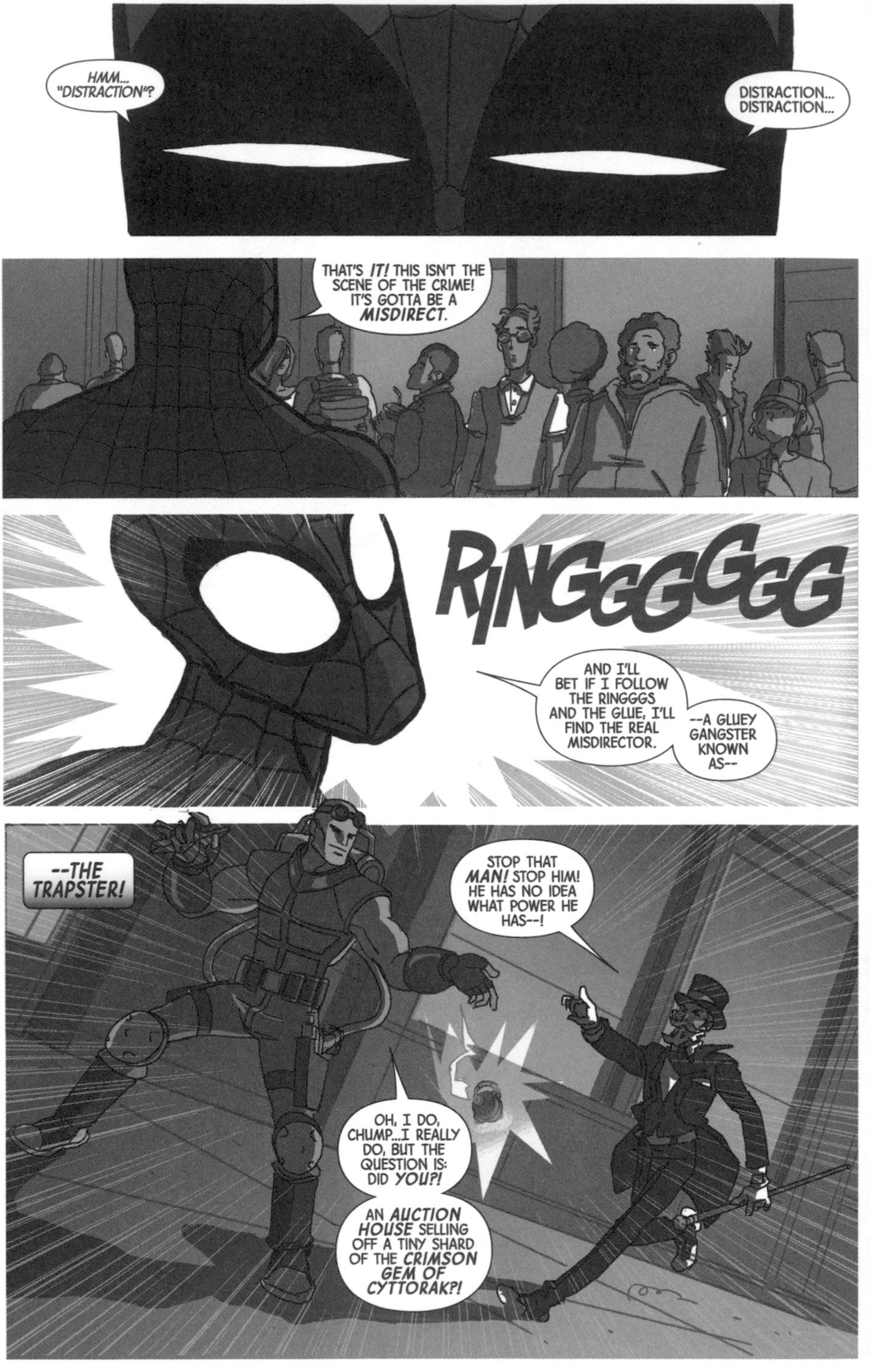
HMM... "DISTRACTION"?
DISTRACTION... DISTRACTION...
THAT'S IT! THIS ISN'T THE SCENE OF THE CRIME! IT'S GOTTA BE A MISDIRECT.
RINGGGGGG
AND I'LL BET IF I FOLLOW THE RINGGGS AND THE GLUE, I'LL FIND THE REAL MISDIRECTOR.
--A GLUEY GANGSTER KNOWN AS--
--THE TRAPSTER!
STOP THAT MAN! STOP HIM! HE HAS NO IDEA WHAT POWER HE HAS--!
OH, I DO, CHUMP...I REALLY DO, BUT THE QUESTION IS: DID YOU?!
AN AUCTION HOUSE SELLING OFF A TINY SHARD OF THE CRIMSON GEM OF CYTTORAK?!

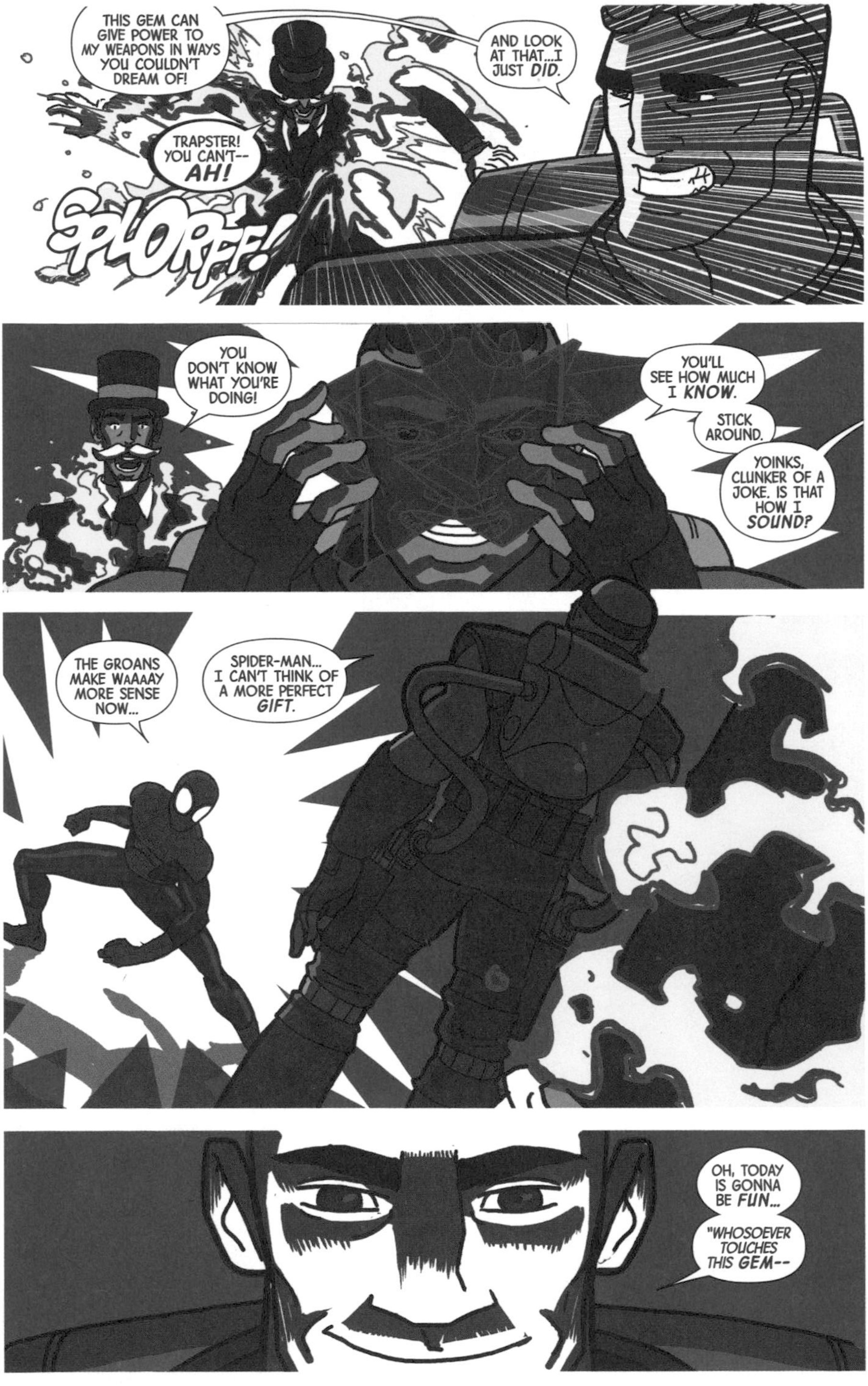
THIS GEM CAN GIVE POWER TO MY WEAPONS IN WAYS YOU COULDN'T DREAM OF!
AND LOOK AT THAT...I JUST DID.
TRAPSTER! YOU CAN'T-- AH!
SPLORFF!
YOU DON'T KNOW WHAT YOU'RE DOING!
YOU'LL SEE HOW MUCH I KNOW.
STICK AROUND.
YOINKS, CLUNKER OF A JOKE. IS THAT HOW I SOUND?
THE GROANS MAKE WAAAAY MORE SENSE NOW...
SPIDER-MAN... I CAN'T THINK OF A MORE PERFECT GIFT.
OH, TODAY IS GONNA BE FUN...
"WHOSOEVER TOUCHES THIS GEM--

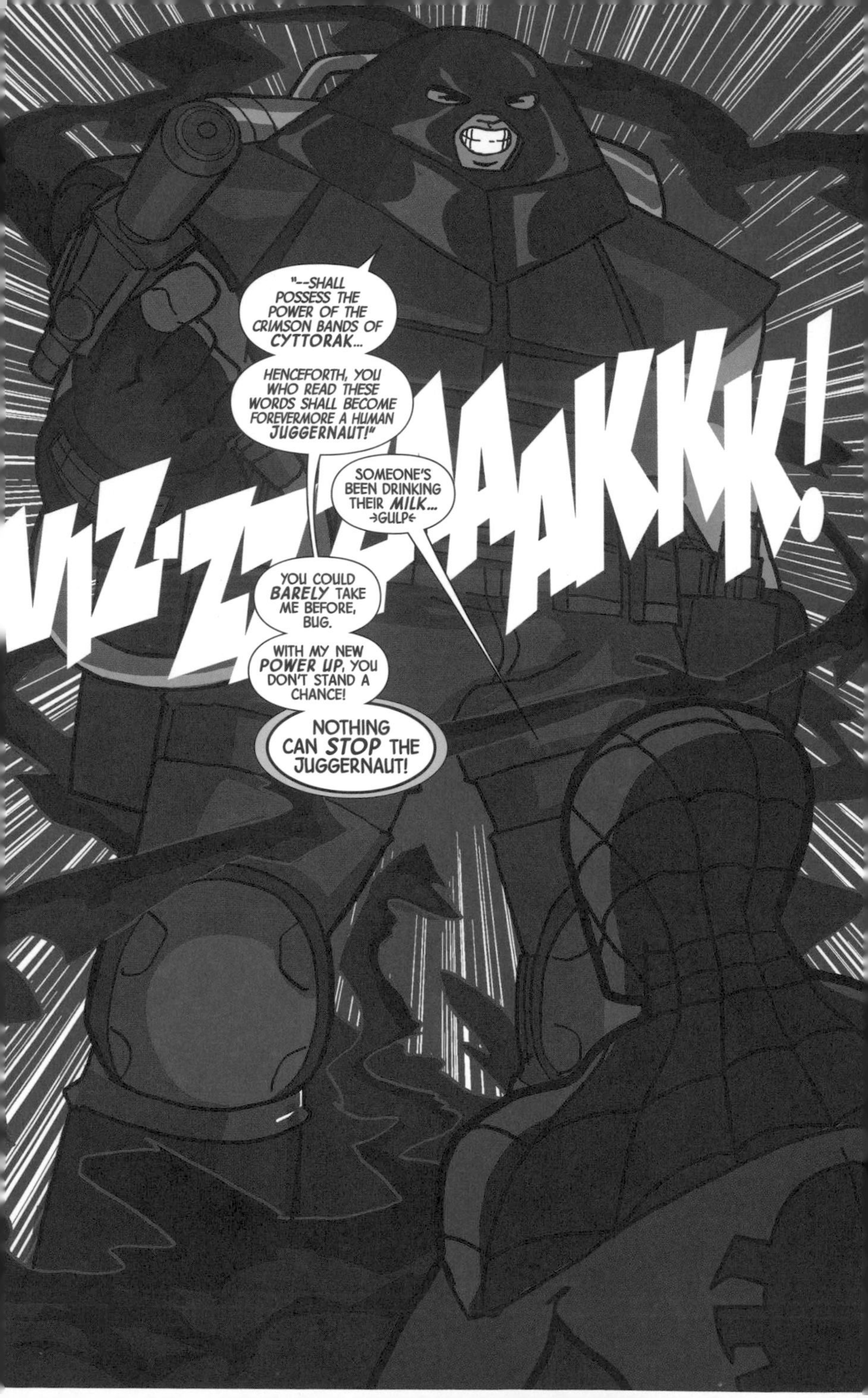
"--SHALL POSSESS THE POWER OF THE CRIMSON BANDS OF CYTTORAK...
HENCEFORTH, YOU WHO READ THESE WORDS SHALL BECOME FOREVERMORE A HUMAN JUGGERNAUT!"
SOMEONE'S BEEN DRINKING THEIR MILK... →GULP←
YOU COULD BARELY TAKE ME BEFORE, BUG.
WITH MY NEW POWER UP, YOU DON'T STAND A CHANCE!
NOTHING CAN STOP THE JUGGERNAUT!

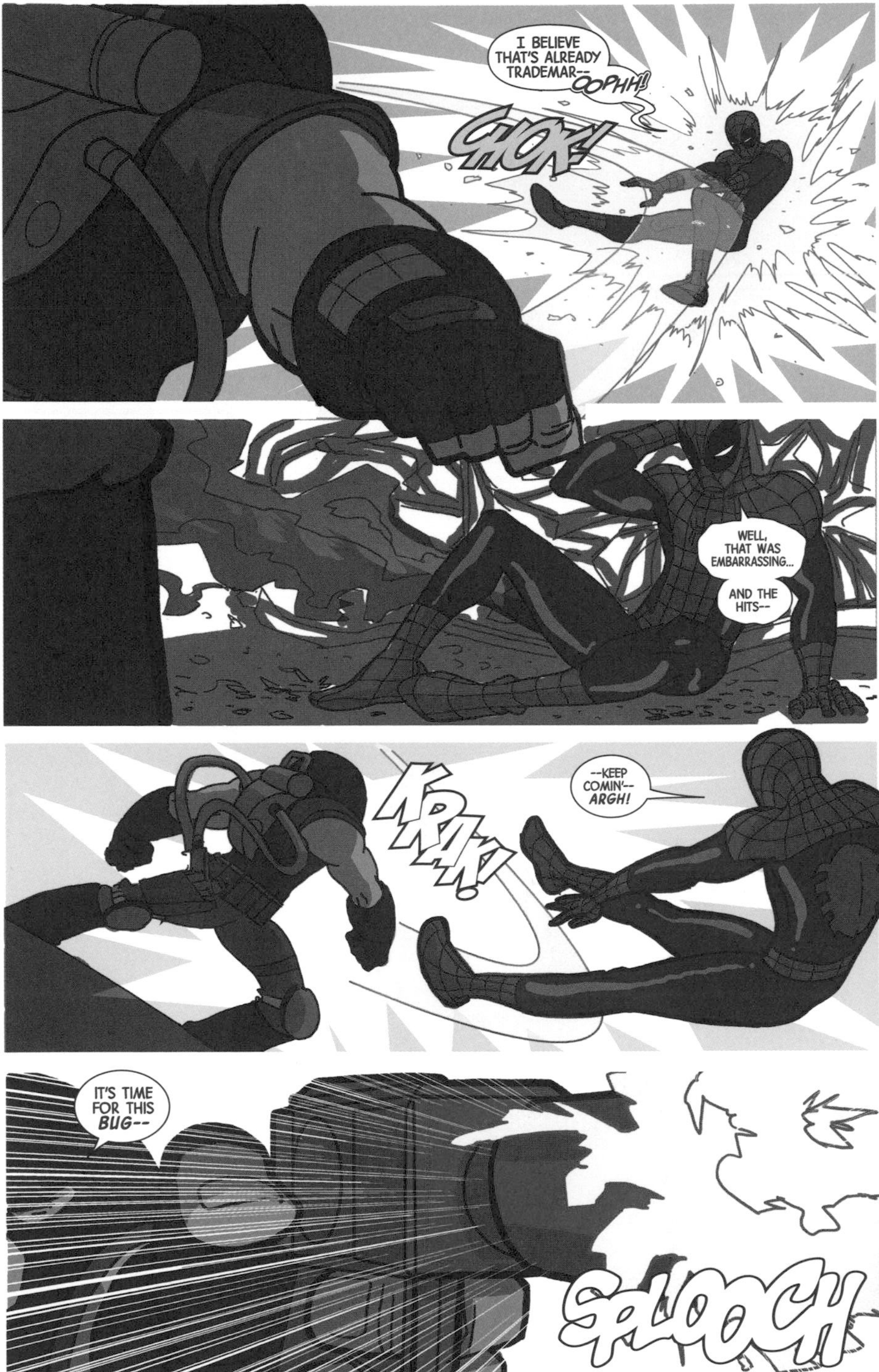
I BELIEVE THAT'S ALREADY TRADEMAR--OOPHH!
CHOK!
WELL, THAT WAS EMBARRASSING...
AND THE HITS--
KRAK!
--KEEP COMIN'--ARGH!
IT'S TIME FOR THIS BUG--
SPLOOCH

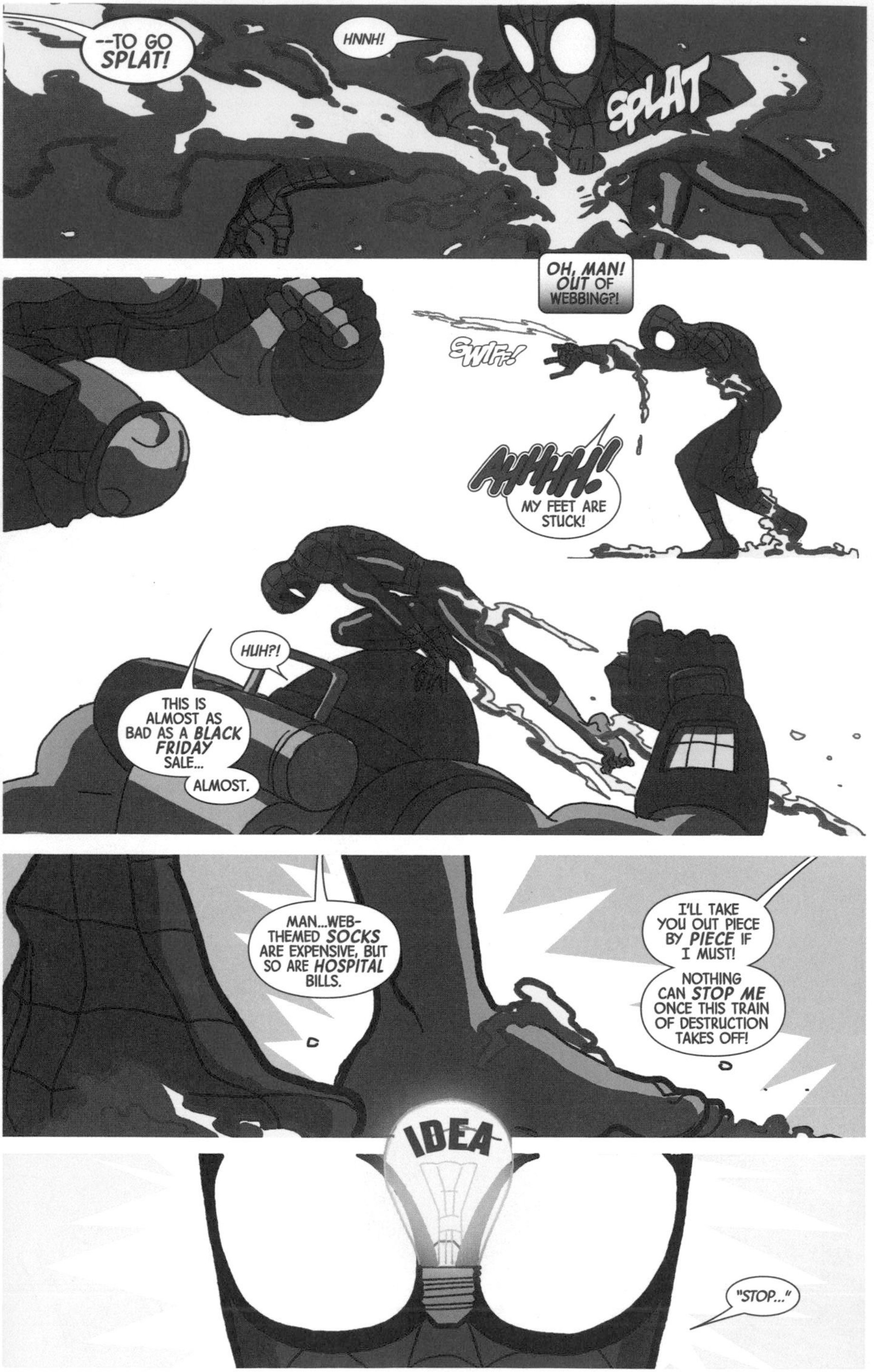
--TO GO SPLAT!
HNNH!
SPLAT
OH, MAN! OUT OF WEBBING?!
SWIFF!
AHHHH!
MY FEET ARE STUCK!
HUH?!
THIS IS ALMOST AS BAD AS A BLACK FRIDAY SALE...
ALMOST.
MAN...WEB-THEMED SOCKS ARE EXPENSIVE, BUT SO ARE HOSPITAL BILLS.
I'LL TAKE YOU OUT PIECE BY PIECE IF I MUST!
NOTHING CAN STOP ME ONCE THIS TRAIN OF DESTRUCTION TAKES OFF!
IDEA
"STOP..."

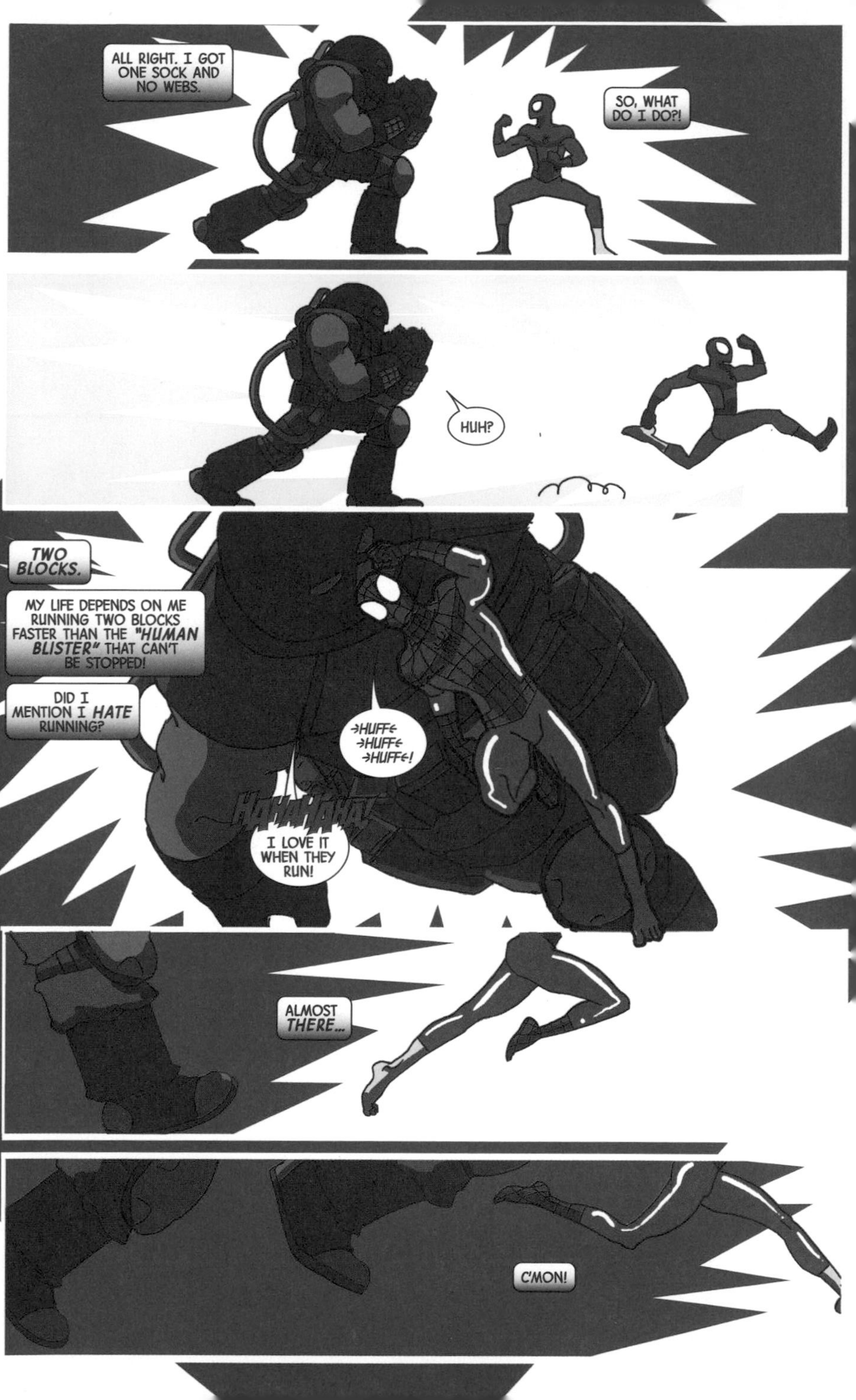
ALL RIGHT. I GOT ONE SOCK AND NO WEBS.
SO, WHAT DO I DO?!
HUH?
TWO BLOCKS.
MY LIFE DEPENDS ON ME RUNNING TWO BLOCKS FASTER THAN THE "HUMAN BLISTER" THAT CAN'T BE STOPPED!
DID I MENTION I HATE RUNNING?
→HUFF← →HUFF← →HUFF←!
HAHAHAHA!
I LOVE IT WHEN THEY RUN!
ALMOST THERE...
C'MON!

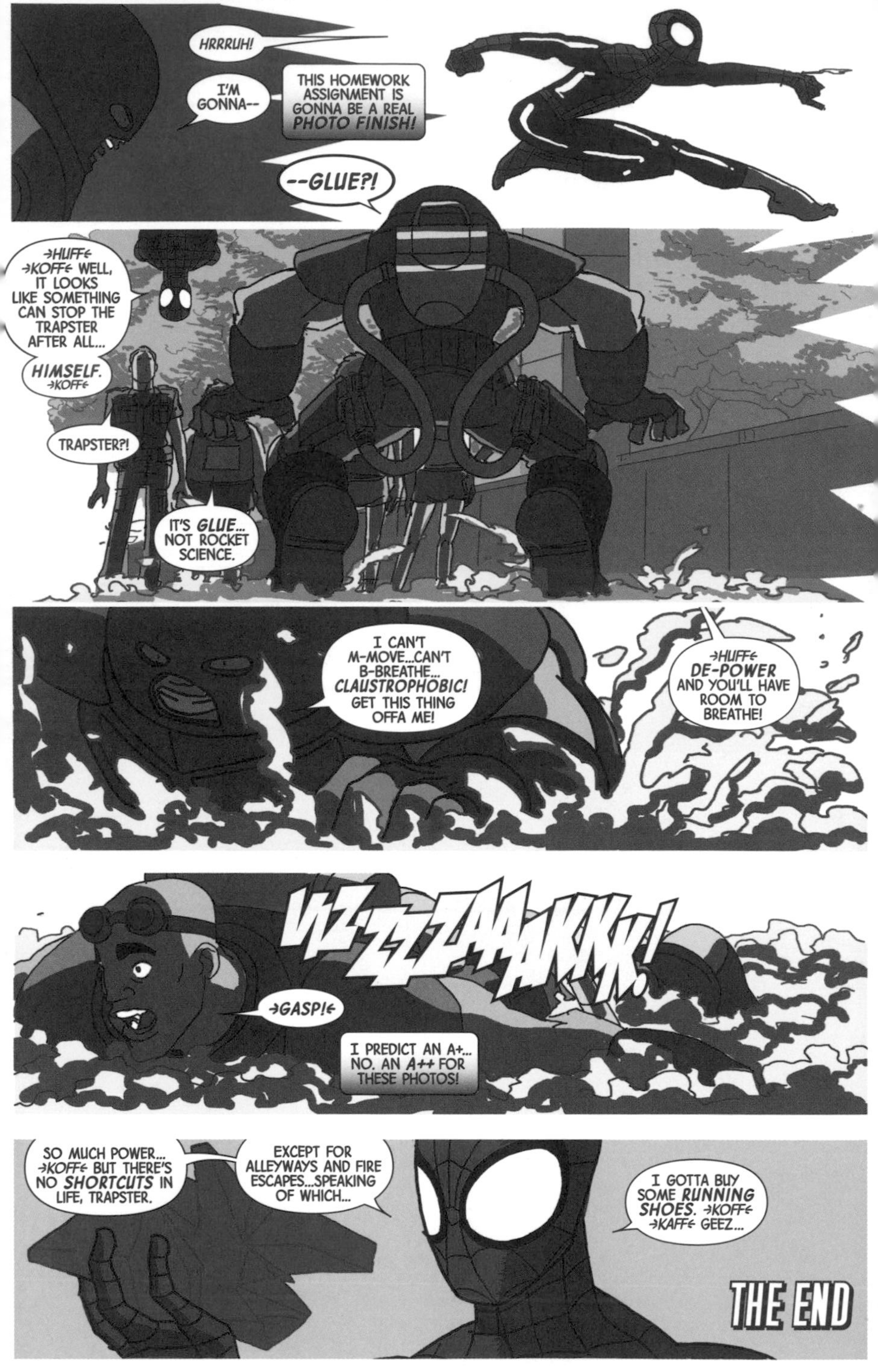
HRRRUH!
I'M GONNA--
THIS HOMEWORK ASSIGNMENT IS GONNA BE A REAL PHOTO FINISH!
--GLUE?!
→HUFF← →KOFF← WELL, IT LOOKS LIKE SOMETHING CAN STOP THE TRAPSTER AFTER ALL...
HIMSELF. →KOFF←
TRAPSTER?!
IT'S GLUE... NOT ROCKET SCIENCE.
I CAN'T M-MOVE...CAN'T B-BREATHE... CLAUSTROPHOBIC! GET THIS THING OFFA ME!
→HUFF← DE-POWER AND YOU'LL HAVE ROOM TO BREATHE!
VZZZZAAAKKK!
→GASP!←
I PREDICT AN A+... NO. AN A++ FOR THESE PHOTOS!
SO MUCH POWER... →KOFF← BUT THERE'S NO SHORTCUTS IN LIFE, TRAPSTER.
EXCEPT FOR ALLEYWAYS AND FIRE ESCAPES...SPEAKING OF WHICH...
I GOTTA BUY SOME RUNNING SHOES. →KOFF← →KAFF← GEEZ...
THE END

6

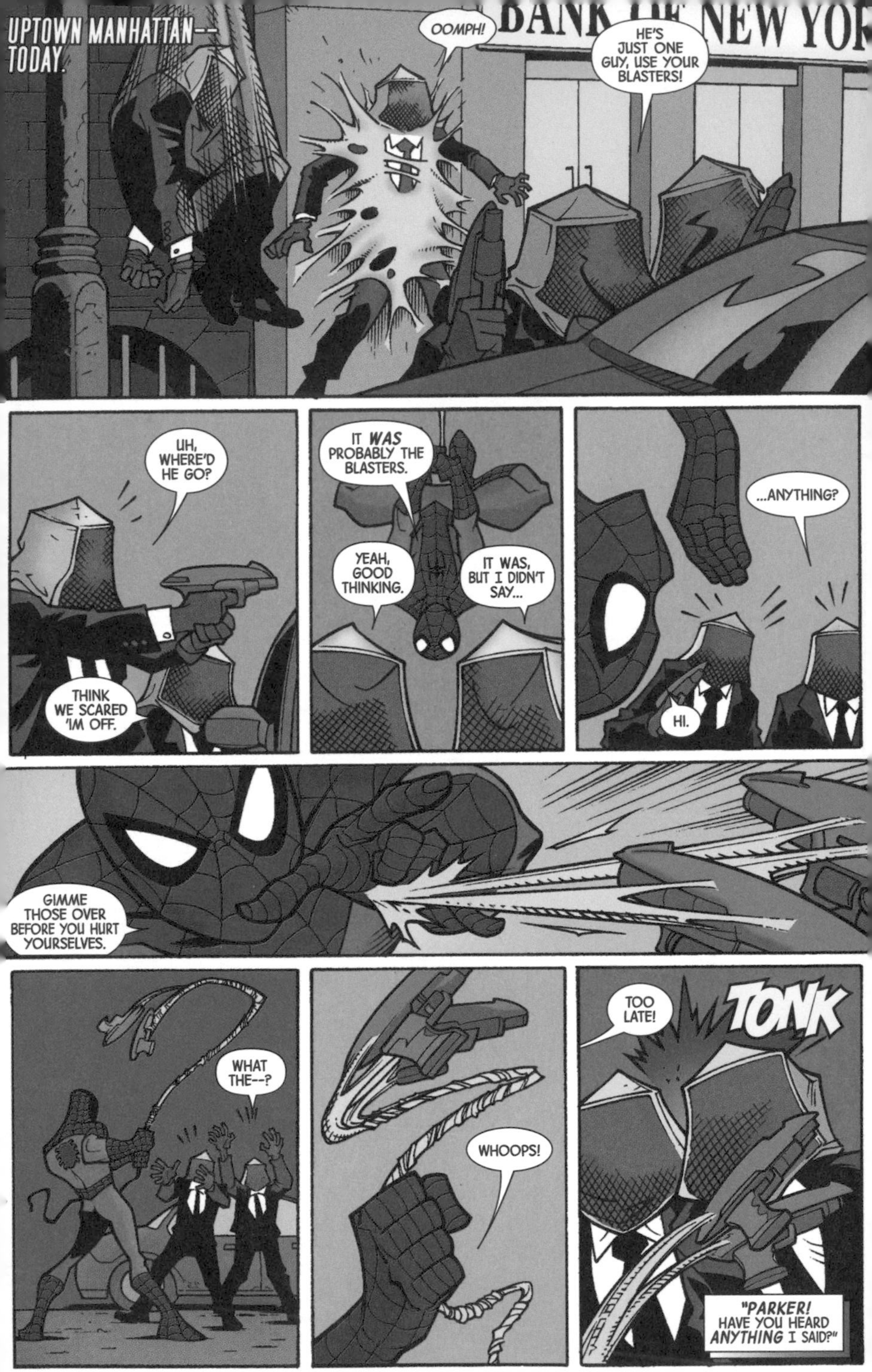
UPTOWN MANHATTAN--
TODAY.
OOMPH!
BANK OF NEW YOR
HE'S JUST ONE GUY, USE YOUR BLASTERS!
UH, WHERE'D HE GO?
THINK WE SCARED 'IM OFF.
IT *WAS* PROBABLY THE BLASTERS.
YEAH, GOOD THINKING.
IT WAS, BUT I DIDN'T SAY...
...ANYTHING?
HI.
GIMME THOSE OVER BEFORE YOU HURT YOURSELVES.
WHAT THE--?
WHOOPS!
TOO LATE!
TONK
"PARKER! HAVE YOU HEARD *ANYTHING* I SAID?"

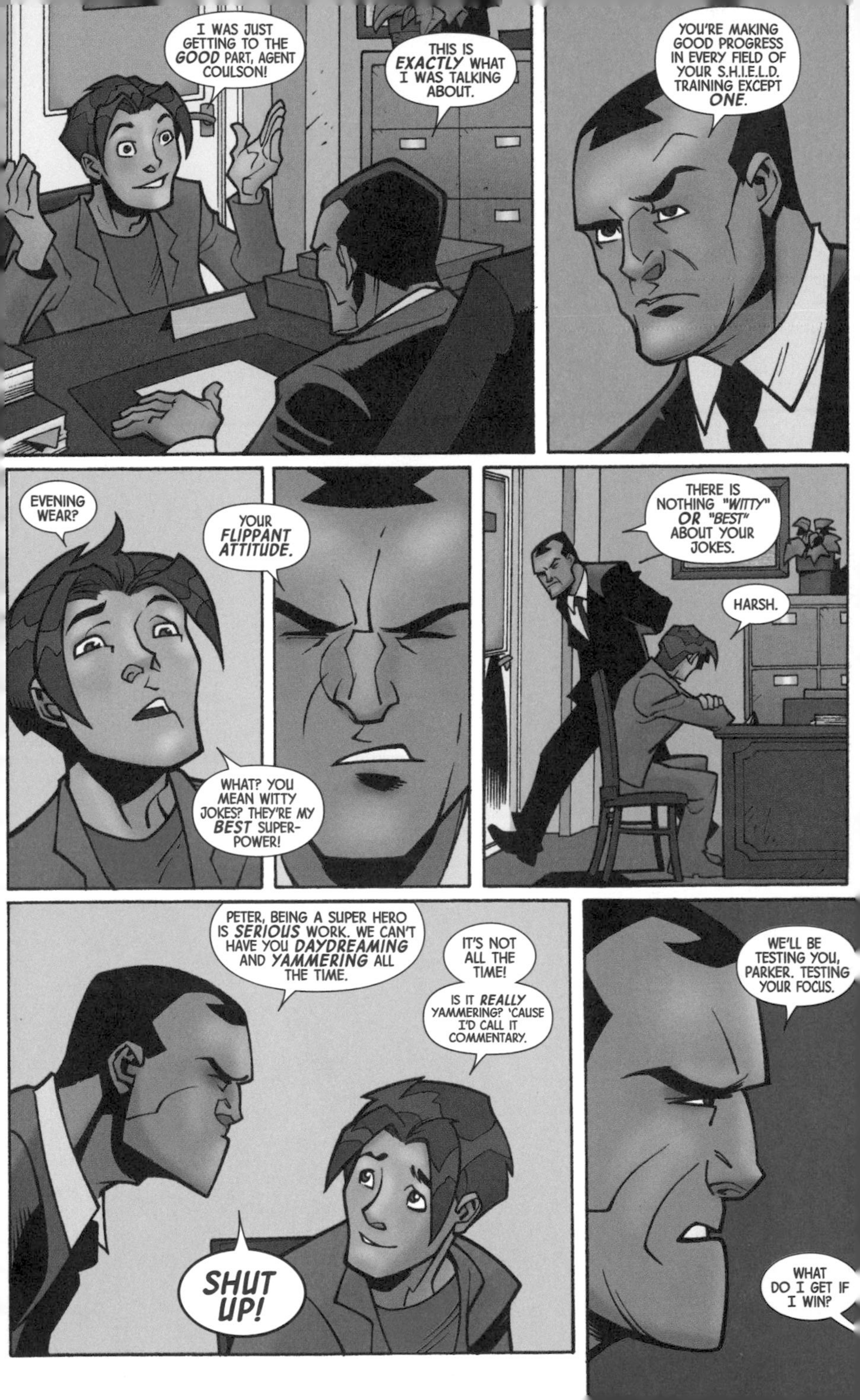
I WAS JUST GETTING TO THE GOOD PART, AGENT COULSON!
THIS IS EXACTLY WHAT I WAS TALKING ABOUT.
YOU'RE MAKING GOOD PROGRESS IN EVERY FIELD OF YOUR S.H.I.E.L.D. TRAINING EXCEPT ONE.
EVENING WEAR?
YOUR FLIPPANT ATTITUDE.
WHAT? YOU MEAN WITTY JOKES? THEY'RE MY BEST SUPER-POWER!
THERE IS NOTHING "WITTY" OR "BEST" ABOUT YOUR JOKES.
HARSH.
PETER, BEING A SUPER HERO IS SERIOUS WORK. WE CAN'T HAVE YOU DAYDREAMING AND YAMMERING ALL THE TIME.
IT'S NOT ALL THE TIME!
IS IT REALLY YAMMERING? 'CAUSE I'D CALL IT COMMENTARY.
SHUT UP!
WE'LL BE TESTING YOU, PARKER. TESTING YOUR FOCUS.
WHAT DO I GET IF I WIN?

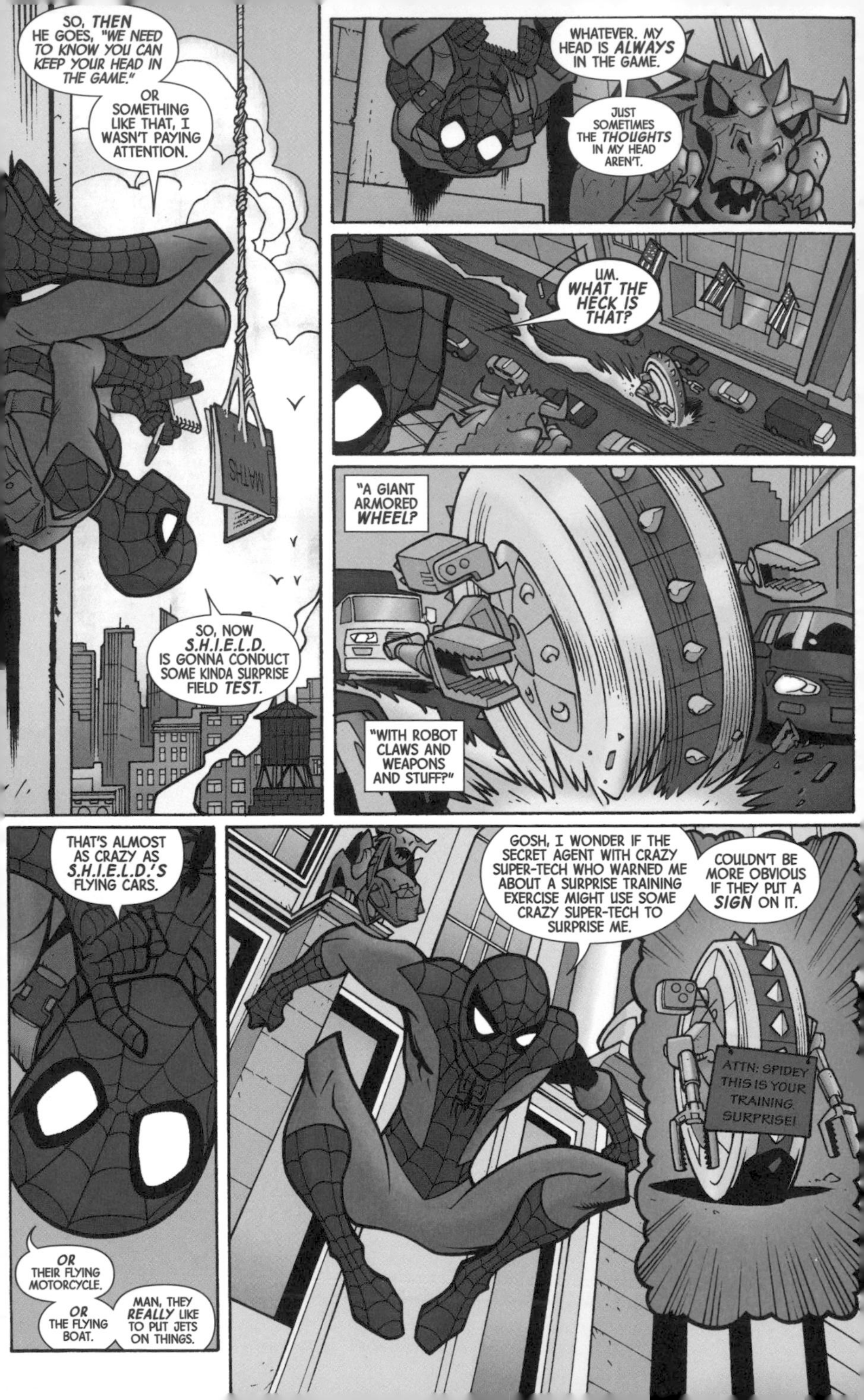
SO, THEN HE GOES, "WE NEED TO KNOW YOU CAN KEEP YOUR HEAD IN THE GAME."
OR SOMETHING LIKE THAT, I WASN'T PAYING ATTENTION.
MATHS
SO, NOW S.H.I.E.L.D. IS GONNA CONDUCT SOME KINDA SURPRISE FIELD TEST.
WHATEVER. MY HEAD IS ALWAYS IN THE GAME.
JUST SOMETIMES THE THOUGHTS IN MY HEAD AREN'T.
UM. WHAT THE HECK IS THAT?
"A GIANT ARMORED WHEEL?
"WITH ROBOT CLAWS AND WEAPONS AND STUFF?"
THAT'S ALMOST AS CRAZY AS S.H.I.E.L.D.'S FLYING CARS.
OR THEIR FLYING MOTORCYCLE.
OR THE FLYING BOAT.
MAN, THEY REALLY LIKE TO PUT JETS ON THINGS.
GOSH, I WONDER IF THE SECRET AGENT WITH CRAZY SUPER-TECH WHO WARNED ME ABOUT A SURPRISE TRAINING EXERCISE MIGHT USE SOME CRAZY SUPER-TECH TO SURPRISE ME.
COULDN'T BE MORE OBVIOUS IF THEY PUT A SIGN ON IT.
ATTN: SPIDEY THIS IS YOUR TRAINING SURPRISE!

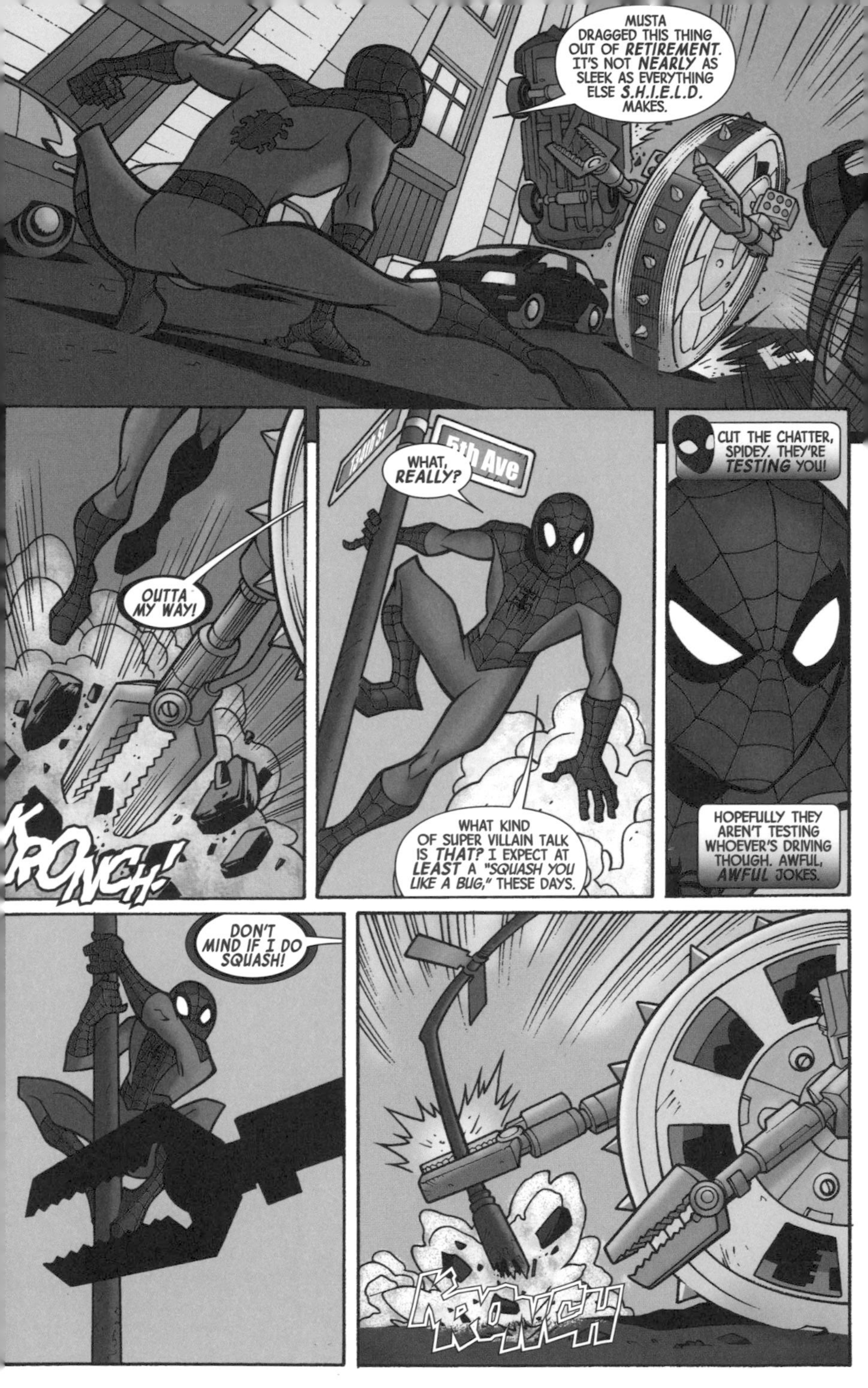

MUSTA DRAGGED THIS THING OUT OF RETIREMENT. IT'S NOT NEARLY AS SLEEK AS EVERYTHING ELSE S.H.I.E.L.D. MAKES.
OUTTA MY WAY!
KRONCH!
134th St
5th Ave
WHAT, REALLY?
WHAT KIND OF SUPER VILLAIN TALK IS THAT? I EXPECT AT LEAST A "SQUASH YOU LIKE A BUG," THESE DAYS.
CUT THE CHATTER, SPIDEY. THEY'RE TESTING YOU!
HOPEFULLY THEY AREN'T TESTING WHOEVER'S DRIVING THOUGH. AWFUL, AWFUL JOKES.
DON'T MIND IF I DO SQUASH!
KRONCH

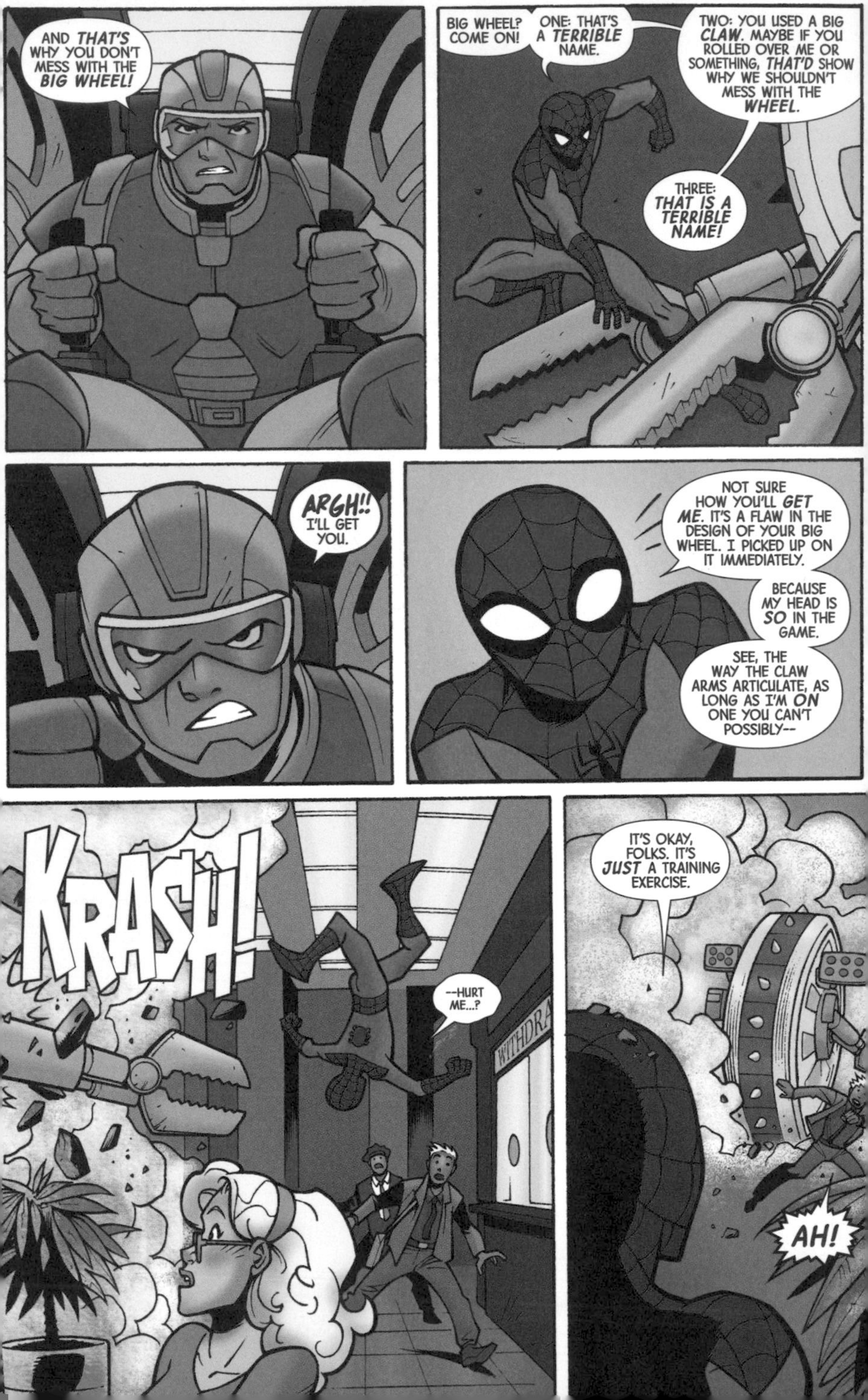
AND THAT'S WHY YOU DON'T MESS WITH THE BIG WHEEL!
BIG WHEEL? COME ON!
ONE: THAT'S A TERRIBLE NAME.
TWO: YOU USED A BIG CLAW. MAYBE IF YOU ROLLED OVER ME OR SOMETHING, THAT'D SHOW WHY WE SHOULDN'T MESS WITH THE WHEEL.
THREE: THAT IS A TERRIBLE NAME!
ARGH!! I'LL GET YOU.
NOT SURE HOW YOU'LL GET ME. IT'S A FLAW IN THE DESIGN OF YOUR BIG WHEEL. I PICKED UP ON IT IMMEDIATELY.
BECAUSE MY HEAD IS SO IN THE GAME.
SEE, THE WAY THE CLAW ARMS ARTICULATE, AS LONG AS I'M ON ONE YOU CAN'T POSSIBLY--
KRASH!
--HURT ME...?
WITHDRA
IT'S OKAY, FOLKS. IT'S JUST A TRAINING EXERCISE.
AH!

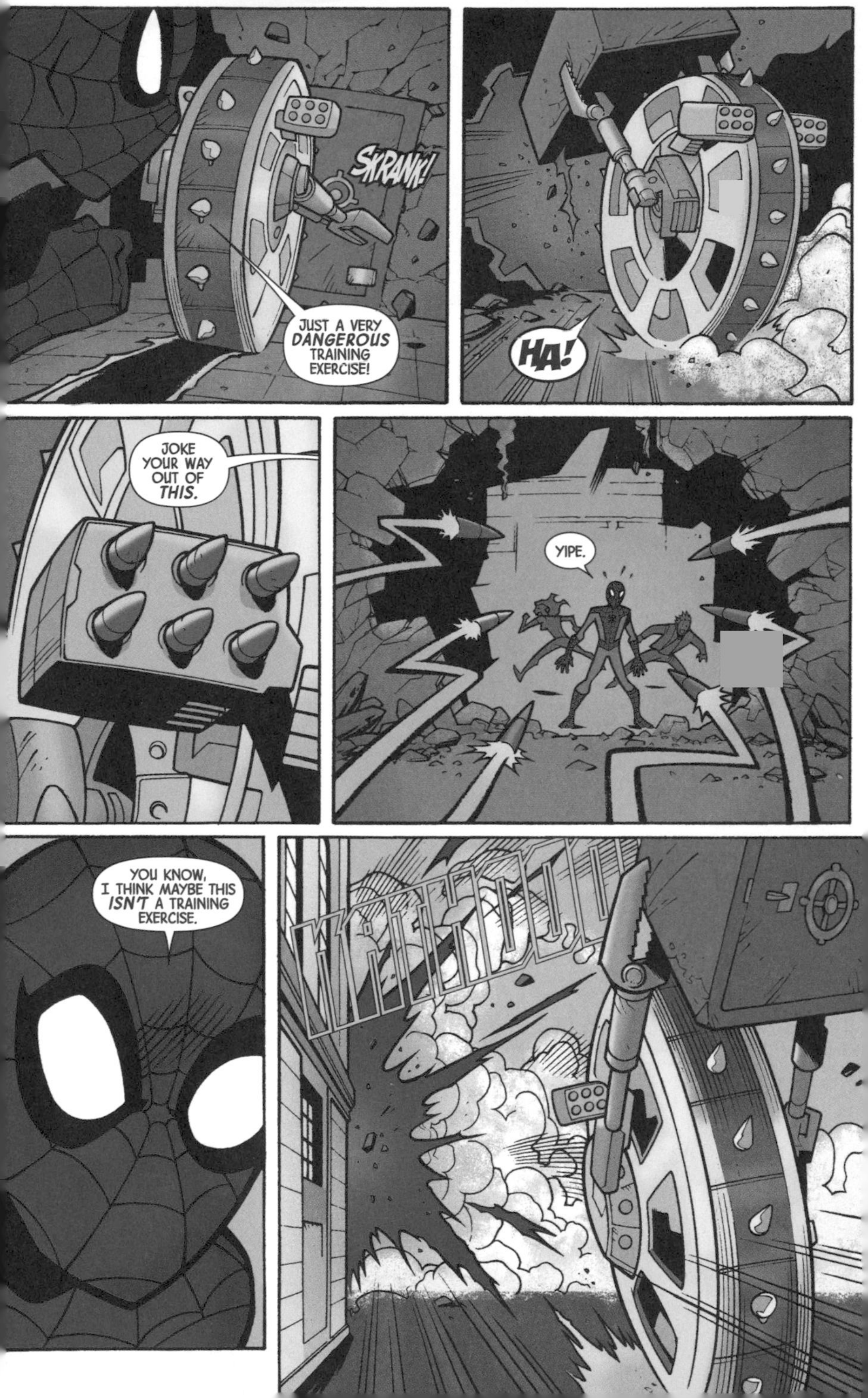
SKRANK!
JUST A VERY DANGEROUS TRAINING EXERCISE!
HA!
JOKE YOUR WAY OUT OF THIS.
YIPE.
YOU KNOW, I THINK MAYBE THIS ISN'T A TRAINING EXERCISE.

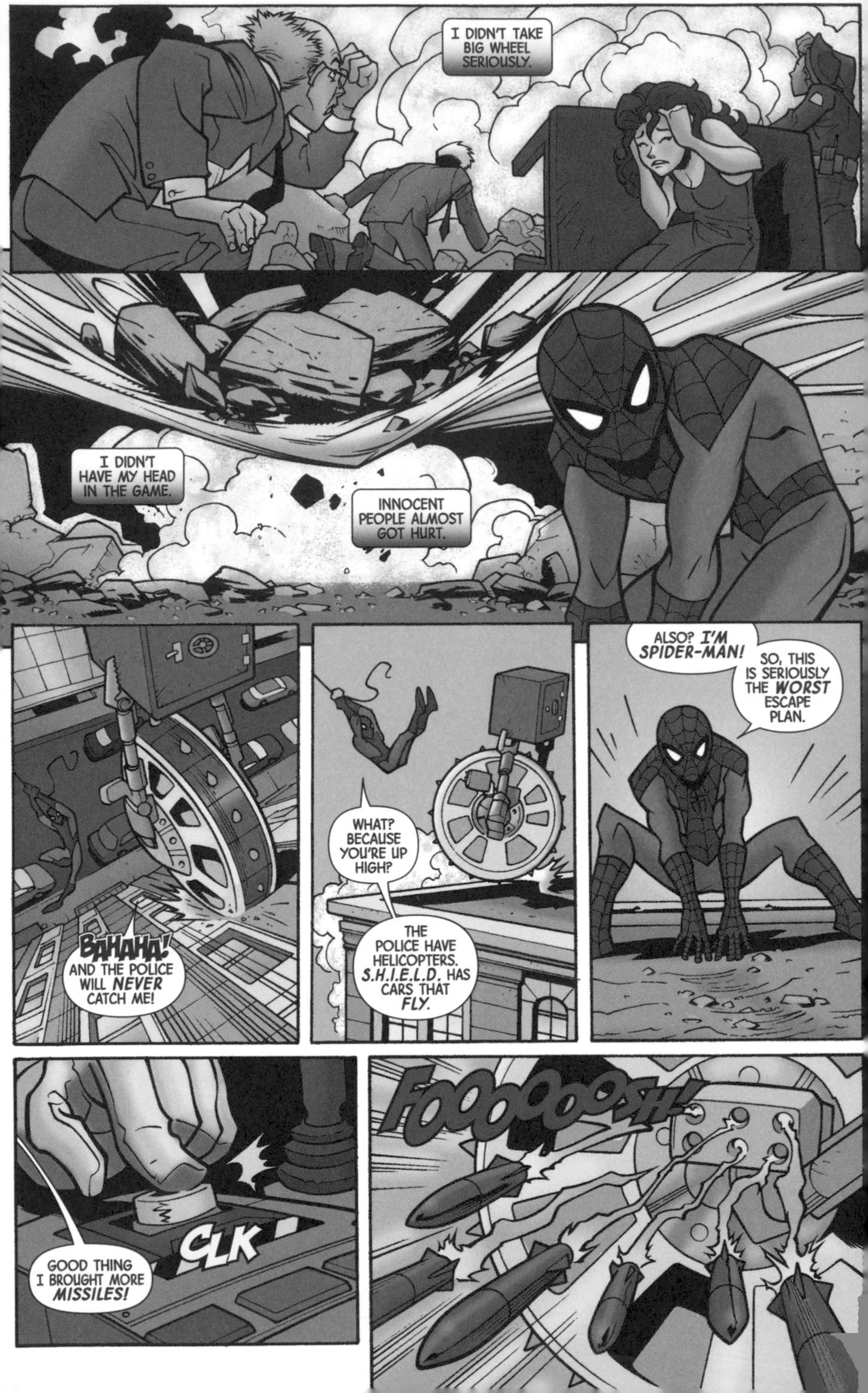
I DIDN'T TAKE BIG WHEEL SERIOUSLY.
I DIDN'T HAVE MY HEAD IN THE GAME.
INNOCENT PEOPLE ALMOST GOT HURT.
BAHAHA!
AND THE POLICE WILL NEVER CATCH ME!
WHAT? BECAUSE YOU'RE UP HIGH?
THE POLICE HAVE HELICOPTERS. S.H.I.E.L.D. HAS CARS THAT FLY.
ALSO? I'M SPIDER-MAN!
SO, THIS IS SERIOUSLY THE WORST ESCAPE PLAN.
CLK
GOOD THING I BROUGHT MORE MISSILES!
FOOOOOOSH!

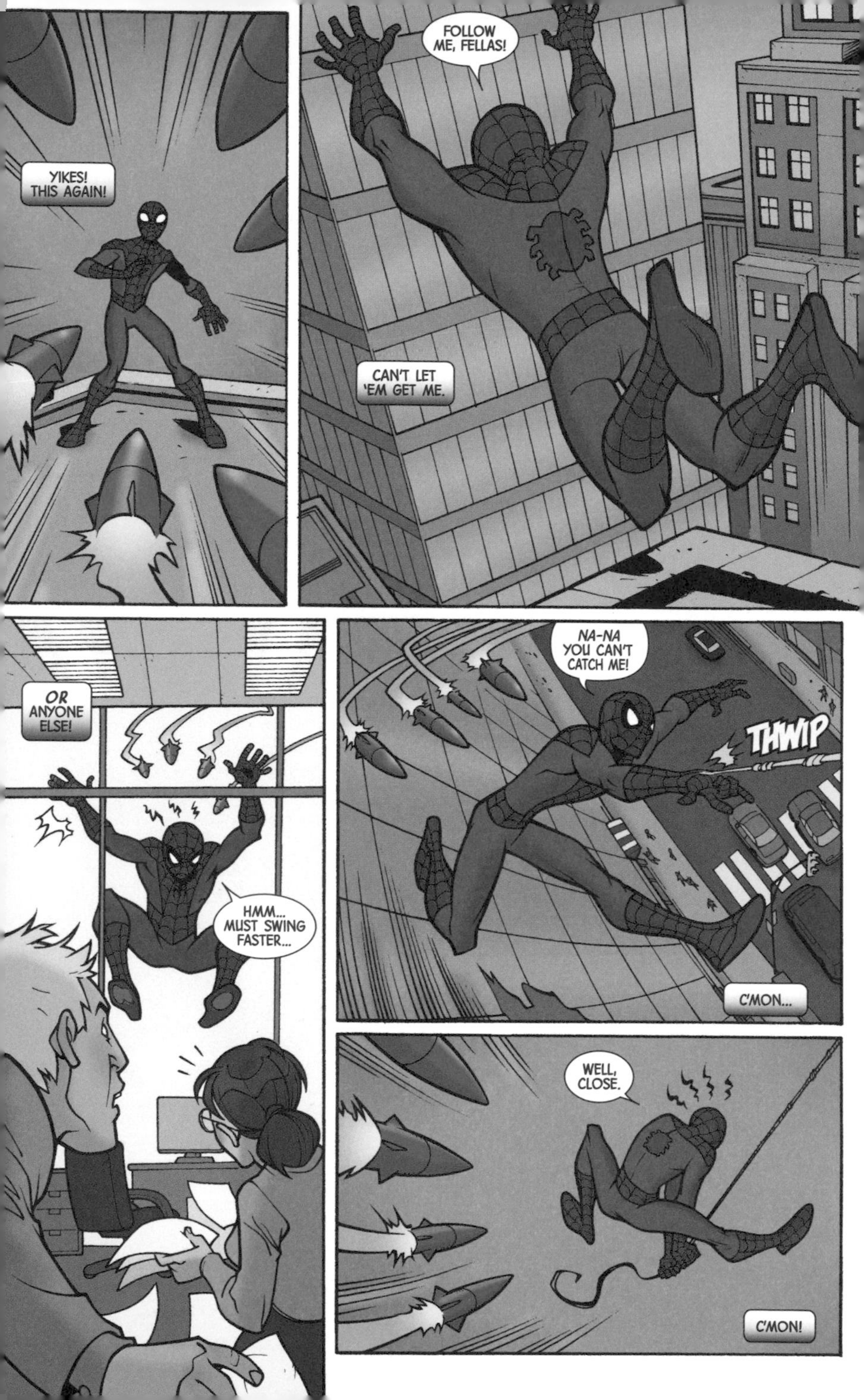
YIKES! THIS AGAIN!
FOLLOW ME, FELLAS!
CAN'T LET 'EM GET ME.
OR ANYONE ELSE!
HMM... MUST SWING FASTER...
NA-NA YOU CAN'T CATCH ME!
THWIP
C'MON...
WELL, CLOSE.
C'MON!

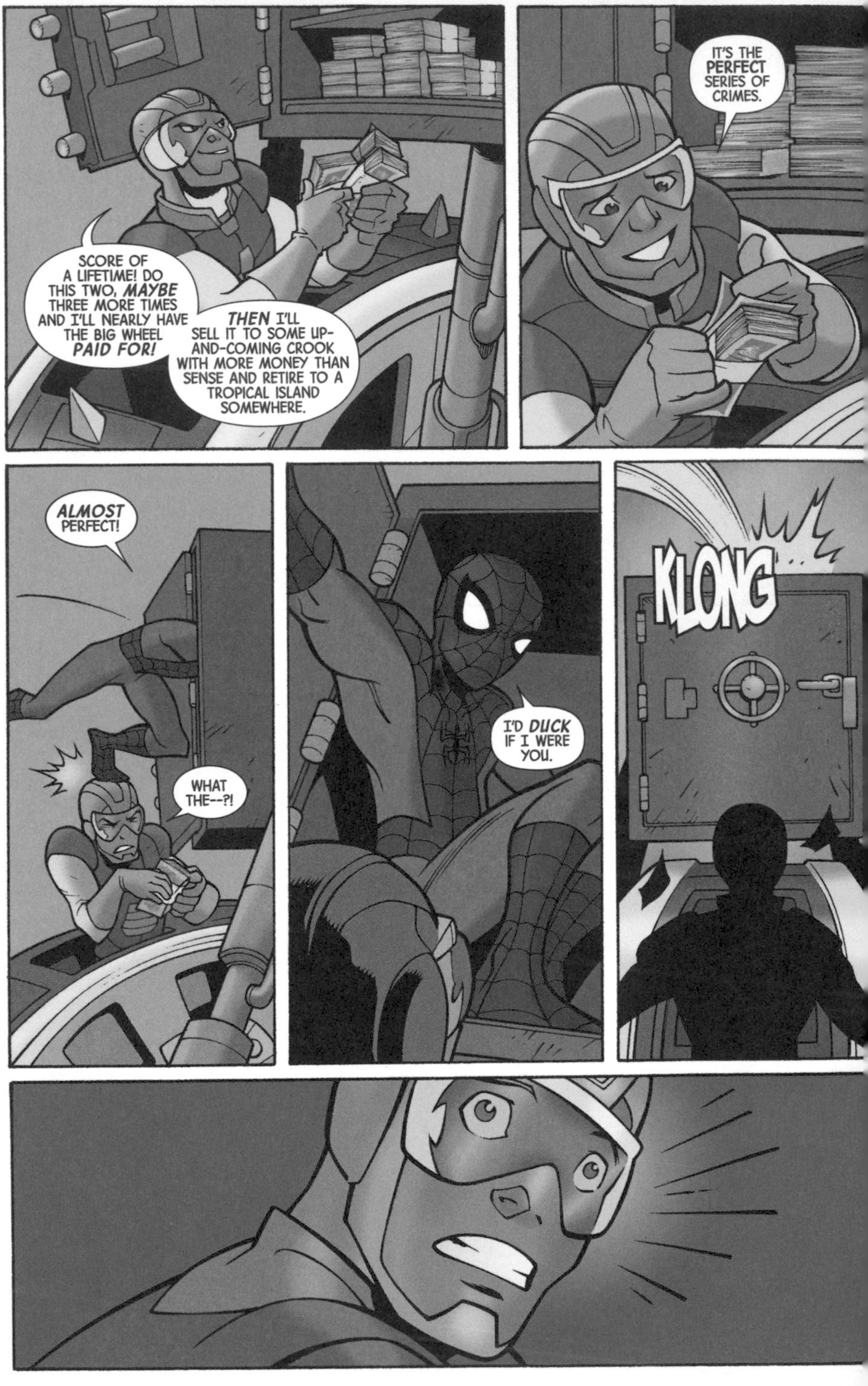
SCORE OF A LIFETIME! DO THIS TWO, MAYBE THREE MORE TIMES AND I'LL NEARLY HAVE THE BIG WHEEL PAID FOR!
THEN I'LL SELL IT TO SOME UP-AND-COMING CROOK WITH MORE MONEY THAN SENSE AND RETIRE TO A TROPICAL ISLAND SOMEWHERE.
IT'S THE PERFECT SERIES OF CRIMES.
ALMOST PERFECT!
WHAT THE--?!
I'D DUCK IF I WERE YOU.
KLONG

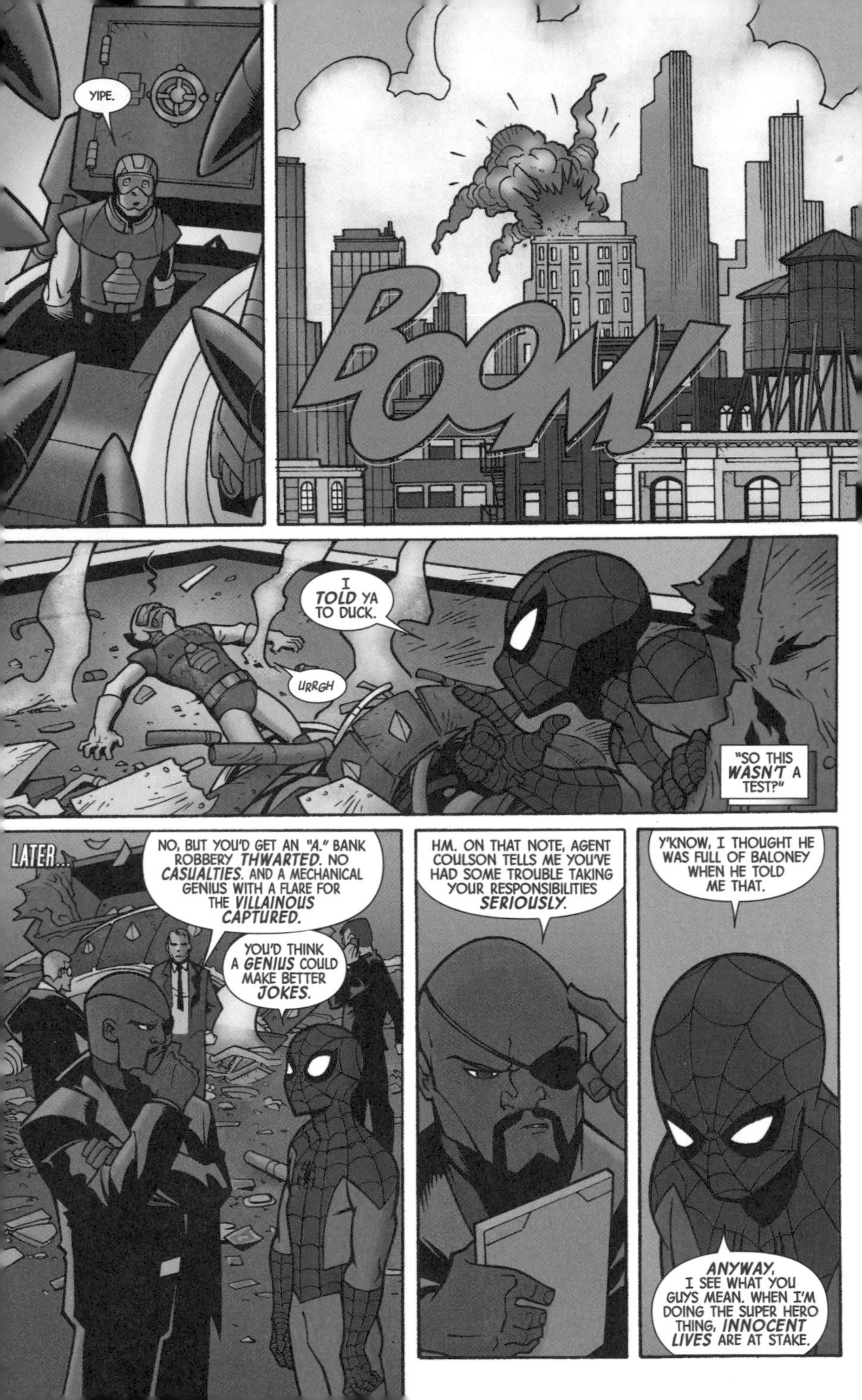
YIPE.
BOOM!
I TOLD YA TO DUCK.
URRGH
"SO THIS WASN'T A TEST?"
LATER...
NO, BUT YOU'D GET AN "A." BANK ROBBERY THWARTED. NO CASUALTIES. AND A MECHANICAL GENIUS WITH A FLARE FOR THE VILLAINOUS CAPTURED.
YOU'D THINK A GENIUS COULD MAKE BETTER JOKES.
HM. ON THAT NOTE, AGENT COULSON TELLS ME YOU'VE HAD SOME TROUBLE TAKING YOUR RESPONSIBILITIES SERIOUSLY.
Y'KNOW, I THOUGHT HE WAS FULL OF BALONEY WHEN HE TOLD ME THAT.
ANYWAY, I SEE WHAT YOU GUYS MEAN. WHEN I'M DOING THE SUPER HERO THING, INNOCENT LIVES ARE AT STAKE.

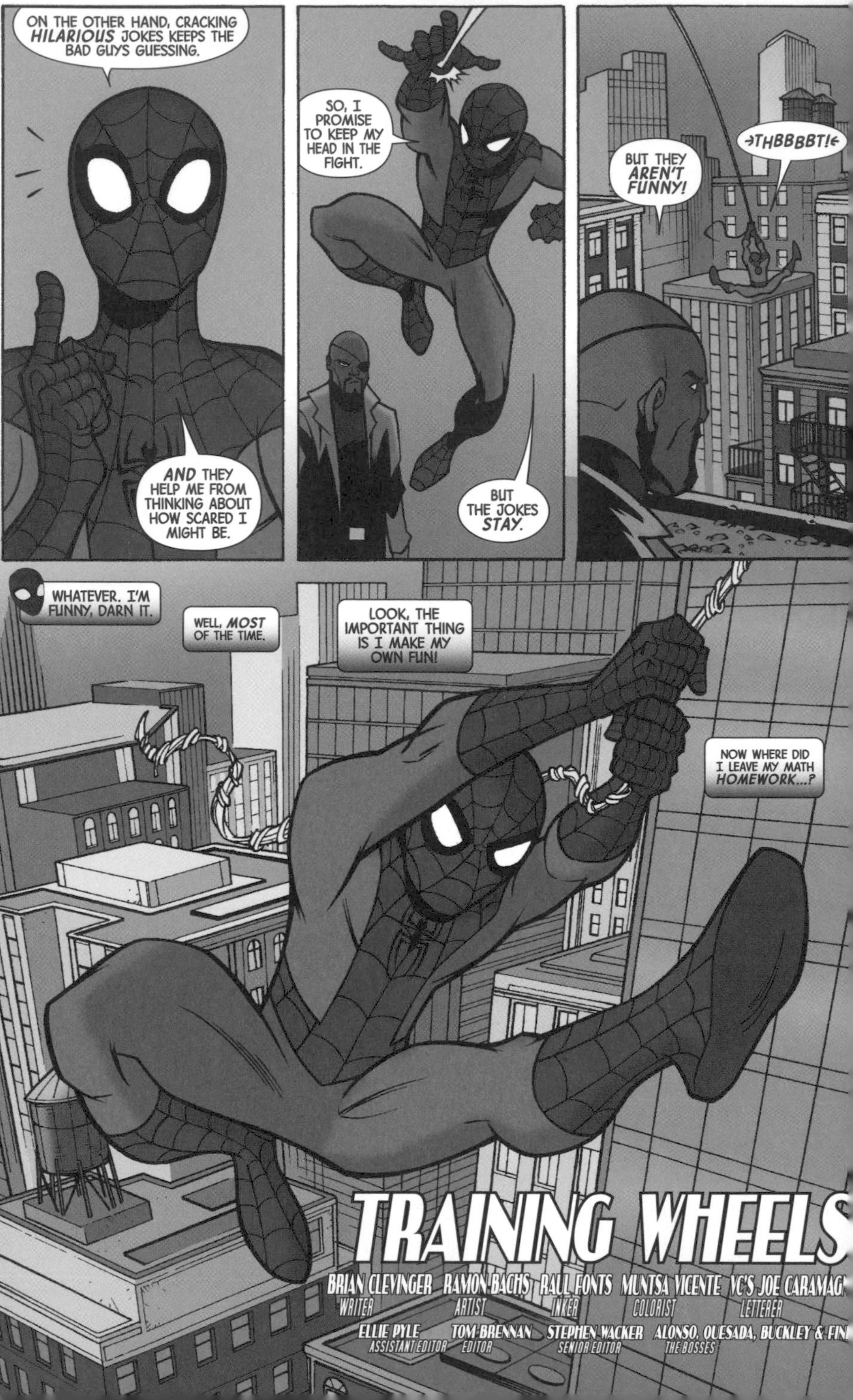
ON THE OTHER HAND, CRACKING HILARIOUS JOKES KEEPS THE BAD GUYS GUESSING.
AND THEY HELP ME FROM THINKING ABOUT HOW SCARED I MIGHT BE.
SO, I PROMISE TO KEEP MY HEAD IN THE FIGHT.
BUT THE JOKES STAY.
BUT THEY AREN'T FUNNY!
THBBBBT!
WHATEVER. I'M FUNNY, DARN IT.
WELL, MOST OF THE TIME.
LOOK, THE IMPORTANT THING IS I MAKE MY OWN FUN!
NOW WHERE DID I LEAVE MY MATH HOMEWORK...?
TRAINING WHEELS
BRIAN CLEVINGER WRITER
RAMON BACHS ARTIST
RAUL FONTS INKER
MUNTSA VICENTE COLORIST
VC'S JOE CARAMAGI LETTERER
ELLIE PYLE ASSISTANT EDITOR
TOM BRENNAN EDITOR
STEPHEN WACKER SENIOR EDITOR
ALONSO, QUESADA, BUCKLEY & FIN THE BOSSES

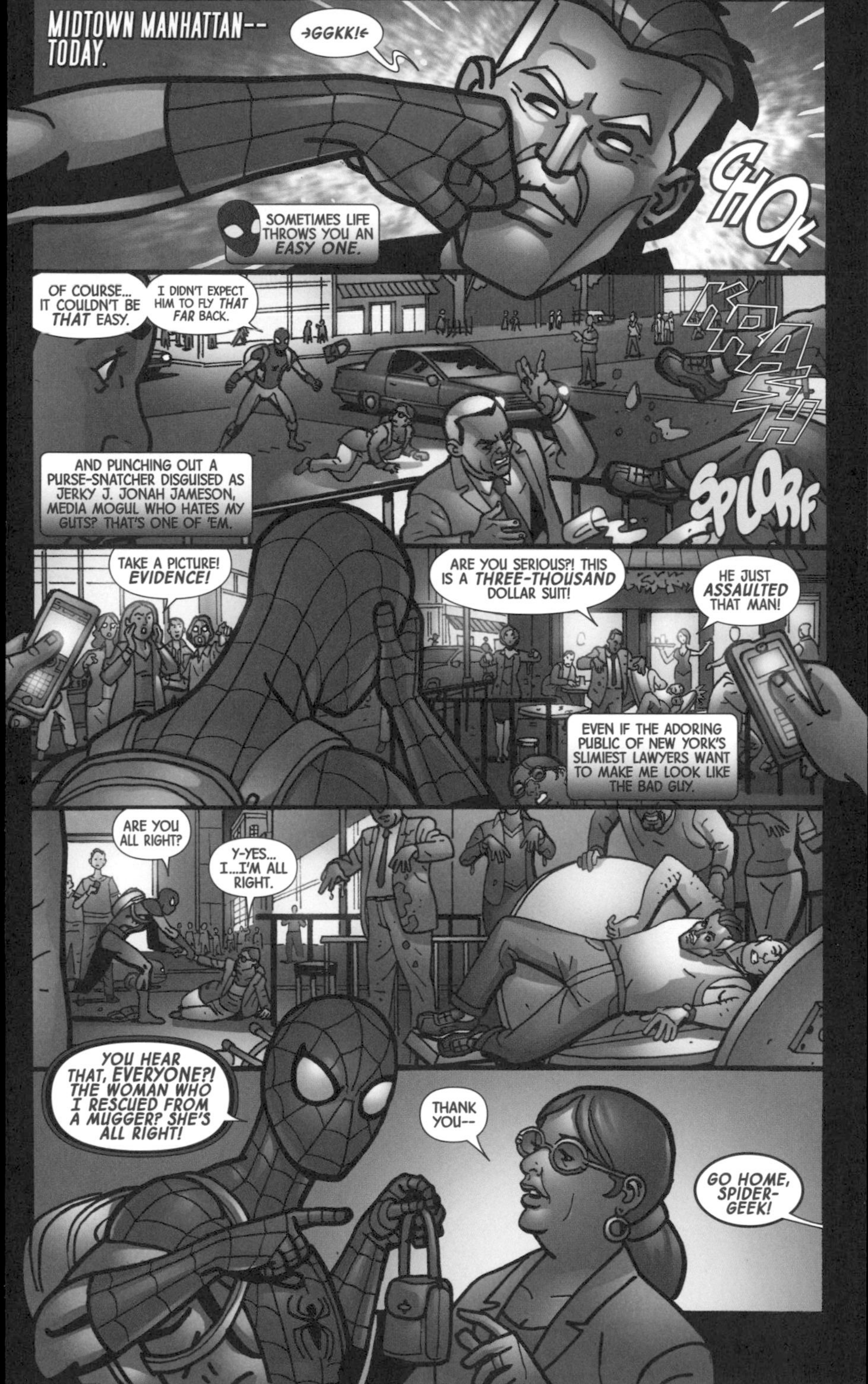

MIDTOWN MANHATTAN-- TODAY.
GGKK!
CHOK
SOMETIMES LIFE THROWS YOU AN EASY ONE.
OF COURSE... IT COULDN'T BE THAT EASY.
I DIDN'T EXPECT HIM TO FLY THAT FAR BACK.
KRASH
AND PUNCHING OUT A PURSE-SNATCHER DISGUISED AS JERKY J. JONAH JAMESON, MEDIA MOGUL WHO HATES MY GUTS? THAT'S ONE OF 'EM.
SPLORF
TAKE A PICTURE! EVIDENCE!
ARE YOU SERIOUS?! THIS IS A THREE-THOUSAND DOLLAR SUIT!
HE JUST ASSAULTED THAT MAN!
EVEN IF THE ADORING PUBLIC OF NEW YORK'S SLIMIEST LAWYERS WANT TO MAKE ME LOOK LIKE THE BAD GUY.
ARE YOU ALL RIGHT?
Y-YES... I...I'M ALL RIGHT.
YOU HEAR THAT, EVERYONE?! THE WOMAN WHO I RESCUED FROM A MUGGER? SHE'S ALL RIGHT!
THANK YOU--
GO HOME, SPIDER-GEEK!

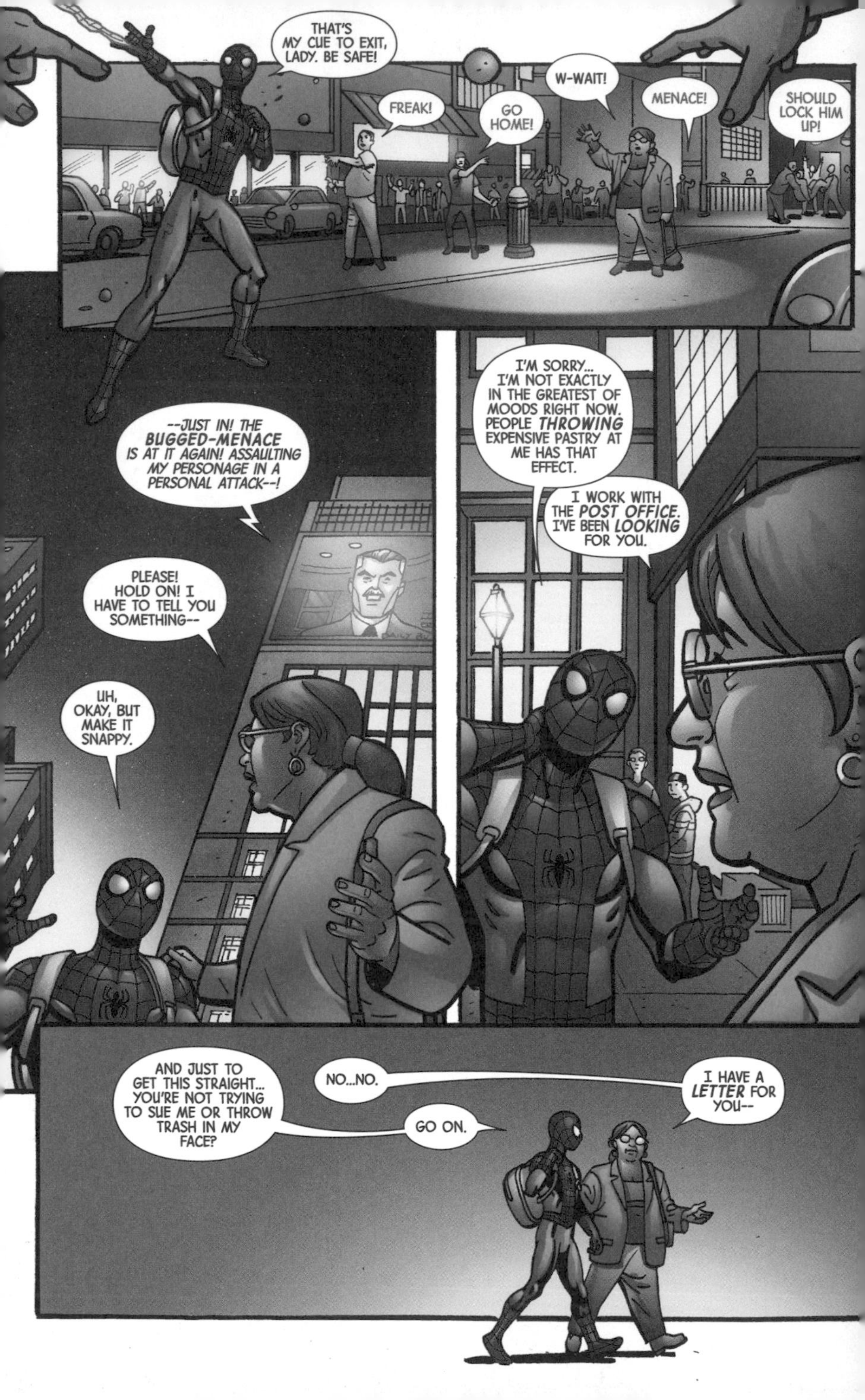
THAT'S MY CUE TO EXIT, LADY. BE SAFE!
FREAK!
GO HOME!
W-WAIT!
MENACE!
SHOULD LOCK HIM UP!
--JUST IN! THE BUGGED-MENACE IS AT IT AGAIN! ASSAULTING MY PERSONAGE IN A PERSONAL ATTACK--!
PLEASE! HOLD ON! I HAVE TO TELL YOU SOMETHING--
UH, OKAY, BUT MAKE IT SNAPPY.
I'M SORRY... I'M NOT EXACTLY IN THE GREATEST OF MOODS RIGHT NOW. PEOPLE THROWING EXPENSIVE PASTRY AT ME HAS THAT EFFECT.
I WORK WITH THE POST OFFICE. I'VE BEEN LOOKING FOR YOU.
AND JUST TO GET THIS STRAIGHT... YOU'RE NOT TRYING TO SUE ME OR THROW TRASH IN MY FACE?
NO...NO.
GO ON.
I HAVE A LETTER FOR YOU--

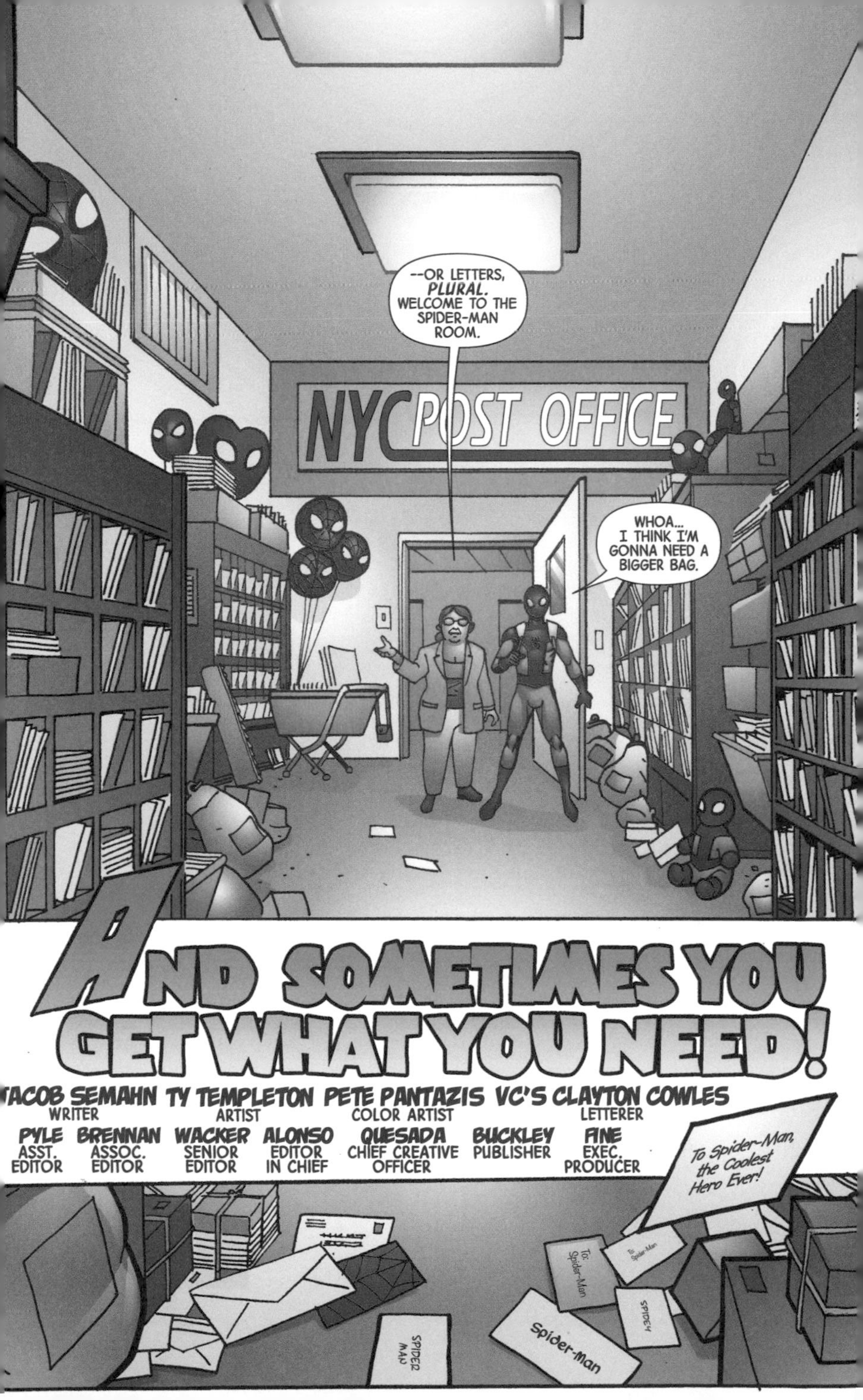
--OR LETTERS, PLURAL. WELCOME TO THE SPIDER-MAN ROOM.
NYC POST OFFICE
WHOA... I THINK I'M GONNA NEED A BIGGER BAG.
AND SOMETIMES YOU GET WHAT YOU NEED!
JACOB SEMAHN WRITER
TY TEMPLETON ARTIST
PETE PANTAZIS COLOR ARTIST
VC'S CLAYTON COWLES LETTERER
PYLE ASST. EDITOR
BRENNAN ASSOC. EDITOR
WACKER SENIOR EDITOR
ALONSO EDITOR IN CHIEF
QUESADA CHIEF CREATIVE OFFICER
BUCKLEY PUBLISHER
FINE EXEC. PRODUCER
To Spider-Man, the Coolest Hero Ever!
To: Spider-Man
To: Spider-Man
SPIDEY
Spider-Man
SPIDER MAN

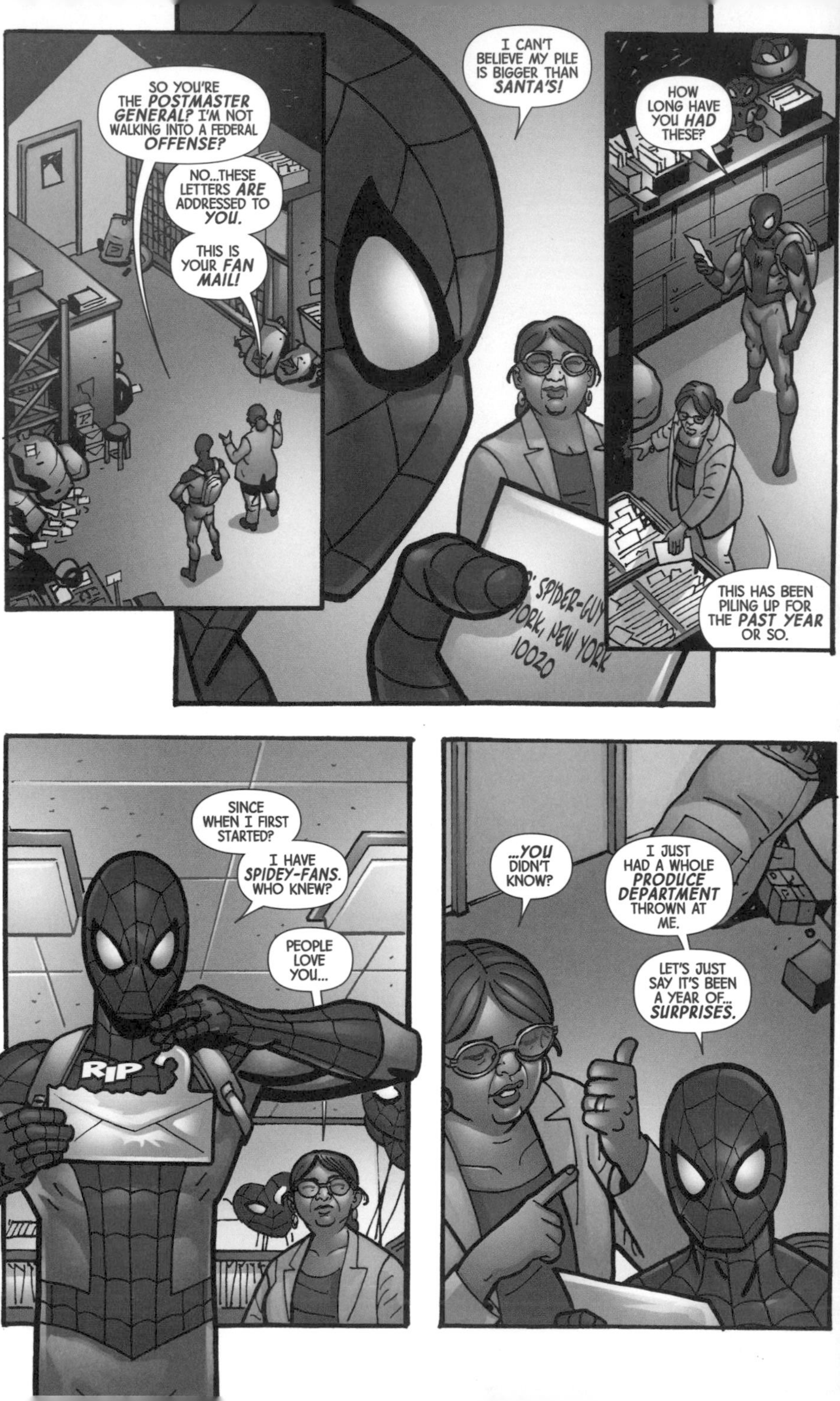

SO YOU'RE THE POSTMASTER GENERAL? I'M NOT WALKING INTO A FEDERAL OFFENSE?
NO...THESE LETTERS ARE ADDRESSED TO YOU.
THIS IS YOUR FAN MAIL!
I CAN'T BELIEVE MY PILE IS BIGGER THAN SANTA'S!
SPIDER-GUY
NEW YORK
10020
HOW LONG HAVE YOU HAD THESE?
THIS HAS BEEN PILING UP FOR THE PAST YEAR OR SO.
SINCE WHEN I FIRST STARTED?
I HAVE SPIDEY-FANS. WHO KNEW?
PEOPLE LOVE YOU...
RIP
...YOU DIDN'T KNOW?
I JUST HAD A WHOLE PRODUCE DEPARTMENT THROWN AT ME.
LET'S JUST SAY IT'S BEEN A YEAR OF... SURPRISES.

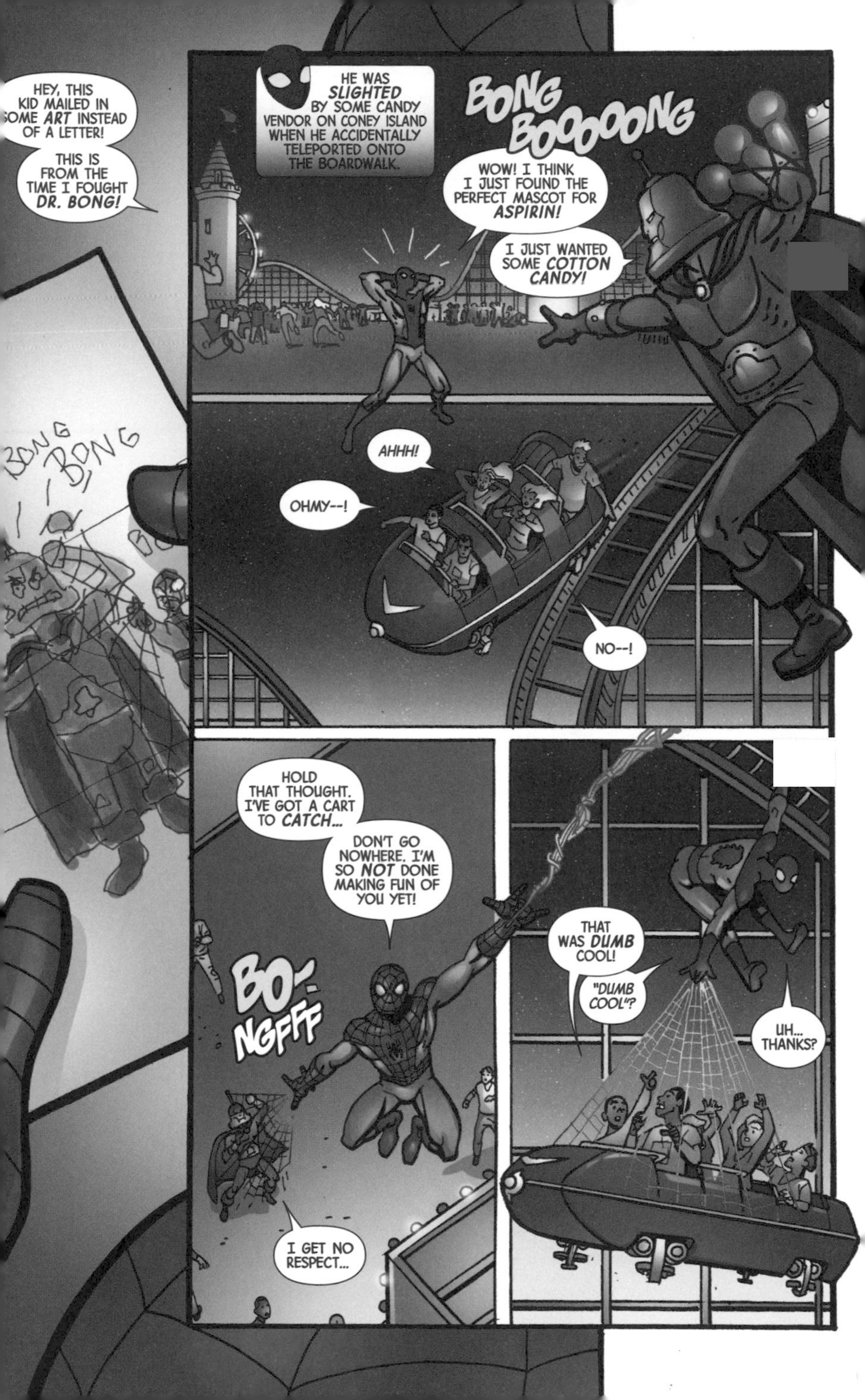
HEY, THIS KID MAILED IN SOME ART INSTEAD OF A LETTER!
THIS IS FROM THE TIME I FOUGHT DR. BONG!
BONG BONG
HE WAS SLIGHTED BY SOME CANDY VENDOR ON CONEY ISLAND WHEN HE ACCIDENTALLY TELEPORTED ONTO THE BOARDWALK.
BONG BOOOOONG
WOW! I THINK I JUST FOUND THE PERFECT MASCOT FOR ASPIRIN!
I JUST WANTED SOME COTTON CANDY!
AHHH!
OHMY--!
NO--!
HOLD THAT THOUGHT. I'VE GOT A CART TO CATCH...
DON'T GO NOWHERE. I'M SO NOT DONE MAKING FUN OF YOU YET!
BO-NGFFF
I GET NO RESPECT...
THAT WAS DUMB COOL!
"DUMB COOL"?
UH... THANKS?

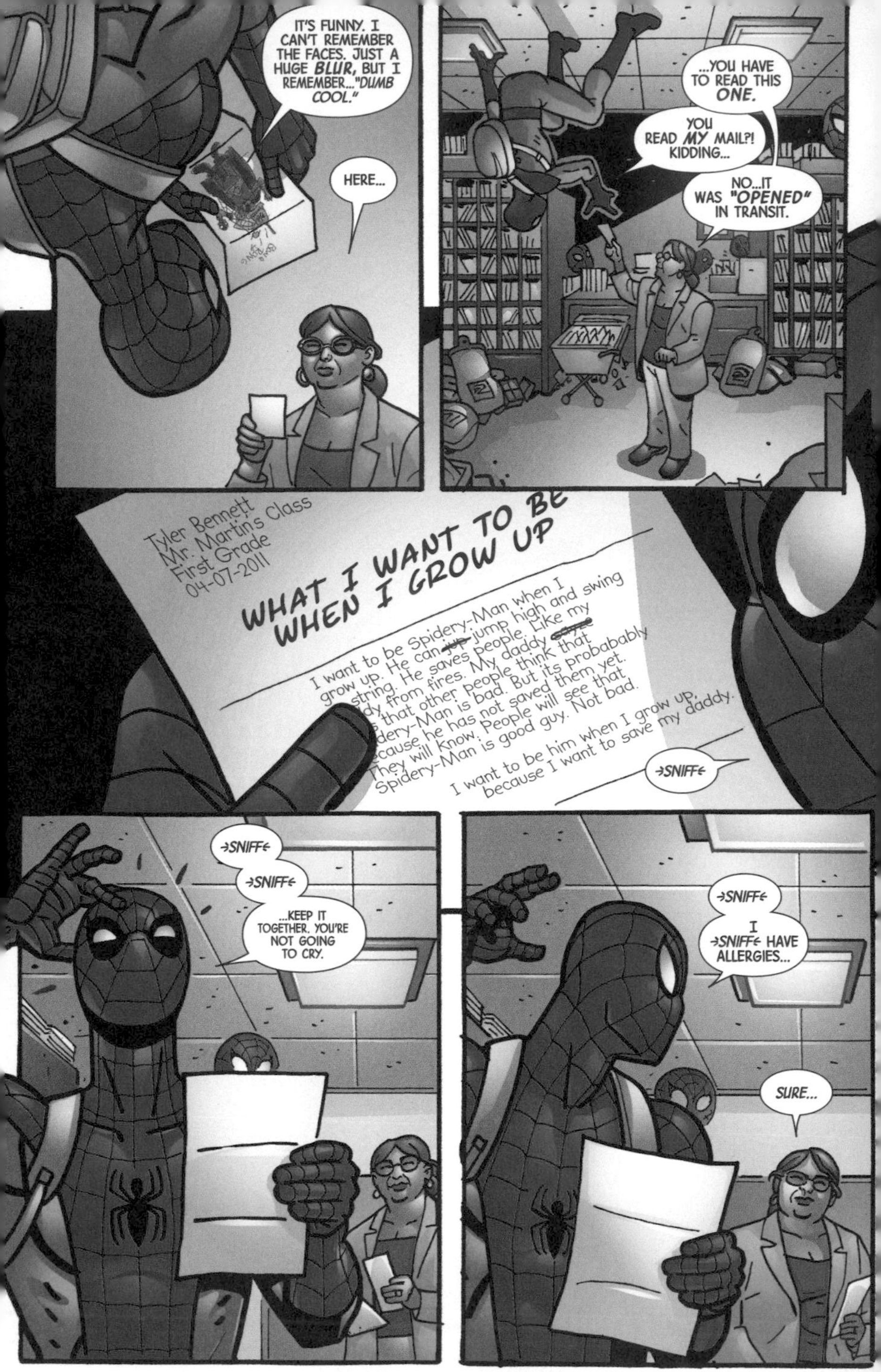
IT'S FUNNY. I CAN'T REMEMBER THE FACES. JUST A HUGE *BLUR*, BUT I REMEMBER..."*DUMB COOL.*"
HERE...
...YOU HAVE TO READ THIS *ONE.*
YOU READ *MY* MAIL?! KIDDING...
NO...IT WAS *"OPENED"* IN TRANSIT.
Tyler Bennett
Mr. Martin's Class
First Grade
04-07-2011
WHAT I WANT TO BE WHEN I GROW UP
I want to be Spidery-Man when I
grow up. He can ~~jup~~ jump high and swing
string. He saves people. Like my
dy from fires. My daddy
that other people think that
dery-Man is bad. But its probabably
ecause he has not saved them yet.
They will Know. People will see that
Spidery-Man is good guy. Not bad.
I want to be him when I grow up,
because I want to save my daddy.
→SNIFF←
→SNIFF←
→SNIFF←
...KEEP IT TOGETHER. YOU'RE NOT GOING TO CRY.
→SNIFF←
I →SNIFF← HAVE ALLERGIES...
SURE...

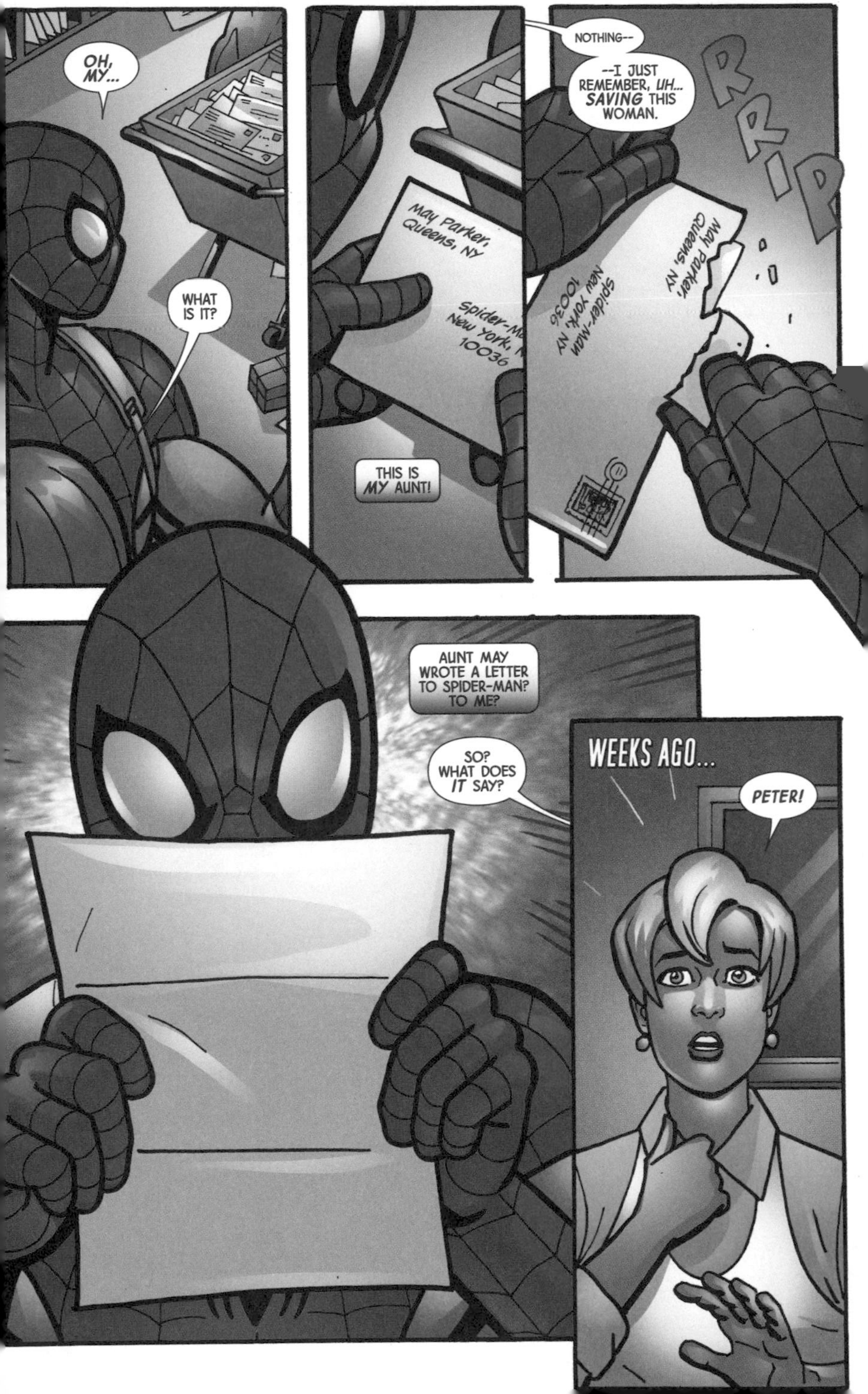

OH, MY...
WHAT IS IT?
May Parker, Queens, NY
Spider-Man New York, NY 10036
THIS IS MY AUNT!
NOTHING--
--I JUST REMEMBER, UH... SAVING THIS WOMAN.
RRIP
AUNT MAY WROTE A LETTER TO SPIDER-MAN? TO ME?
SO? WHAT DOES IT SAY?
WEEKS AGO...
PETER!

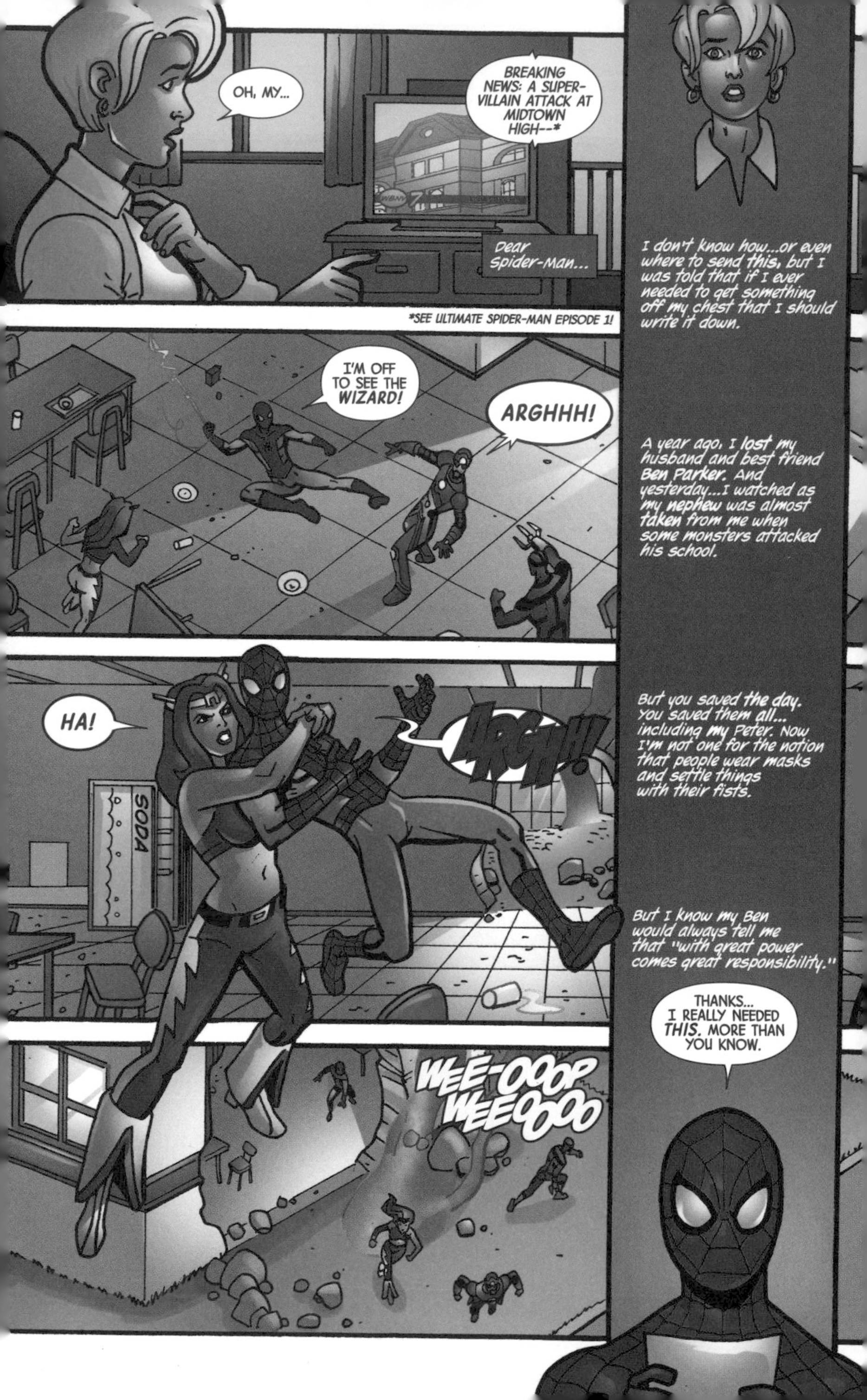
OH, MY...
BREAKING NEWS: A SUPER-VILLAIN ATTACK AT MIDTOWN HIGH--*
Dear Spider-Man...
I don't know how...or even where to send this, but I was told that if I ever needed to get something off my chest that I should write it down.
*SEE ULTIMATE SPIDER-MAN EPISODE 1!
I'M OFF TO SEE THE WIZARD!
ARGHHH!
A year ago, I lost my husband and best friend Ben Parker. And yesterday...I watched as my nephew was almost taken from me when some monsters attacked his school.
HA!
ARGHH!
SODA
But you saved the day. You saved them all... including my Peter. Now I'm not one for the notion that people wear masks and settle things with their fists.
But I know my Ben would always tell me that "with great power comes great responsibility."
WEE-OOOP WEEOOOO
THANKS... I REALLY NEEDED THIS. MORE THAN YOU KNOW.

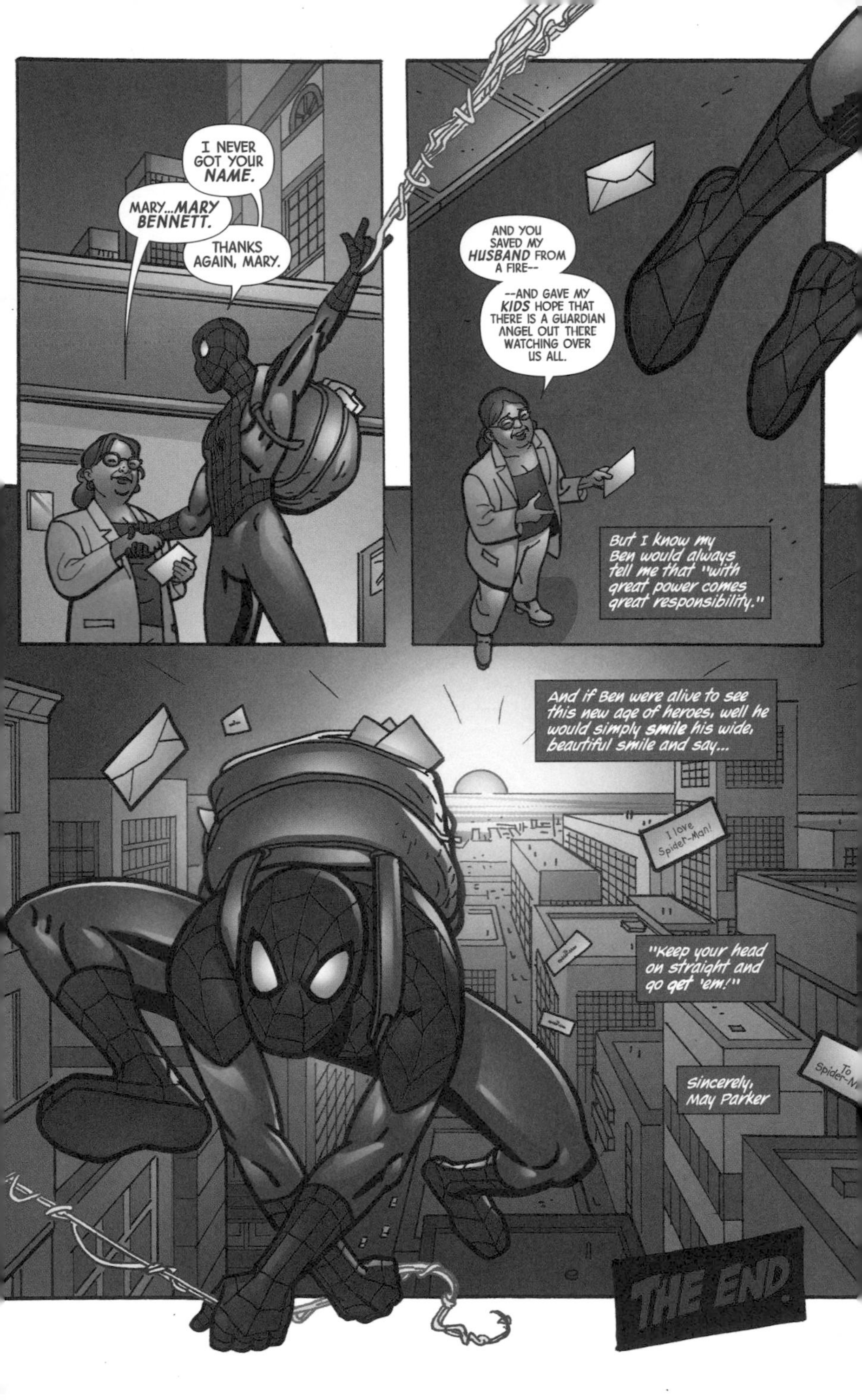
I NEVER GOT YOUR NAME.
MARY...MARY BENNETT.
THANKS AGAIN, MARY.
AND YOU SAVED MY HUSBAND FROM A FIRE--
--AND GAVE MY KIDS HOPE THAT THERE IS A GUARDIAN ANGEL OUT THERE WATCHING OVER US ALL.
But I know my Ben would always tell me that "with great power comes great responsibility."
And if Ben were alive to see this new age of heroes, well he would simply smile his wide, beautiful smile and say...
I love Spider-Man!
"Keep your head on straight and go get 'em!"
Sincerely, May Parker
THE END.

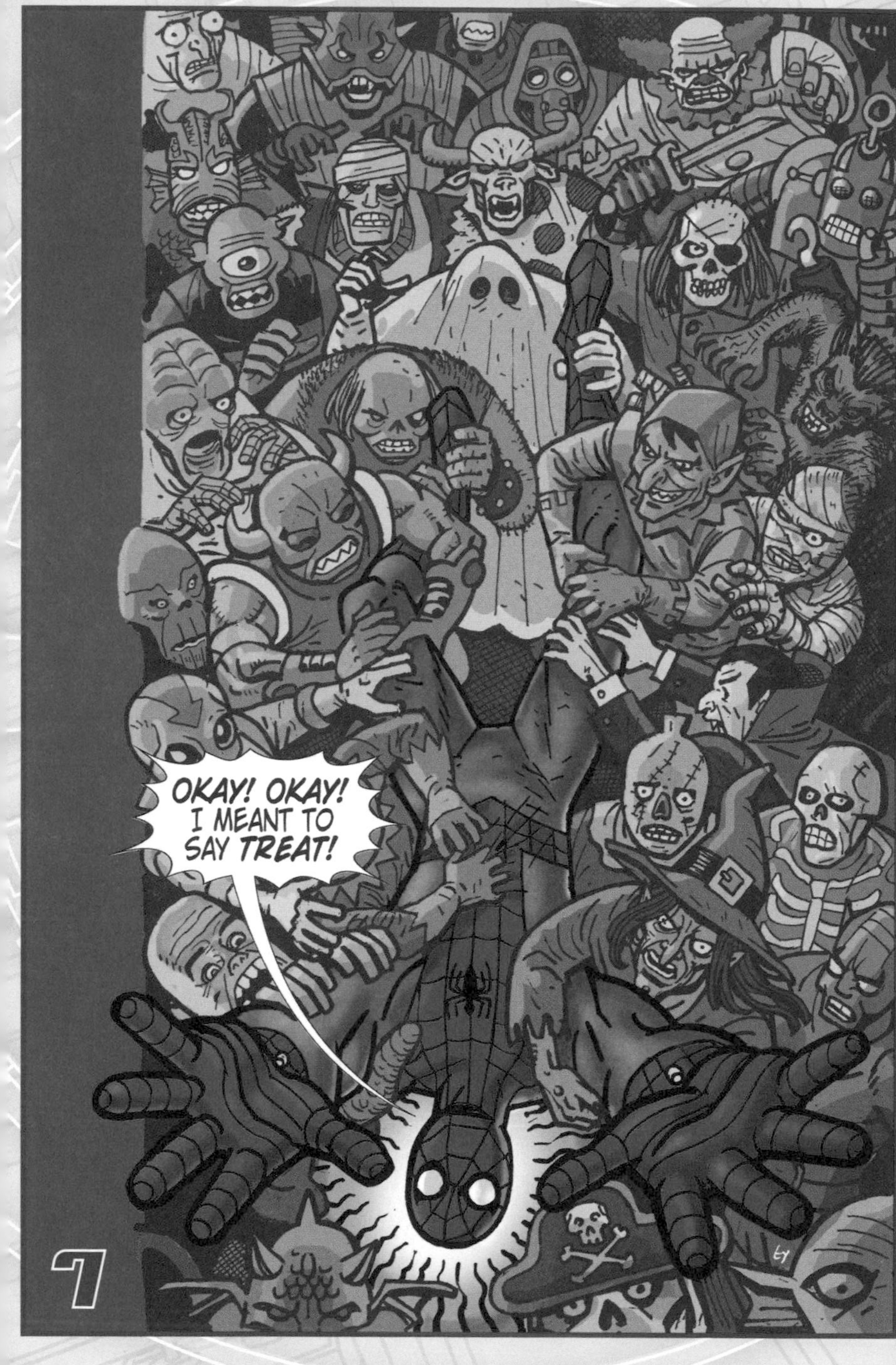
OKAY! OKAY! I MEANT TO SAY TREAT!

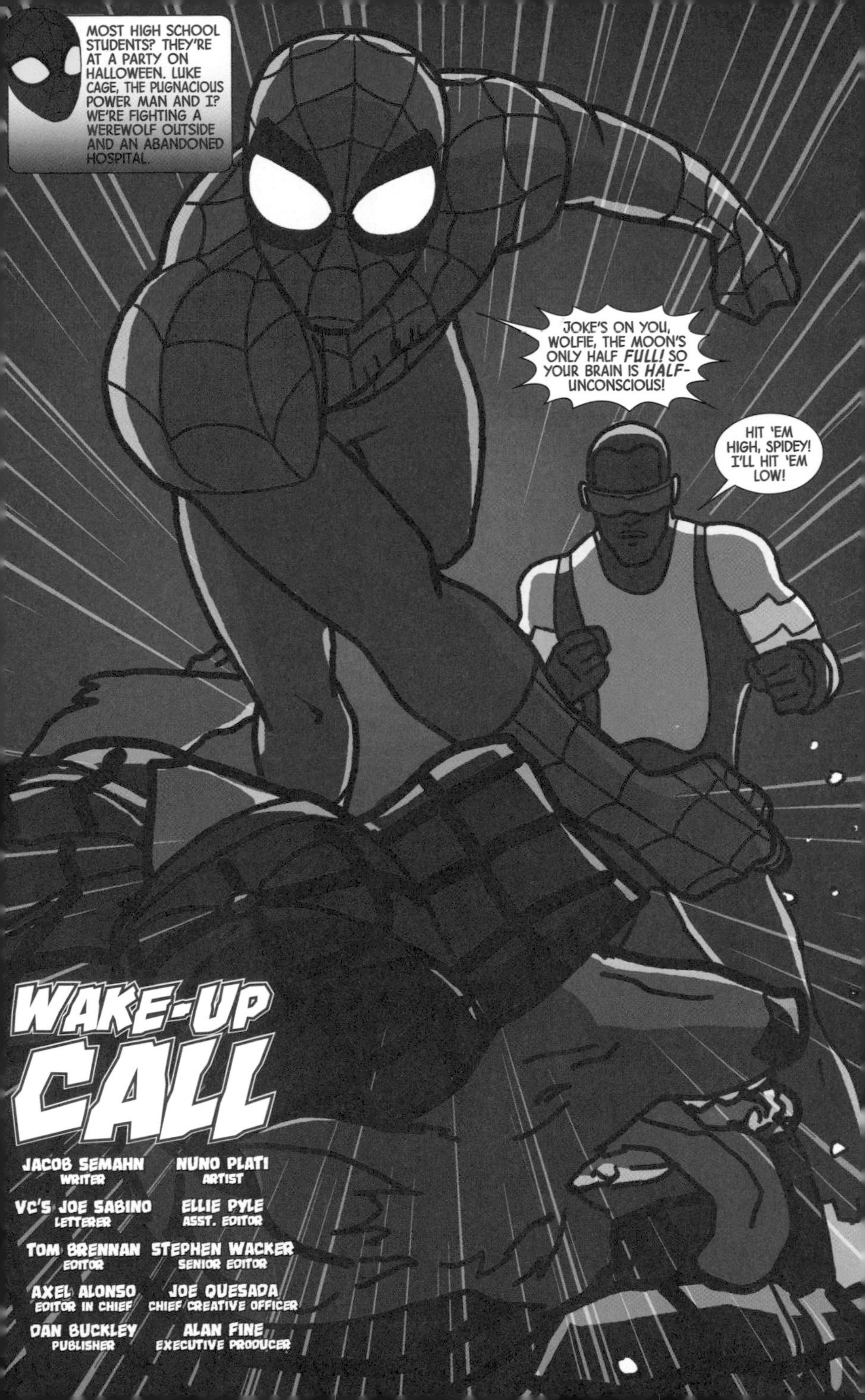
MOST HIGH SCHOOL STUDENTS? THEY'RE AT A PARTY ON HALLOWEEN. LUKE CAGE, THE PUGNACIOUS POWER MAN AND I? WE'RE FIGHTING A WEREWOLF OUTSIDE AND AN ABANDONED HOSPITAL.
JOKE'S ON YOU, WOLFIE, THE MOON'S ONLY HALF FULL! SO YOUR BRAIN IS HALF-UNCONSCIOUS!
HIT 'EM HIGH, SPIDEY! I'LL HIT 'EM LOW!
WAKE-UP CALL
JACOB SEMAHN WRITER
NUNO PLATI ARTIST
VC'S JOE SABINO LETTERER
ELLIE PYLE ASST. EDITOR
TOM BRENNAN EDITOR
STEPHEN WACKER SENIOR EDITOR
AXEL ALONSO EDITOR IN CHIEF
JOE QUESADA CHIEF CREATIVE OFFICER
DAN BUCKLEY PUBLISHER
ALAN FINE EXECUTIVE PRODUCER

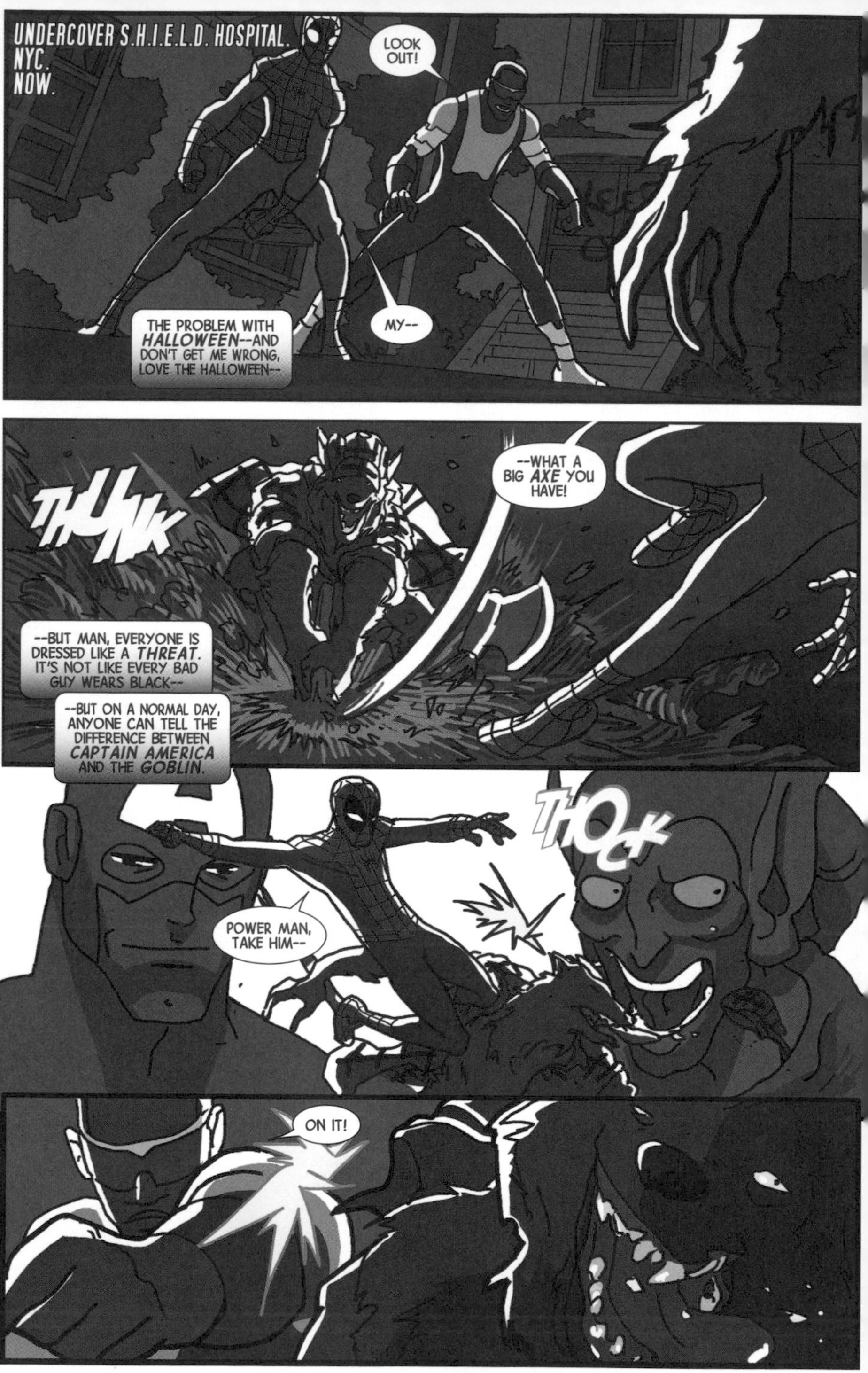
UNDERCOVER S.H.I.E.L.D. HOSPITAL.
NYC.
NOW.
LOOK OUT!
THE PROBLEM WITH HALLOWEEN--AND DON'T GET ME WRONG, LOVE THE HALLOWEEN--
MY--
THUNK
--WHAT A BIG AXE YOU HAVE!
--BUT MAN, EVERYONE IS DRESSED LIKE A THREAT. IT'S NOT LIKE EVERY BAD GUY WEARS BLACK--
--BUT ON A NORMAL DAY, ANYONE CAN TELL THE DIFFERENCE BETWEEN CAPTAIN AMERICA AND THE GOBLIN.
THOCK
POWER MAN, TAKE HIM--
ON IT!

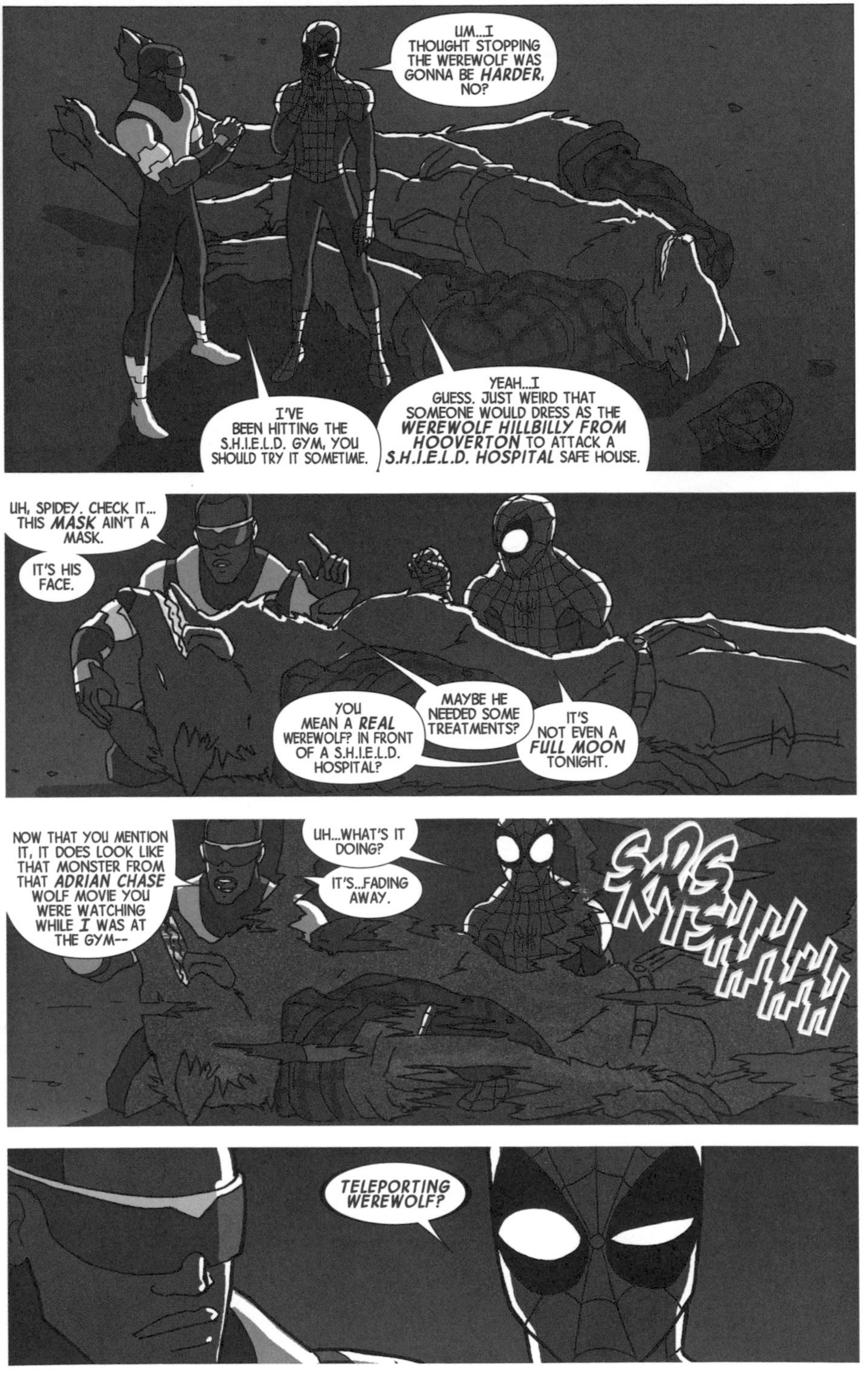
UM...I THOUGHT STOPPING THE WEREWOLF WAS GONNA BE HARDER, NO?
I'VE BEEN HITTING THE S.H.I.E.L.D. GYM, YOU SHOULD TRY IT SOMETIME.
YEAH...I GUESS. JUST WEIRD THAT SOMEONE WOULD DRESS AS THE WEREWOLF HILLBILLY FROM HOOVERTON TO ATTACK A S.H.I.E.L.D. HOSPITAL SAFE HOUSE.
UH, SPIDEY. CHECK IT... THIS MASK AIN'T A MASK.
IT'S HIS FACE.
YOU MEAN A REAL WEREWOLF? IN FRONT OF A S.H.I.E.L.D. HOSPITAL?
MAYBE HE NEEDED SOME TREATMENTS?
IT'S NOT EVEN A FULL MOON TONIGHT.
NOW THAT YOU MENTION IT, IT DOES LOOK LIKE THAT MONSTER FROM THAT ADRIAN CHASE WOLF MOVIE YOU WERE WATCHING WHILE I WAS AT THE GYM--
UH...WHAT'S IT DOING?
IT'S...FADING AWAY.
SKRSHHHHH
TELEPORTING WEREWOLF?

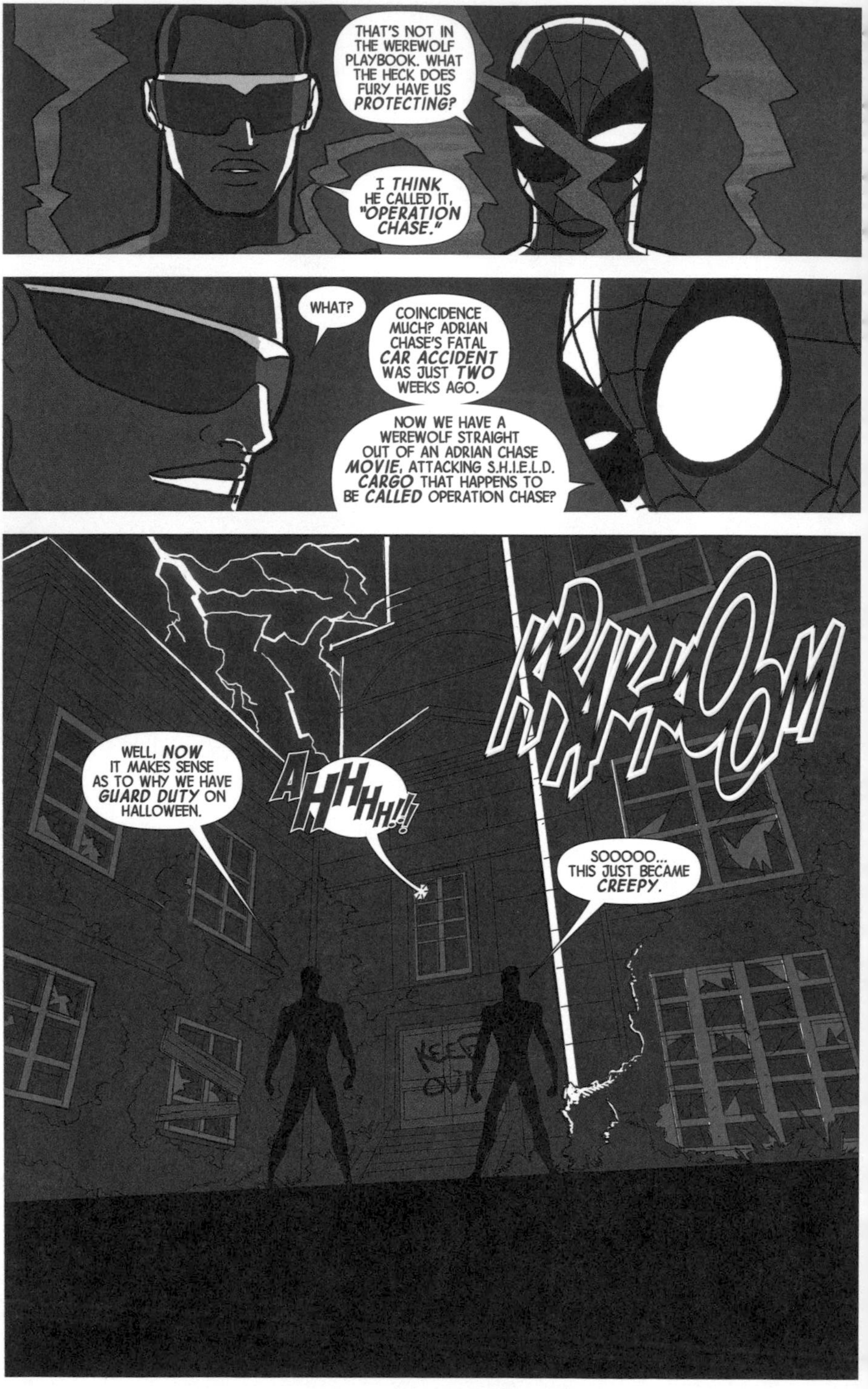
THAT'S NOT IN THE WEREWOLF PLAYBOOK. WHAT THE HECK DOES FURY HAVE US PROTECTING?
I THINK HE CALLED IT, "OPERATION CHASE."
WHAT?
COINCIDENCE MUCH? ADRIAN CHASE'S FATAL CAR ACCIDENT WAS JUST TWO WEEKS AGO.
NOW WE HAVE A WEREWOLF STRAIGHT OUT OF AN ADRIAN CHASE MOVIE, ATTACKING S.H.I.E.L.D. CARGO THAT HAPPENS TO BE CALLED OPERATION CHASE?
KRAKOOM
WELL, NOW IT MAKES SENSE AS TO WHY WE HAVE GUARD DUTY ON HALLOWEEN.
AHHHH!!
SOOOOO... THIS JUST BECAME CREEPY.
KEEP OUT

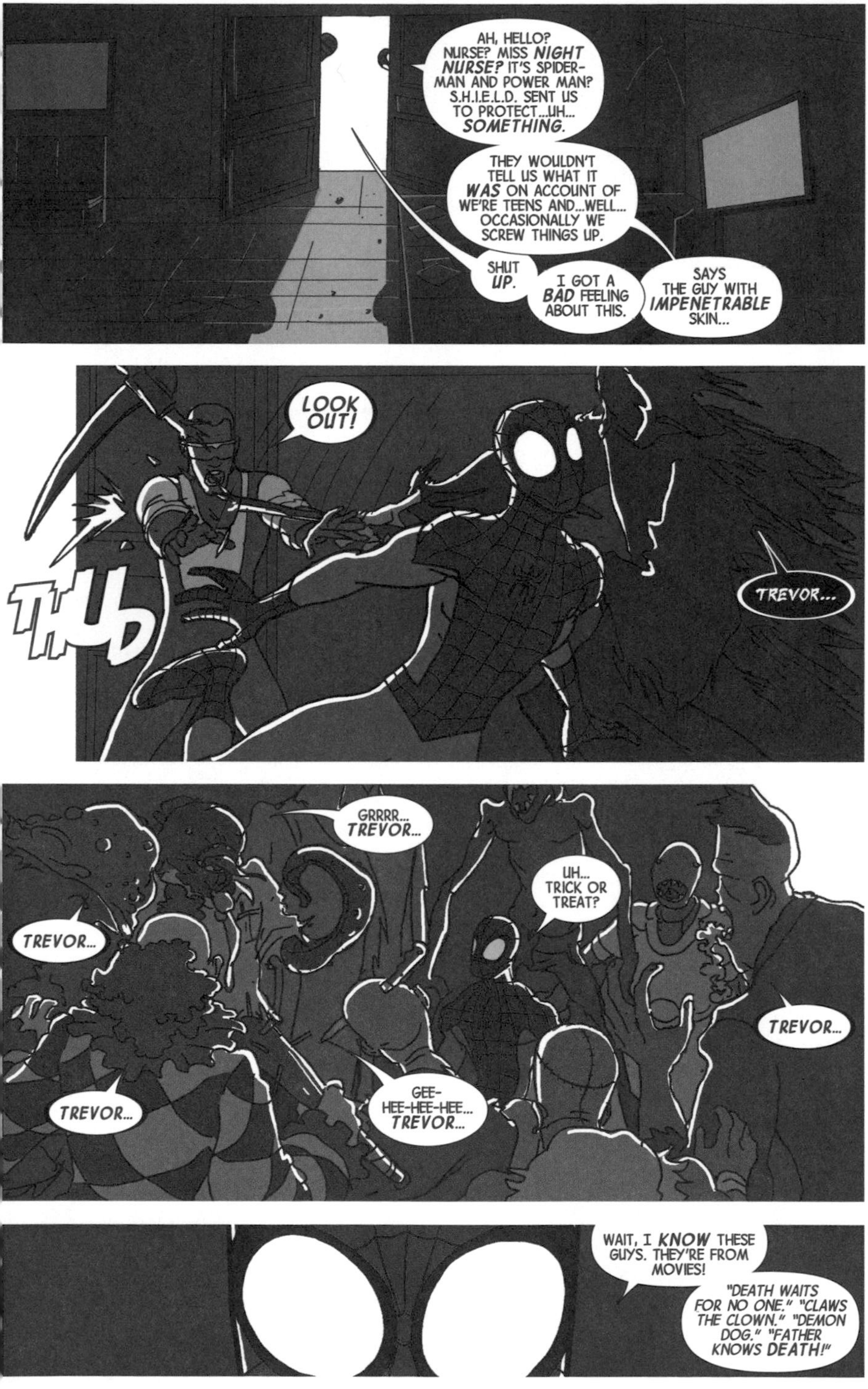
AH, HELLO? NURSE? MISS NIGHT NURSE? IT'S SPIDER-MAN AND POWER MAN? S.H.I.E.L.D. SENT US TO PROTECT...UH... SOMETHING.
THEY WOULDN'T TELL US WHAT IT WAS ON ACCOUNT OF WE'RE TEENS AND...WELL... OCCASIONALLY WE SCREW THINGS UP.
SHUT UP.
I GOT A BAD FEELING ABOUT THIS.
SAYS THE GUY WITH IMPENETRABLE SKIN...
LOOK OUT!
THUD
TREVOR...
GRRRR... TREVOR...
UH... TRICK OR TREAT?
TREVOR...
TREVOR...
TREVOR...
GEE-HEE-HEE-HEE... TREVOR...
WAIT, I KNOW THESE GUYS. THEY'RE FROM MOVIES!
"DEATH WAITS FOR NO ONE." "CLAWS THE CLOWN." "DEMON DOG." "FATHER KNOWS DEATH!"

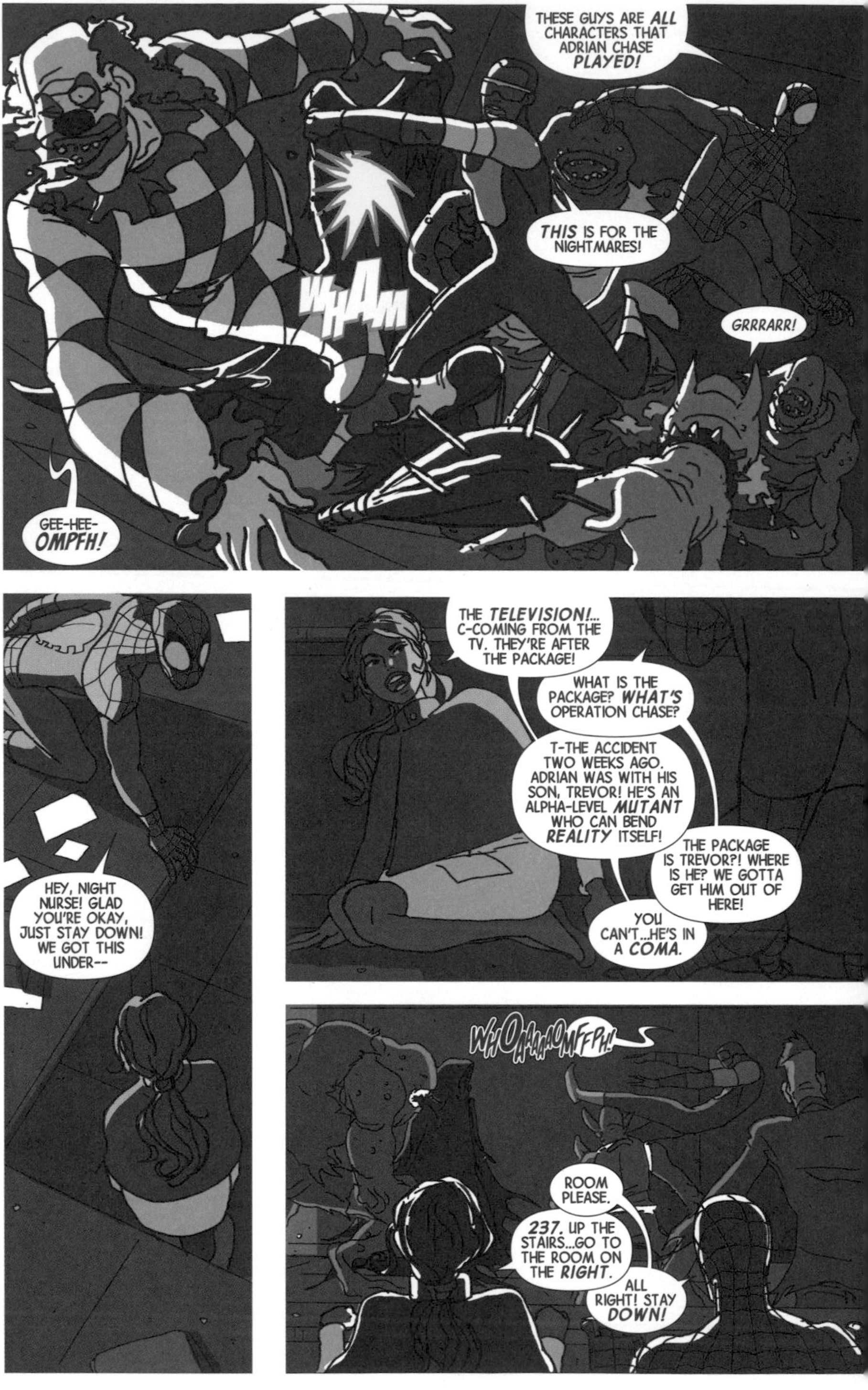
THESE GUYS ARE ALL CHARACTERS THAT ADRIAN CHASE PLAYED!
THIS IS FOR THE NIGHTMARES!
WHAM
GRRRARR!
GEE-HEE-OMPFH!
HEY, NIGHT NURSE! GLAD YOU'RE OKAY, JUST STAY DOWN! WE GOT THIS UNDER--
THE TELEVISION!... C-COMING FROM THE TV. THEY'RE AFTER THE PACKAGE!
WHAT IS THE PACKAGE? WHAT'S OPERATION CHASE?
T-THE ACCIDENT TWO WEEKS AGO. ADRIAN WAS WITH HIS SON, TREVOR! HE'S AN ALPHA-LEVEL MUTANT WHO CAN BEND REALITY ITSELF!
THE PACKAGE IS TREVOR?! WHERE IS HE? WE GOTTA GET HIM OUT OF HERE!
YOU CAN'T...HE'S IN A COMA.
WHOAAAAAOMFFPH!
ROOM PLEASE.
237. UP THE STAIRS...GO TO THE ROOM ON THE RIGHT.
ALL RIGHT! STAY DOWN!

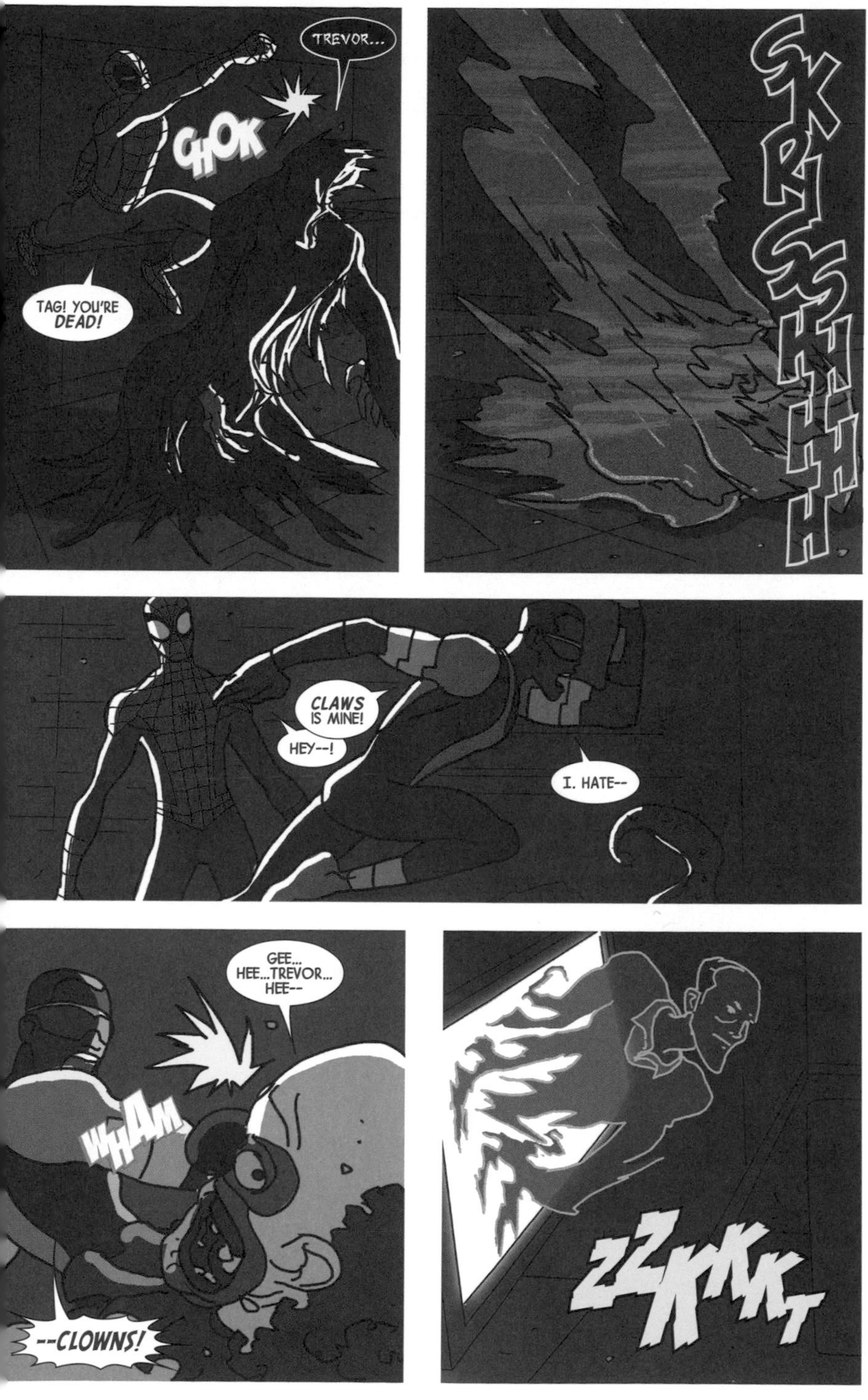
TREVOR...
CHOK
TAG! YOU'RE DEAD!
SKRSSHHHHH
CLAWS IS MINE!
HEY--!
I. HATE--
GEE... HEE...TREVOR... HEE--
WHAM
--CLOWNS!
ZZKKKT

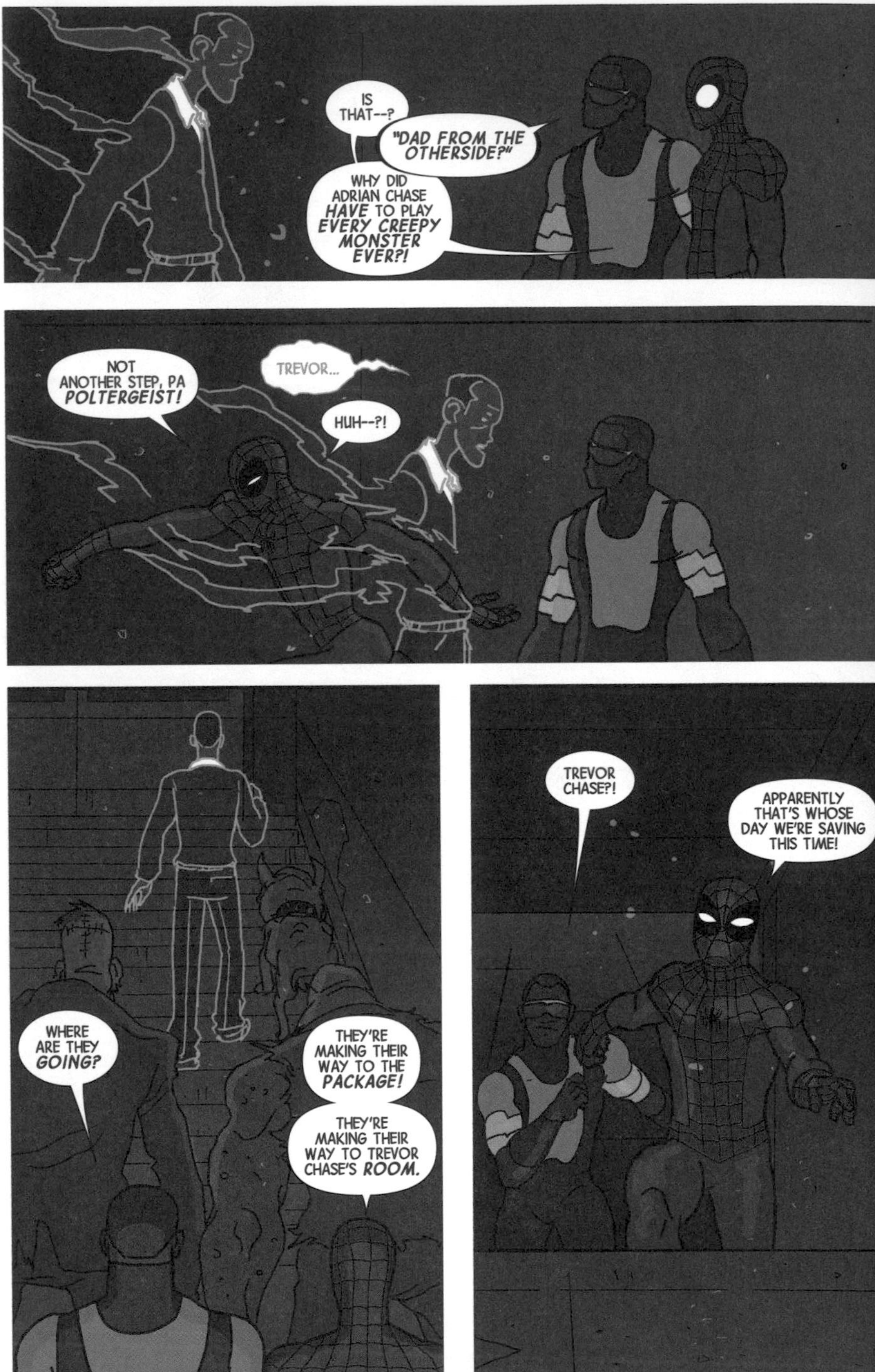

IS THAT--?
"DAD FROM THE OTHERSIDE?"
WHY DID ADRIAN CHASE HAVE TO PLAY EVERY CREEPY MONSTER EVER?!
NOT ANOTHER STEP, PA POLTERGEIST!
TREVOR...
HUH--?!
WHERE ARE THEY GOING?
THEY'RE MAKING THEIR WAY TO THE PACKAGE!
THEY'RE MAKING THEIR WAY TO TREVOR CHASE'S ROOM.
TREVOR CHASE?!
APPARENTLY THAT'S WHOSE DAY WE'RE SAVING THIS TIME!

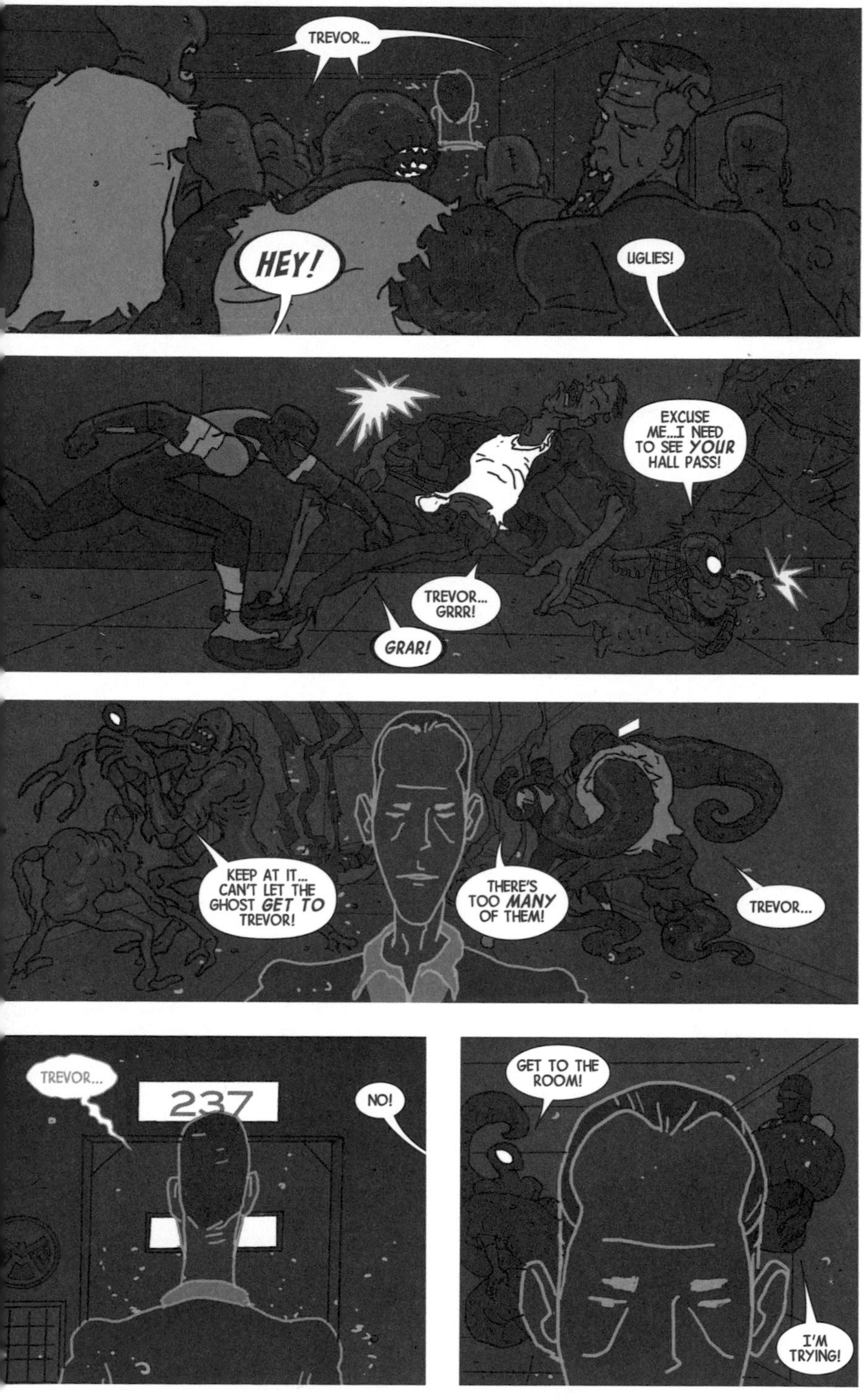
TREVOR...
HEY!
UGLIES!
EXCUSE ME...I NEED TO SEE YOUR HALL PASS!
TREVOR... GRRR!
GRAR!
KEEP AT IT... CAN'T LET THE GHOST GET TO TREVOR!
THERE'S TOO MANY OF THEM!
TREVOR...
TREVOR...
237
NO!
GET TO THE ROOM!
I'M TRYING!

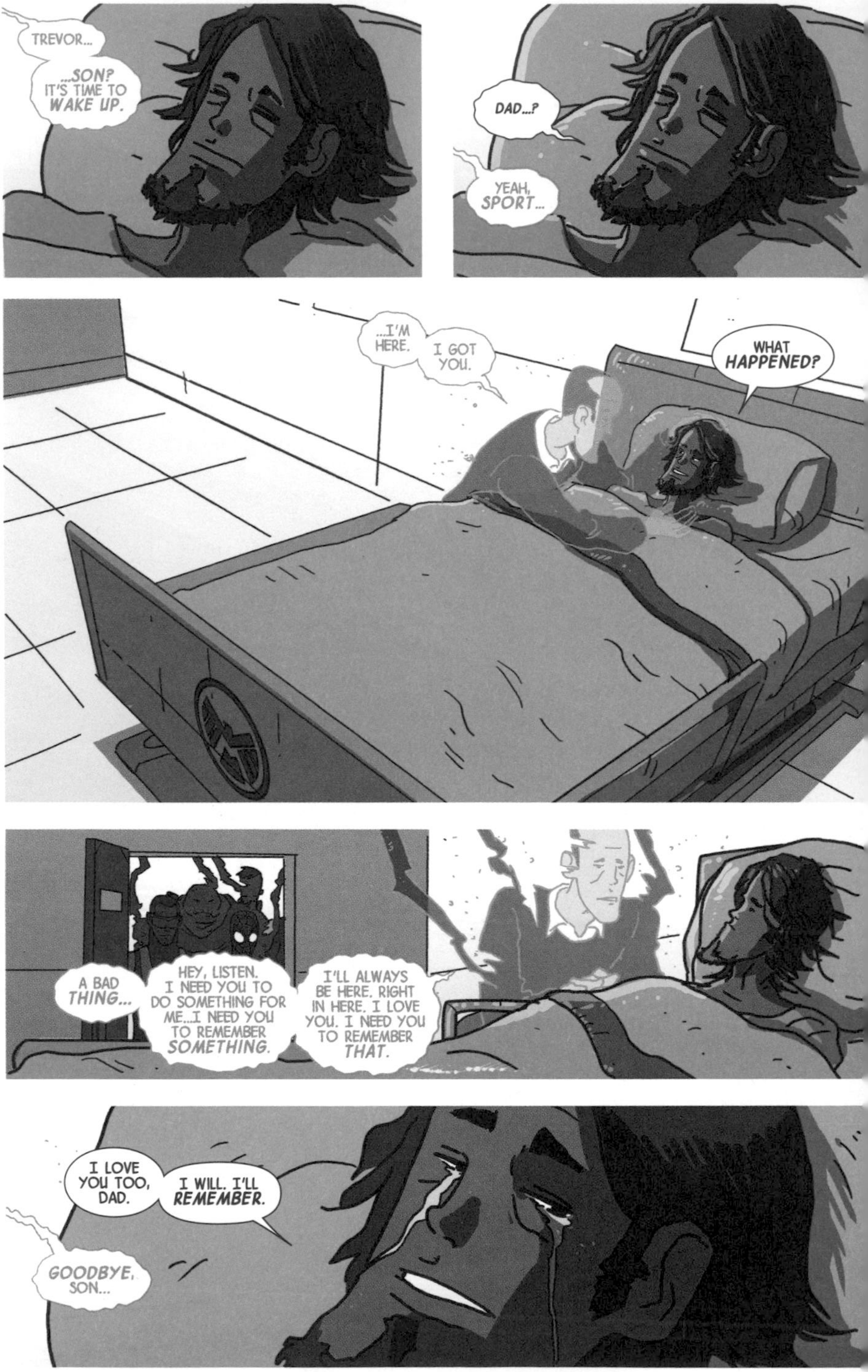
TREVOR...
...SON? IT'S TIME TO WAKE UP.
DAD...?
YEAH, SPORT...
...I'M HERE.
I GOT YOU.
WHAT HAPPENED?
A BAD THING...
HEY, LISTEN. I NEED YOU TO DO SOMETHING FOR ME...I NEED YOU TO REMEMBER SOMETHING.
I'LL ALWAYS BE HERE. RIGHT IN HERE. I LOVE YOU. I NEED YOU TO REMEMBER THAT.
I LOVE YOU TOO, DAD.
I WILL. I'LL REMEMBER.
GOODBYE, SON...

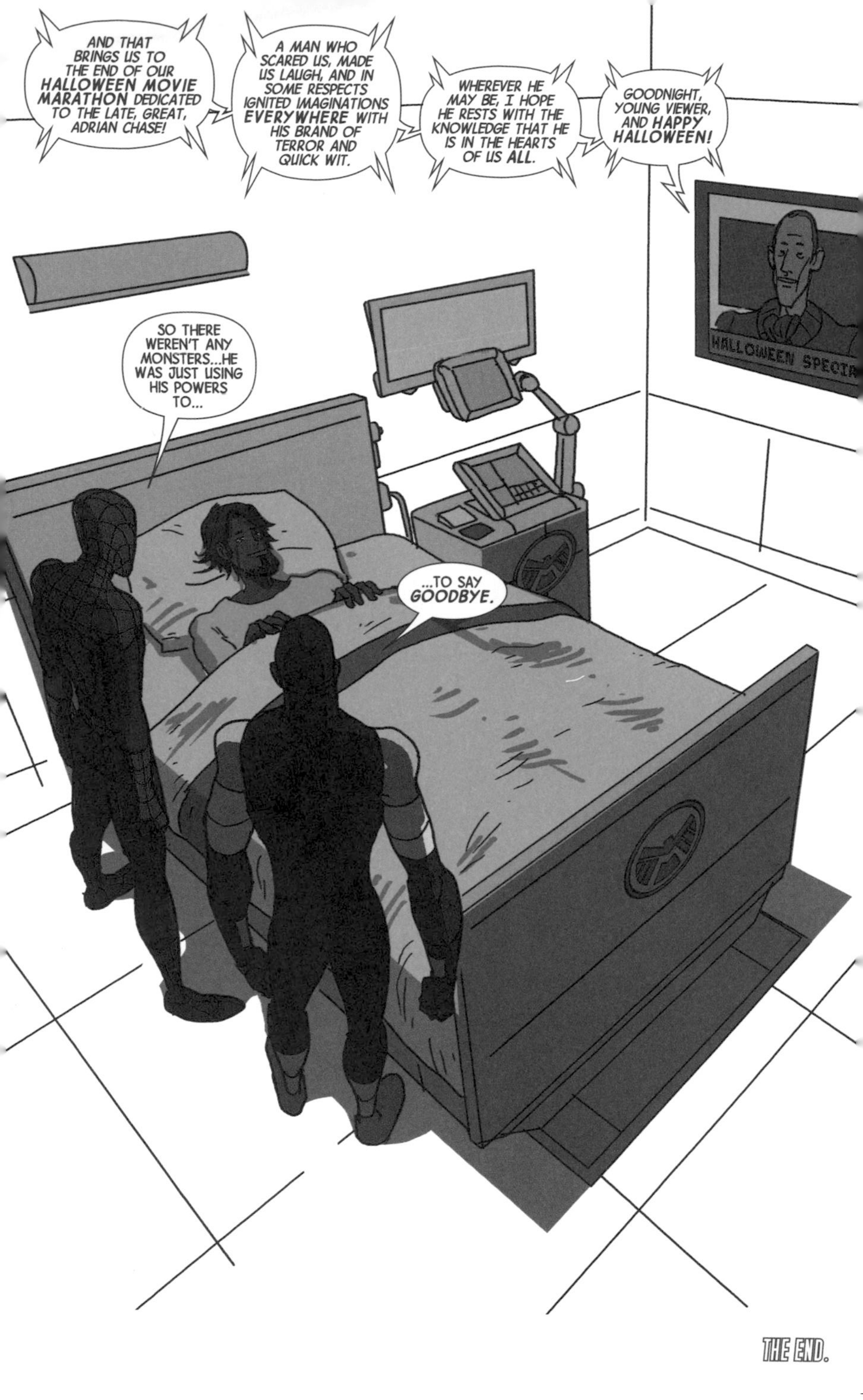
AND THAT BRINGS US TO THE END OF OUR HALLOWEEN MOVIE MARATHON DEDICATED TO THE LATE, GREAT, ADRIAN CHASE!
A MAN WHO SCARED US, MADE US LAUGH, AND IN SOME RESPECTS IGNITED IMAGINATIONS EVERYWHERE WITH HIS BRAND OF TERROR AND QUICK WIT.
WHEREVER HE MAY BE, I HOPE HE RESTS WITH THE KNOWLEDGE THAT HE IS IN THE HEARTS OF US ALL.
GOODNIGHT, YOUNG VIEWER, AND HAPPY HALLOWEEN!
HALLOWEEN SPECIA
SO THERE WEREN'T ANY MONSTERS...HE WAS JUST USING HIS POWERS TO...
...TO SAY GOODBYE.
THE END.

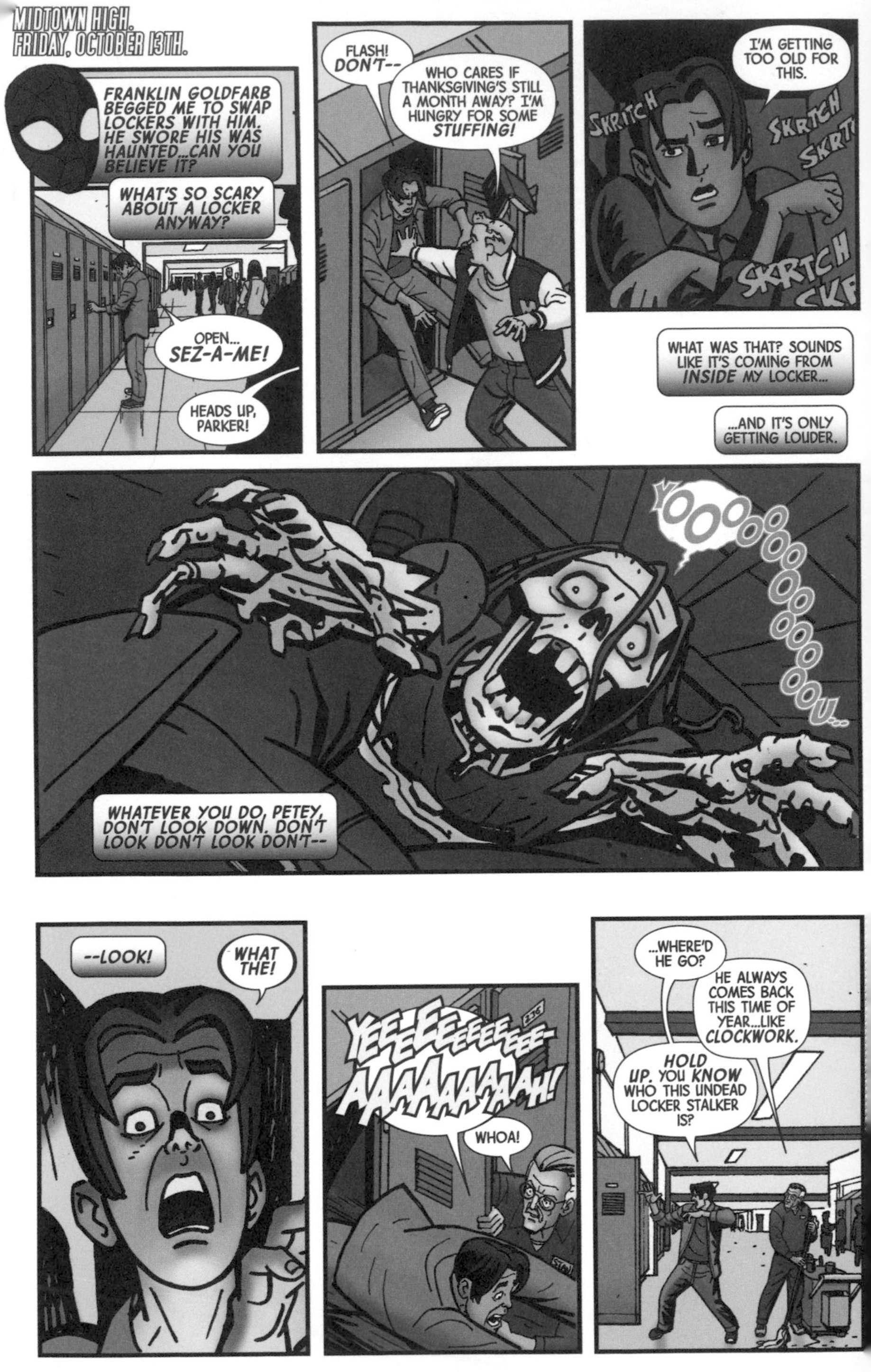
MIDTOWN HIGH.
FRIDAY, OCTOBER 13TH.
FRANKLIN GOLDFARB BEGGED ME TO SWAP LOCKERS WITH HIM. HE SWORE HIS WAS HAUNTED...CAN YOU BELIEVE IT?
WHAT'S SO SCARY ABOUT A LOCKER ANYWAY?
OPEN... SEZ-A-ME!
HEADS UP, PARKER!
FLASH! DON'T--
WHO CARES IF THANKSGIVING'S STILL A MONTH AWAY? I'M HUNGRY FOR SOME STUFFING!
I'M GETTING TOO OLD FOR THIS.
SKRITCH
SKRTCH
SKRTCH
SKRTCH
WHAT WAS THAT? SOUNDS LIKE IT'S COMING FROM INSIDE MY LOCKER...
...AND IT'S ONLY GETTING LOUDER.
YOOOOOOOOOOOOOOU...
WHATEVER YOU DO, PETEY, DON'T LOOK DOWN. DON'T LOOK DON'T LOOK DON'T--
--LOOK!
WHAT THE!
YEEEEEEEEEEEE-AAAAAAAAAH!
WHOA!
...WHERE'D HE GO?
HE ALWAYS COMES BACK THIS TIME OF YEAR...LIKE CLOCKWORK.
HOLD UP. YOU KNOW WHO THIS UNDEAD LOCKER STALKER IS?

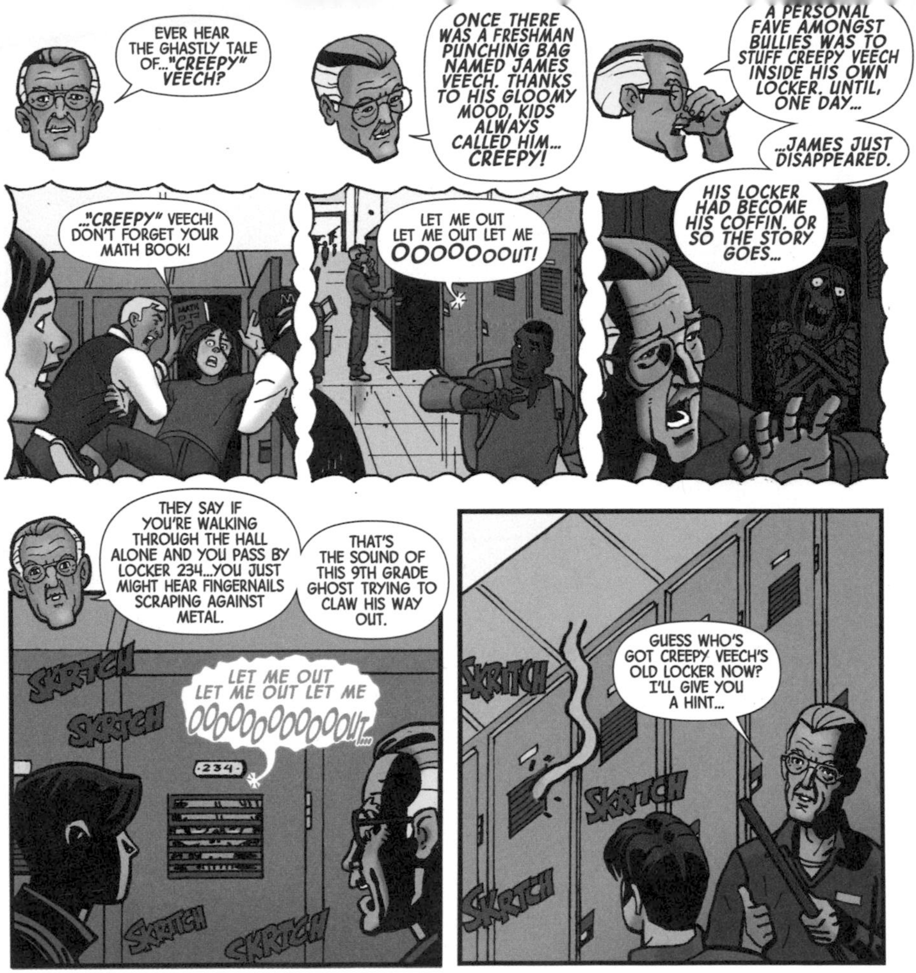
EVER HEAR THE GHASTLY TALE OF..."CREEPY" VEECH?
ONCE THERE WAS A FRESHMAN PUNCHING BAG NAMED JAMES VEECH. THANKS TO HIS GLOOMY MOOD, KIDS ALWAYS CALLED HIM... CREEPY!
A PERSONAL FAVE AMONGST BULLIES WAS TO STUFF CREEPY VEECH INSIDE HIS OWN LOCKER. UNTIL, ONE DAY...
...JAMES JUST DISAPPEARED.
..."CREEPY" VEECH! DON'T FORGET YOUR MATH BOOK!
LET ME OUT LET ME OUT LET ME OOOOOOOUT!
HIS LOCKER HAD BECOME HIS COFFIN. OR SO THE STORY GOES...
THEY SAY IF YOU'RE WALKING THROUGH THE HALL ALONE AND YOU PASS BY LOCKER 234...YOU JUST MIGHT HEAR FINGERNAILS SCRAPING AGAINST METAL.
THAT'S THE SOUND OF THIS 9TH GRADE GHOST TRYING TO CLAW HIS WAY OUT.
SKRTCH
SKRTCH
LET ME OUT LET ME OUT LET ME OOOOOOOOOOOOUT...
234
SKRTCH
SKRTCH
SKRTCH
GUESS WHO'S GOT CREEPY VEECH'S OLD LOCKER NOW? I'LL GIVE YOU A HINT...
SKRTCH
SKRTCH

THERE'S A GHOST IN MY LOCKER!

STORY: CLAY McLEOD CHAPMAN
ART: TY TEMPLETON
COLORS: MUNTSA VICENTE
LETTERS: VC's JOE SABINO
EDITORS: TOM BRENNAN & ELLIE PYLE
SENIOR EDITOR: STEPHEN WACKER
EDITOR IN CHIEF: AXEL ALONSO
CHIEF CREATIVE OFFICER: JOE QUESADA
PUBLISHER: DAN BUCKLEY
EXEC. PRODUCER: ALAN FINE

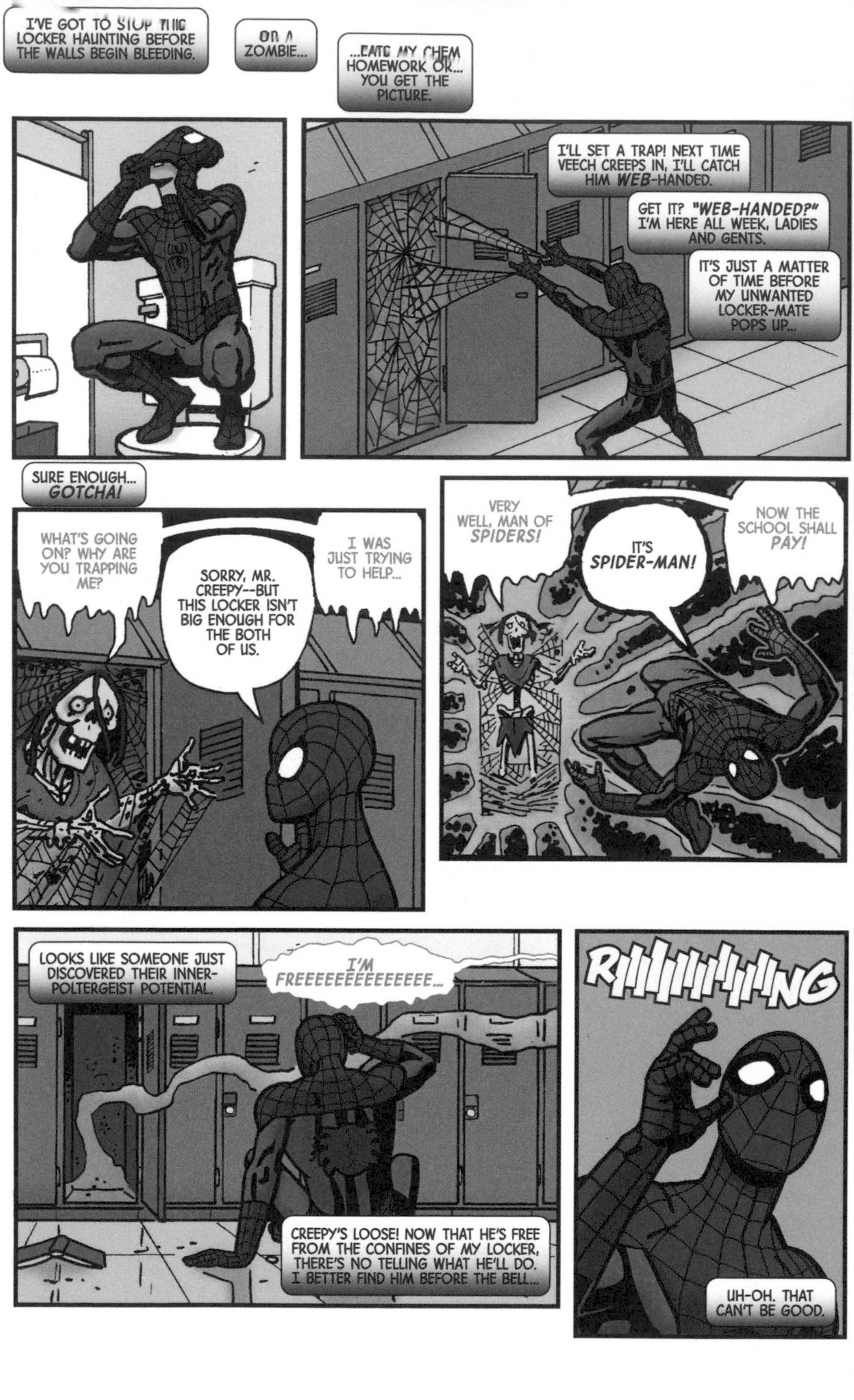
I'VE GOT TO STOP THIS LOCKER HAUNTING BEFORE THE WALLS BEGIN BLEEDING.
OR A ZOMBIE...
...EATS MY CHEM HOMEWORK OR... YOU GET THE PICTURE.
I'LL SET A TRAP! NEXT TIME VEECH CREEPS IN, I'LL CATCH HIM WEB-HANDED.
GET IT? "WEB-HANDED?" I'M HERE ALL WEEK, LADIES AND GENTS.
IT'S JUST A MATTER OF TIME BEFORE MY UNWANTED LOCKER-MATE POPS UP...
SURE ENOUGH... GOTCHA!
WHAT'S GOING ON? WHY ARE YOU TRAPPING ME?
SORRY, MR. CREEPY--BUT THIS LOCKER ISN'T BIG ENOUGH FOR THE BOTH OF US.
I WAS JUST TRYING TO HELP...
VERY WELL, MAN OF SPIDERS!
IT'S SPIDER-MAN!
NOW THE SCHOOL SHALL PAY!
LOOKS LIKE SOMEONE JUST DISCOVERED THEIR INNER-POLTERGEIST POTENTIAL.
I'M FREEEEEEEEEEEEEE...
CREEPY'S LOOSE! NOW THAT HE'S FREE FROM THE CONFINES OF MY LOCKER, THERE'S NO TELLING WHAT HE'LL DO. I BETTER FIND HIM BEFORE THE BELL...
RIIIIIIIIIING
UH-OH. THAT CAN'T BE GOOD.

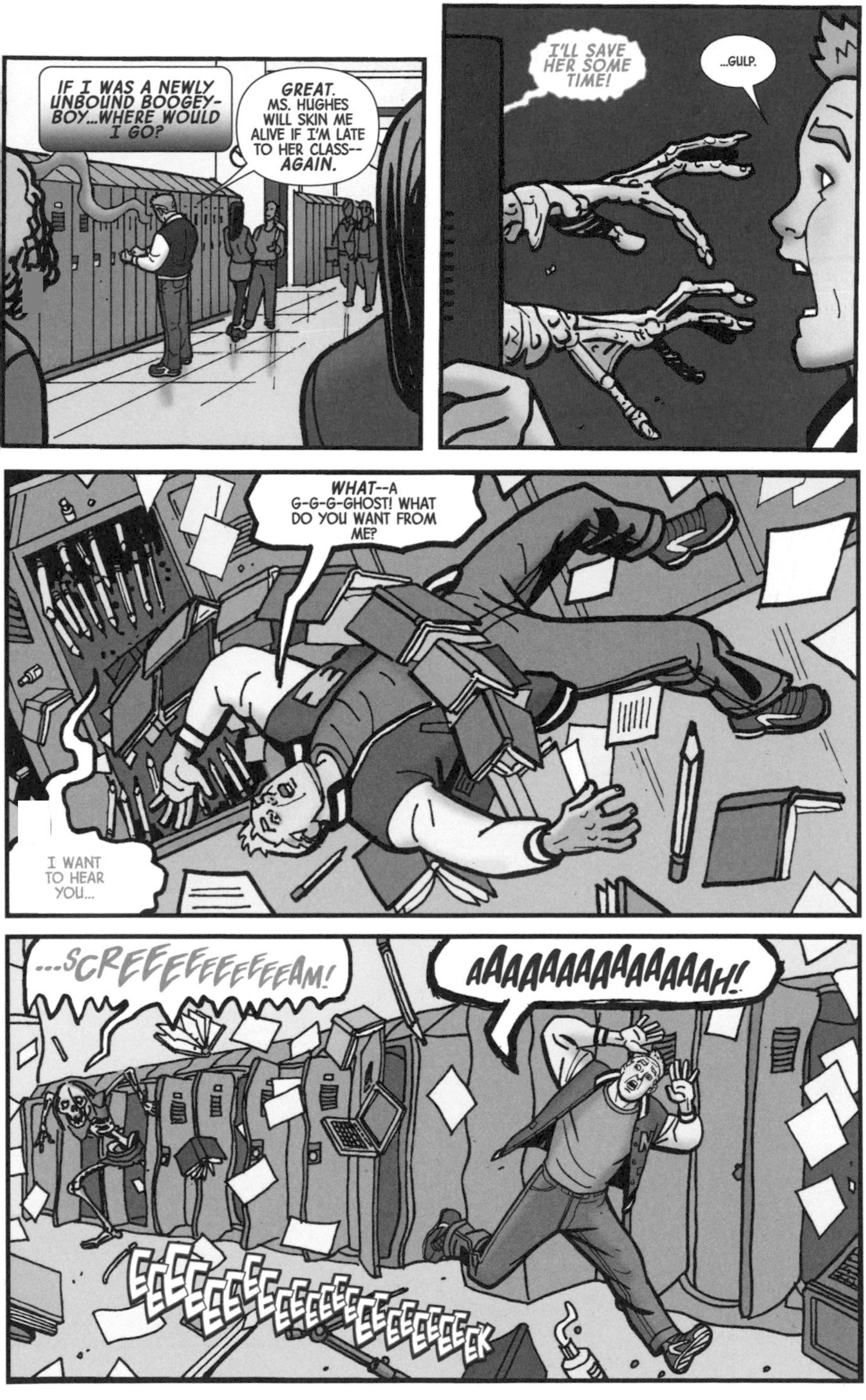
IF I WAS A NEWLY UNBOUND BOOGEY-BOY...WHERE WOULD I GO?
GREAT. MS. HUGHES WILL SKIN ME ALIVE IF I'M LATE TO HER CLASS-- AGAIN.
I'LL SAVE HER SOME TIME!
...GULP.
WHAT--A G-G-G-GHOST! WHAT DO YOU WANT FROM ME?
I WANT TO HEAR YOU...
...SCREEEEEEEEEEAM!
AAAAAAAAAAAAAAAH!
EEEEEEEEEEEEEEEEEEEEEEEEK

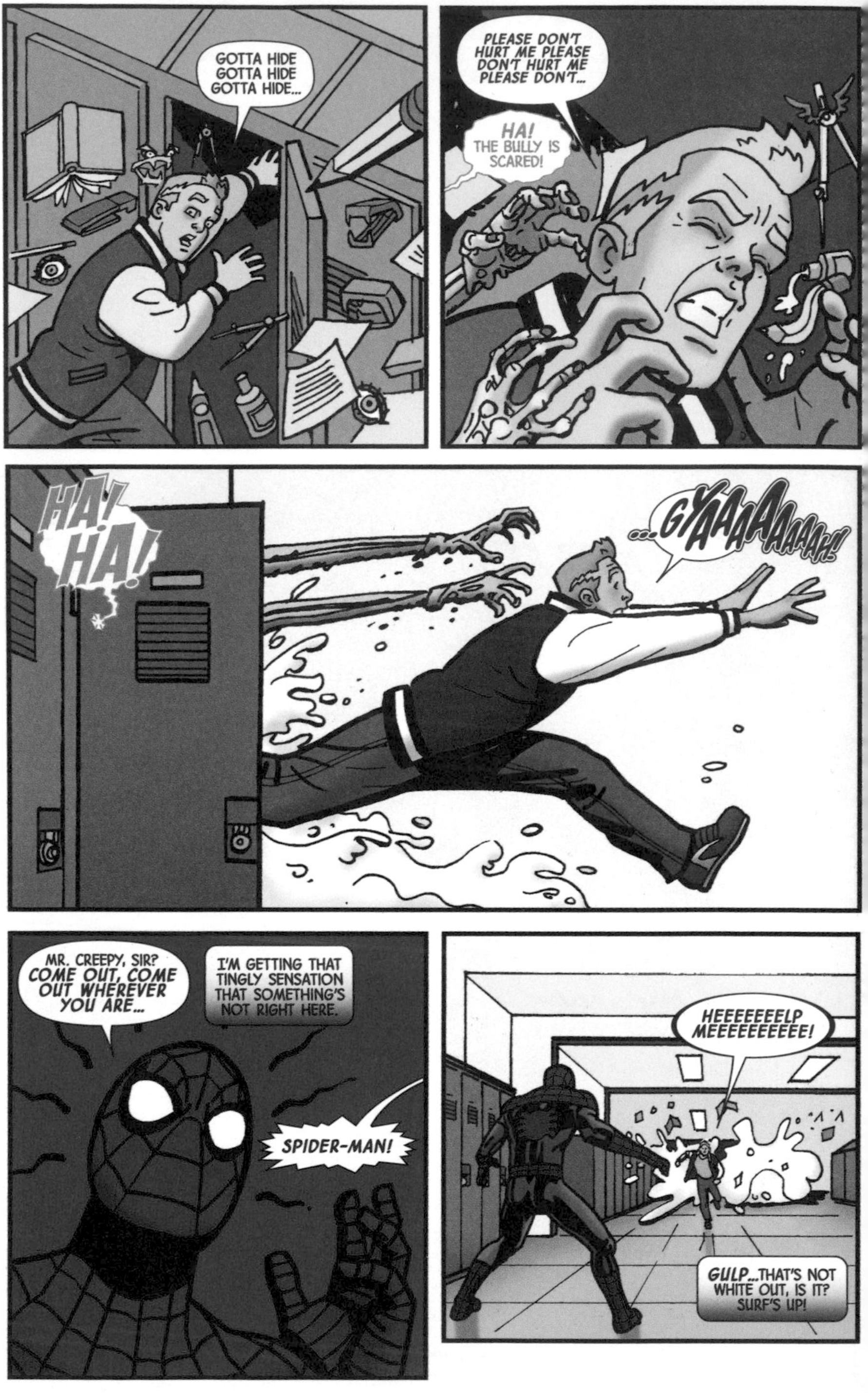
GOTTA HIDE GOTTA HIDE GOTTA HIDE...
PLEASE DON'T HURT ME PLEASE DON'T HURT ME PLEASE DON'T...
HA! THE BULLY IS SCARED!
HA! HA!
...GYAAAAAAAAH!!
MR. CREEPY, SIR? COME OUT, COME OUT WHEREVER YOU ARE...
I'M GETTING THAT TINGLY SENSATION THAT SOMETHING'S NOT RIGHT HERE.
SPIDER-MAN!
HEEEEEEELP MEEEEEEEEEE!
GULP...THAT'S NOT WHITE OUT, IS IT? SURF'S UP!

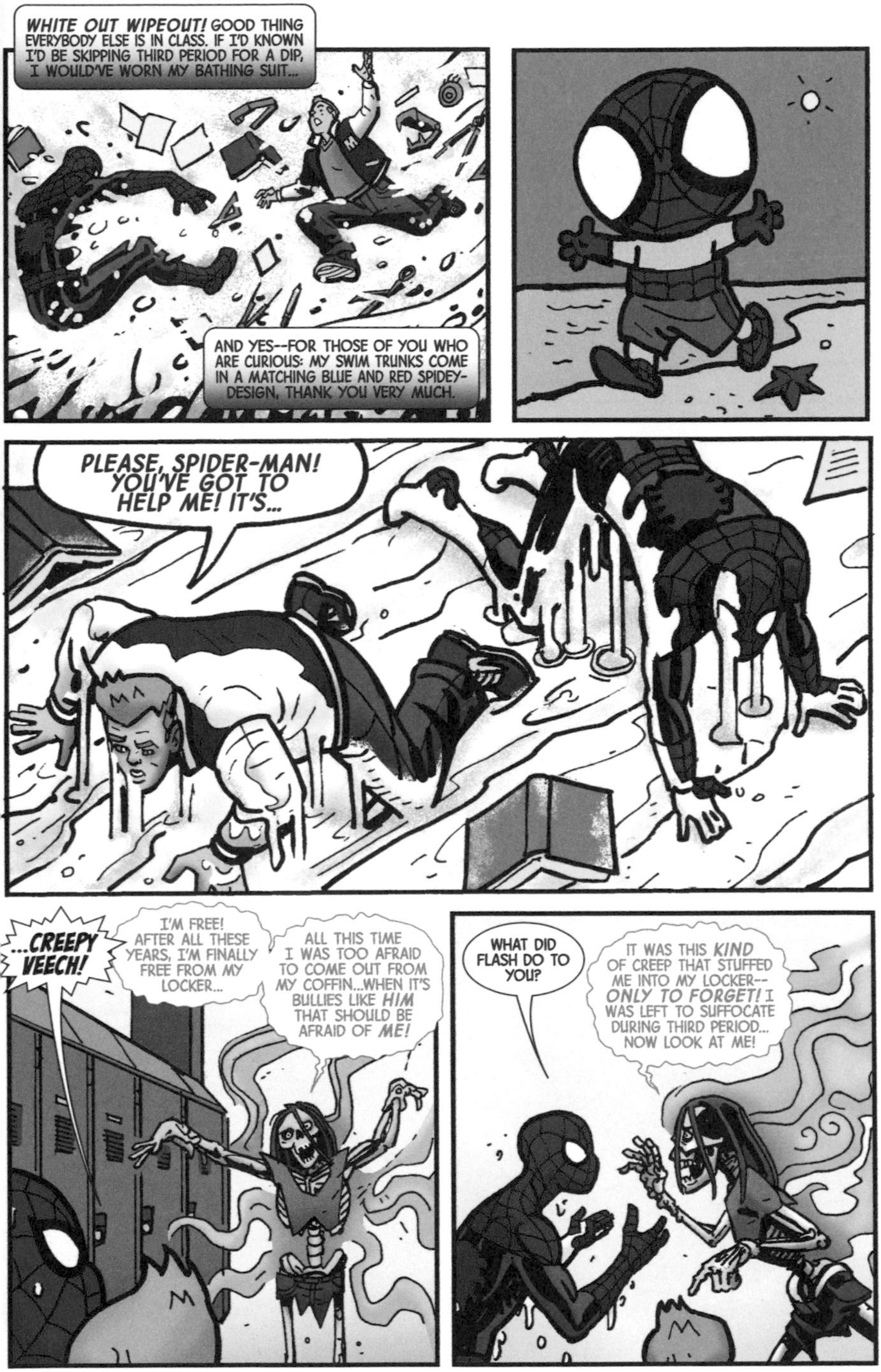
WHITE OUT WIPEOUT! GOOD THING EVERYBODY ELSE IS IN CLASS. IF I'D KNOWN I'D BE SKIPPING THIRD PERIOD FOR A DIP, I WOULD'VE WORN MY BATHING SUIT...
AND YES--FOR THOSE OF YOU WHO ARE CURIOUS: MY SWIM TRUNKS COME IN A MATCHING BLUE AND RED SPIDEY-DESIGN, THANK YOU VERY MUCH.
PLEASE, SPIDER-MAN! YOU'VE GOT TO HELP ME! IT'S...
...CREEPY VEECH!
I'M FREE! AFTER ALL THESE YEARS, I'M FINALLY FREE FROM MY LOCKER...
ALL THIS TIME I WAS TOO AFRAID TO COME OUT FROM MY COFFIN...WHEN IT'S BULLIES LIKE HIM THAT SHOULD BE AFRAID OF ME!
WHAT DID FLASH DO TO YOU?
IT WAS THIS KIND OF CREEP THAT STUFFED ME INTO MY LOCKER--ONLY TO FORGET! I WAS LEFT TO SUFFOCATE DURING THIRD PERIOD... NOW LOOK AT ME!

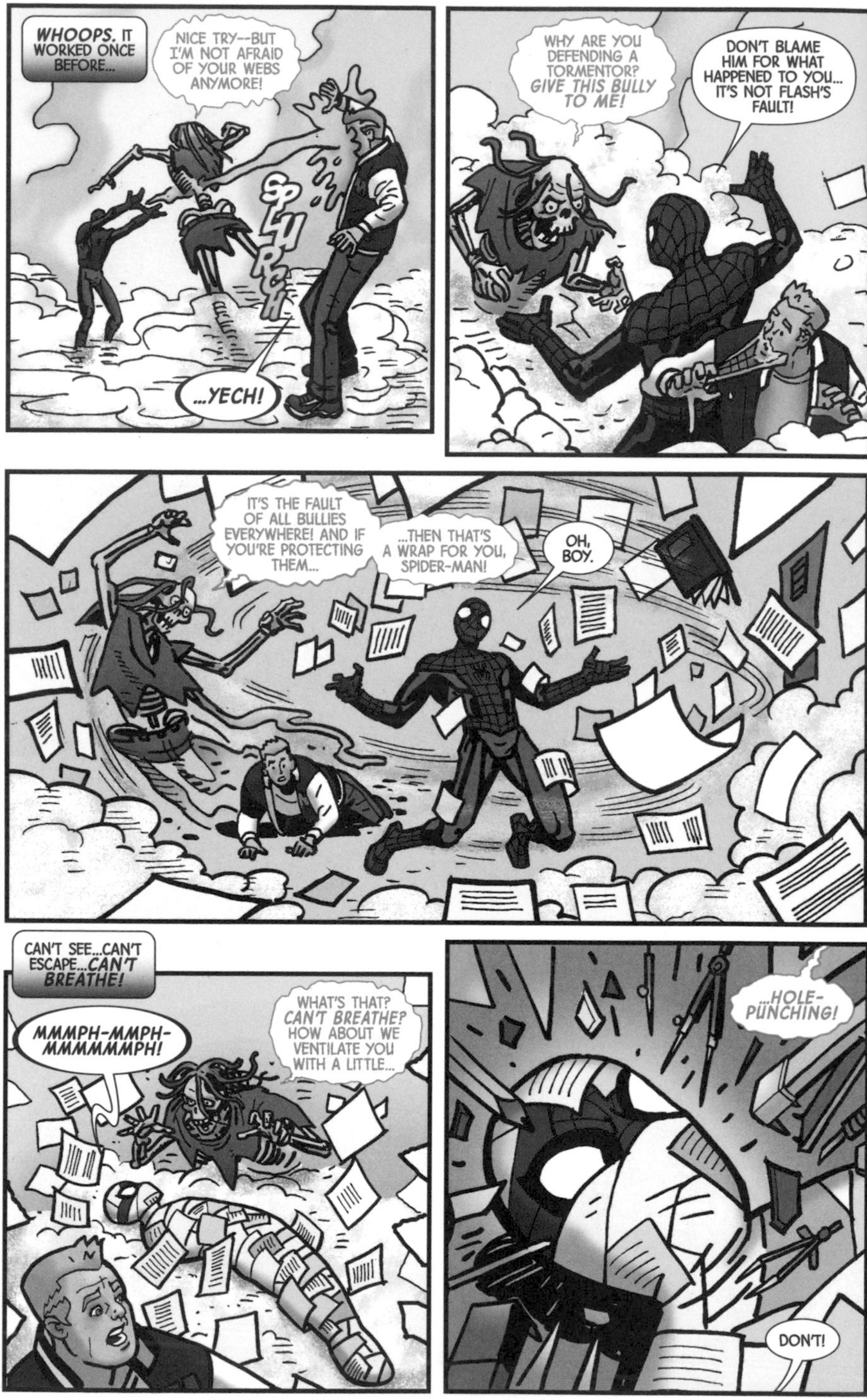
WHOOPS. IT WORKED ONCE BEFORE...
NICE TRY--BUT I'M NOT AFRAID OF YOUR WEBS ANYMORE!
SPLURCH
...YECH!
WHY ARE YOU DEFENDING A TORMENTOR? GIVE THIS BULLY TO ME!
DON'T BLAME HIM FOR WHAT HAPPENED TO YOU... IT'S NOT FLASH'S FAULT!
IT'S THE FAULT OF ALL BULLIES EVERYWHERE! AND IF YOU'RE PROTECTING THEM...
...THEN THAT'S A WRAP FOR YOU, SPIDER-MAN!
OH, BOY.
CAN'T SEE...CAN'T ESCAPE...CAN'T BREATHE!
MMMPH-MMPH-MMMMMMPH!
WHAT'S THAT? CAN'T BREATHE? HOW ABOUT WE VENTILATE YOU WITH A LITTLE...
...HOLE-PUNCHING!
DON'T!

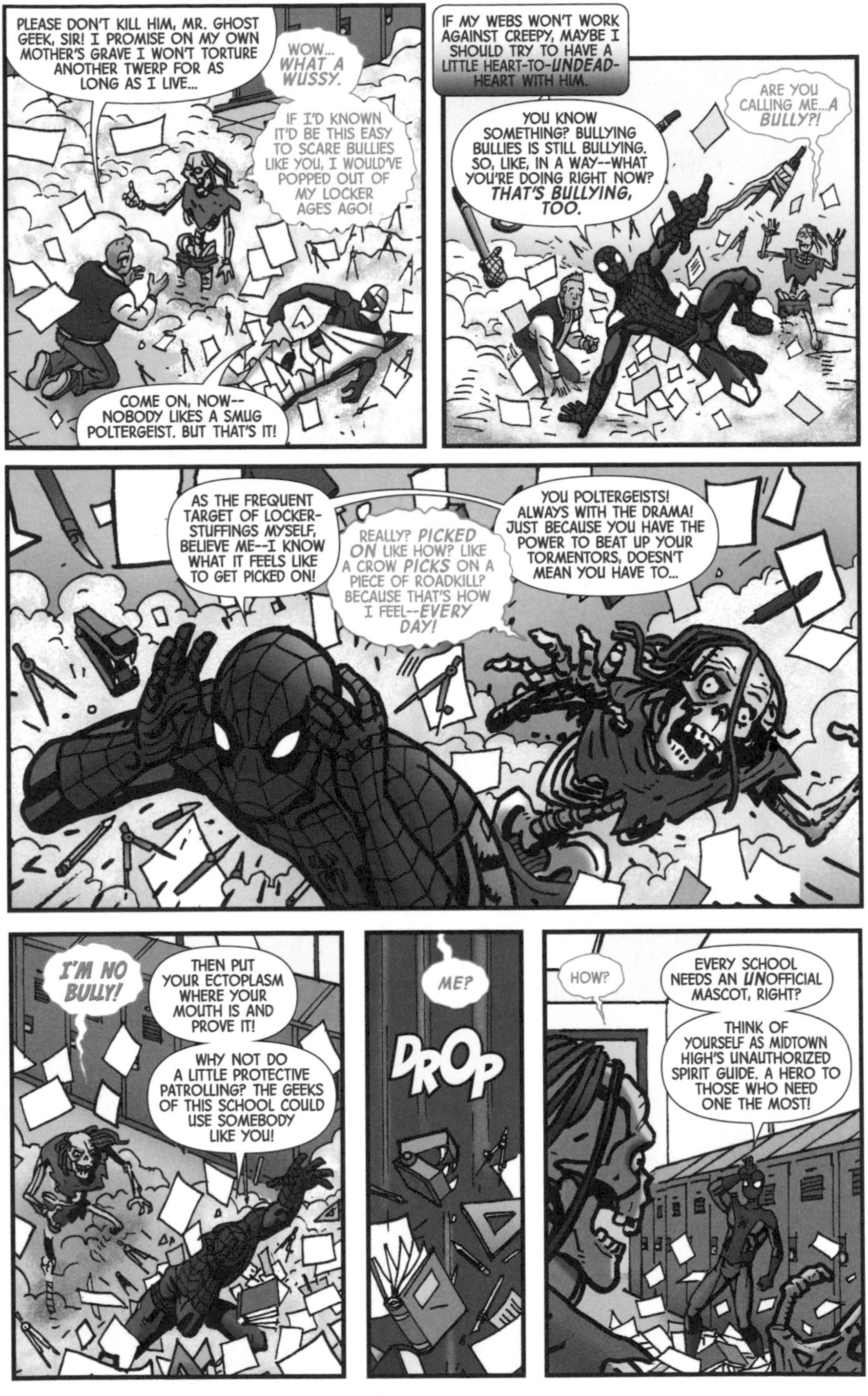

PLEASE DON'T KILL HIM, MR. GHOST GEEK, SIR! I PROMISE ON MY OWN MOTHER'S GRAVE I WON'T TORTURE ANOTHER TWERP FOR AS LONG AS I LIVE...
WOW... WHAT A WUSSY.
IF I'D KNOWN IT'D BE THIS EASY TO SCARE BULLIES LIKE YOU, I WOULD'VE POPPED OUT OF MY LOCKER AGES AGO!
COME ON, NOW-- NOBODY LIKES A SMUG POLTERGEIST. BUT THAT'S IT!
IF MY WEBS WON'T WORK AGAINST CREEPY, MAYBE I SHOULD TRY TO HAVE A LITTLE HEART-TO-UNDEAD-HEART WITH HIM.
YOU KNOW SOMETHING? BULLYING BULLIES IS STILL BULLYING. SO, LIKE, IN A WAY--WHAT YOU'RE DOING RIGHT NOW? THAT'S BULLYING, TOO.
ARE YOU CALLING ME...A BULLY?!
AS THE FREQUENT TARGET OF LOCKER-STUFFINGS MYSELF, BELIEVE ME--I KNOW WHAT IT FEELS LIKE TO GET PICKED ON!
REALLY? PICKED ON LIKE HOW? LIKE A CROW PICKS ON A PIECE OF ROADKILL? BECAUSE THAT'S HOW I FEEL--EVERY DAY!
YOU POLTERGEISTS! ALWAYS WITH THE DRAMA! JUST BECAUSE YOU HAVE THE POWER TO BEAT UP YOUR TORMENTORS, DOESN'T MEAN YOU HAVE TO...
I'M NO BULLY!
THEN PUT YOUR ECTOPLASM WHERE YOUR MOUTH IS AND PROVE IT!
WHY NOT DO A LITTLE PROTECTIVE PATROLLING? THE GEEKS OF THIS SCHOOL COULD USE SOMEBODY LIKE YOU!
ME?
DROP
HOW?
EVERY SCHOOL NEEDS AN UNOFFICIAL MASCOT, RIGHT?
THINK OF YOURSELF AS MIDTOWN HIGH'S UNAUTHORIZED SPIRIT GUIDE. A HERO TO THOSE WHO NEED ONE THE MOST!

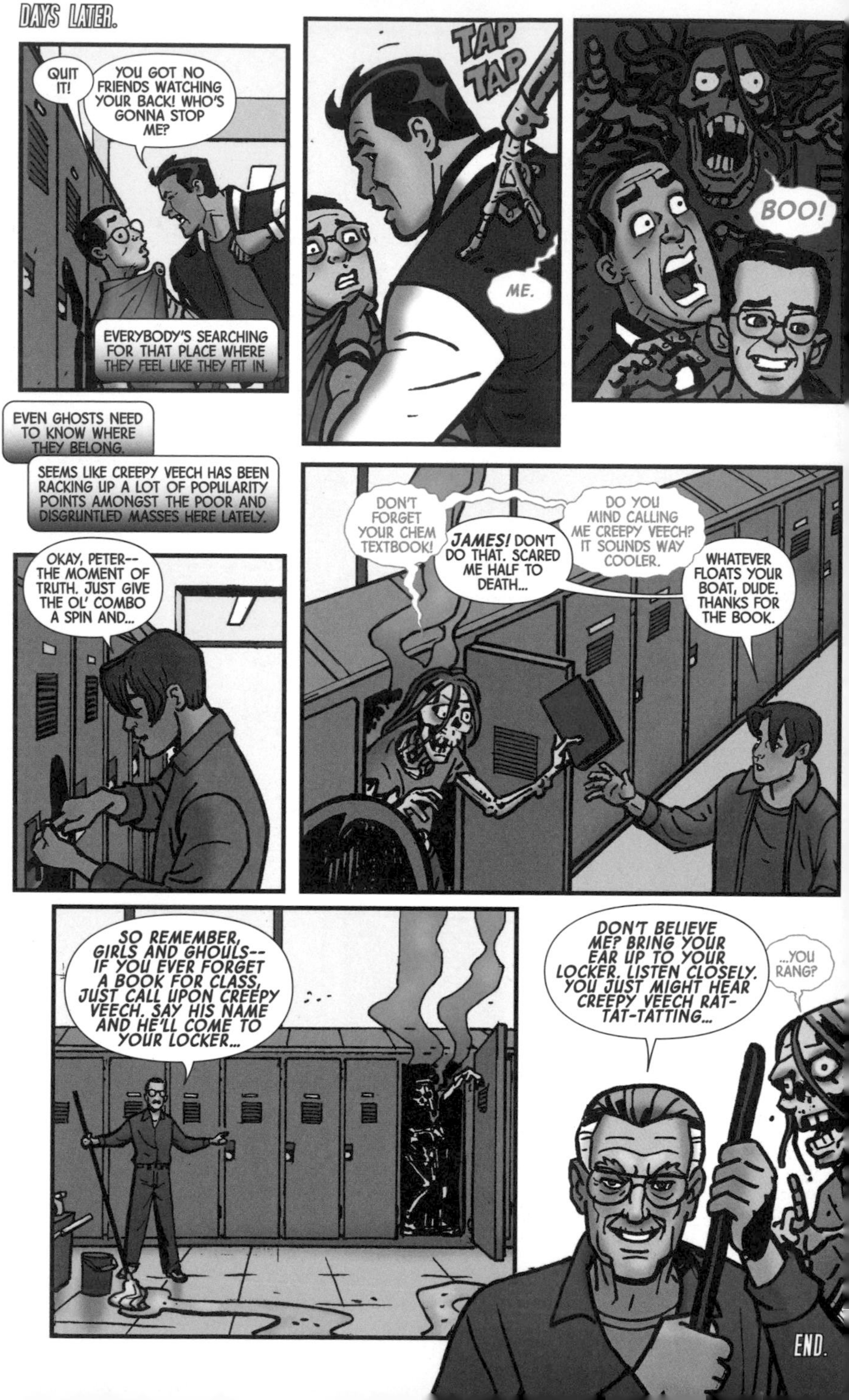
DAYS LATER.
QUIT IT!
YOU GOT NO FRIENDS WATCHING YOUR BACK! WHO'S GONNA STOP ME?
EVERYBODY'S SEARCHING FOR THAT PLACE WHERE THEY FEEL LIKE THEY FIT IN.
TAP TAP
ME.
BOO!
EVEN GHOSTS NEED TO KNOW WHERE THEY BELONG.
SEEMS LIKE CREEPY VEECH HAS BEEN RACKING UP A LOT OF POPULARITY POINTS AMONGST THE POOR AND DISGRUNTLED MASSES HERE LATELY.
OKAY, PETER-- THE MOMENT OF TRUTH. JUST GIVE THE OL' COMBO A SPIN AND...
DON'T FORGET YOUR CHEM TEXTBOOK!
JAMES! DON'T DO THAT. SCARED ME HALF TO DEATH...
DO YOU MIND CALLING ME CREEPY VEECH? IT SOUNDS WAY COOLER.
WHATEVER FLOATS YOUR BOAT, DUDE. THANKS FOR THE BOOK.
SO REMEMBER, GIRLS AND GHOULS-- IF YOU EVER FORGET A BOOK FOR CLASS, JUST CALL UPON CREEPY VEECH. SAY HIS NAME AND HE'LL COME TO YOUR LOCKER...
DON'T BELIEVE ME? BRING YOUR EAR UP TO YOUR LOCKER. LISTEN CLOSELY. YOU JUST MIGHT HEAR CREEPY VEECH RAT-TAT-TATTING...
...YOU RANG?
END.

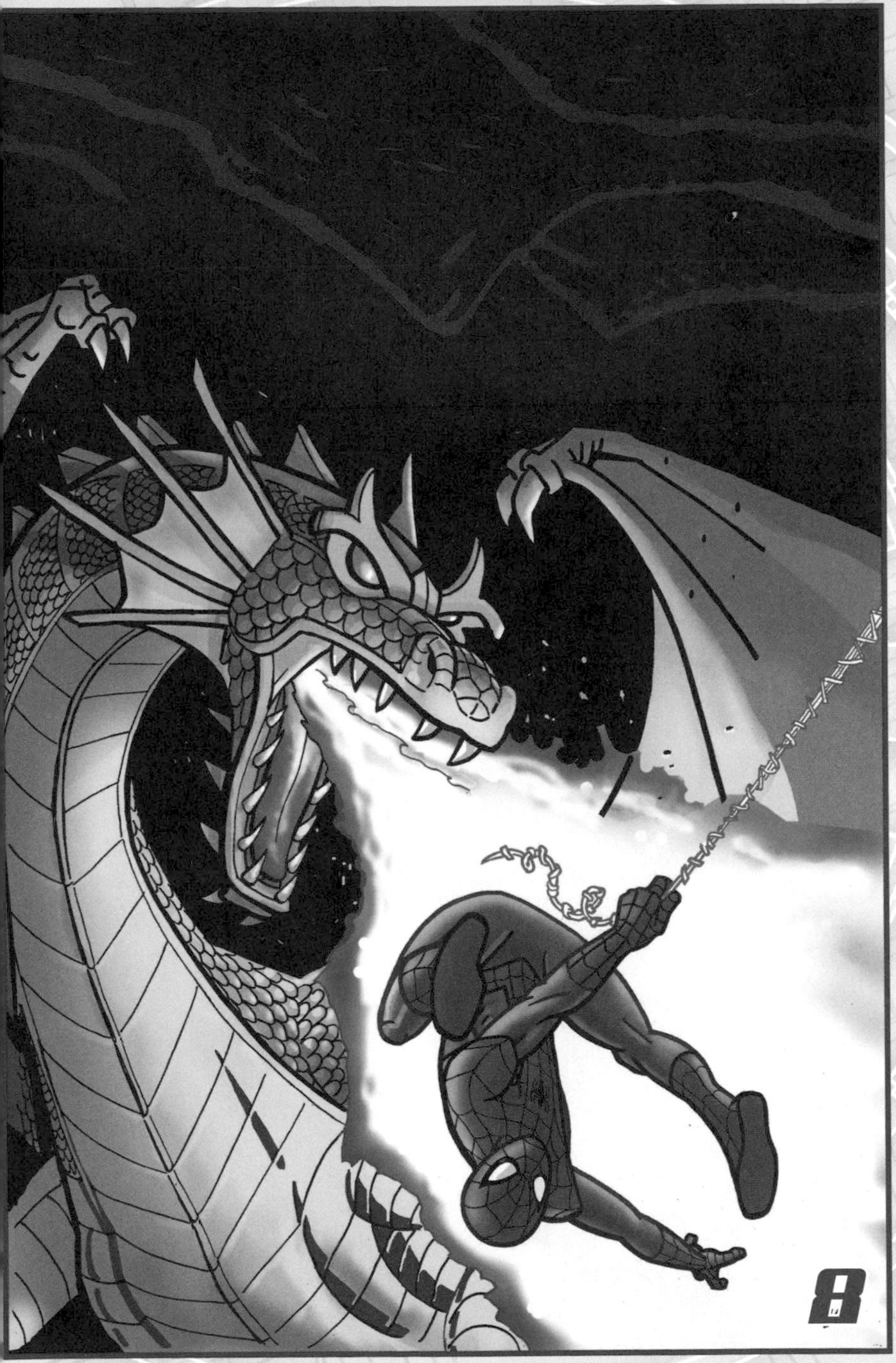
8

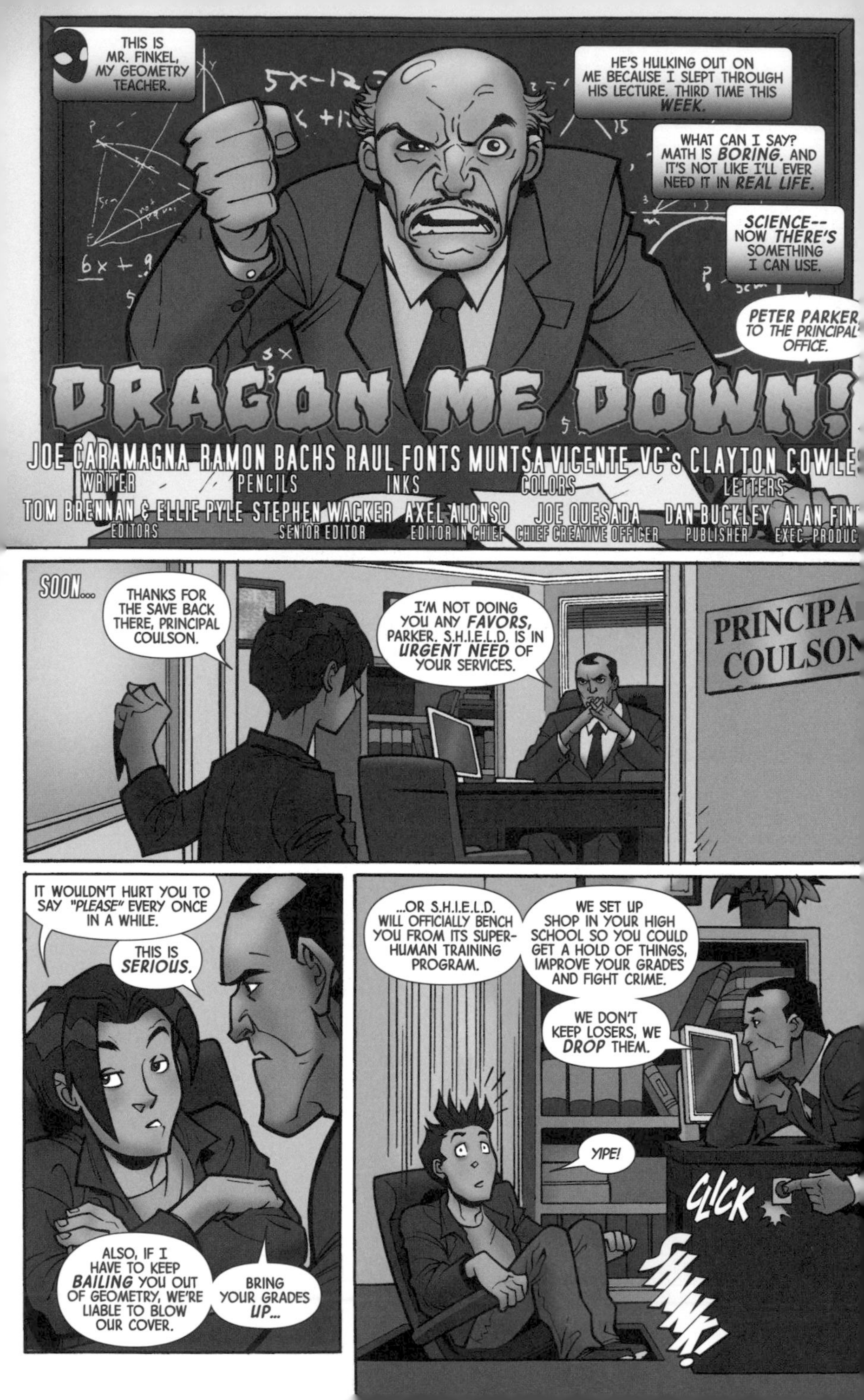
THIS IS MR. FINKEL, MY GEOMETRY TEACHER.
HE'S HULKING OUT ON ME BECAUSE I SLEPT THROUGH HIS LECTURE. THIRD TIME THIS WEEK.
WHAT CAN I SAY? MATH IS BORING. AND IT'S NOT LIKE I'LL EVER NEED IT IN REAL LIFE.
SCIENCE-- NOW THERE'S SOMETHING I CAN USE.
PETER PARKER TO THE PRINCIPAL'S OFFICE.
DRAGON ME DOWN!
JOE CARAMAGNA WRITER RAMON BACHS PENCILS RAUL FONTS INKS MUNTSA VICENTE COLORS VC's CLAYTON COWLES LETTERS
TOM BRENNAN & ELLIE PYLE EDITORS STEPHEN WACKER SENIOR EDITOR AXEL ALONSO EDITOR IN CHIEF JOE QUESADA CHIEF CREATIVE OFFICER DAN BUCKLEY PUBLISHER ALAN FINE EXEC. PRODUCER
SOON...
THANKS FOR THE SAVE BACK THERE, PRINCIPAL COULSON.
I'M NOT DOING YOU ANY FAVORS, PARKER. S.H.I.E.L.D. IS IN URGENT NEED OF YOUR SERVICES.
PRINCIPAL COULSON
IT WOULDN'T HURT YOU TO SAY "PLEASE" EVERY ONCE IN A WHILE.
THIS IS SERIOUS.
ALSO, IF I HAVE TO KEEP BAILING YOU OUT OF GEOMETRY, WE'RE LIABLE TO BLOW OUR COVER.
BRING YOUR GRADES UP...
...OR S.H.I.E.L.D. WILL OFFICIALLY BENCH YOU FROM ITS SUPER-HUMAN TRAINING PROGRAM.
WE SET UP SHOP IN YOUR HIGH SCHOOL SO YOU COULD GET A HOLD OF THINGS, IMPROVE YOUR GRADES AND FIGHT CRIME.
WE DON'T KEEP LOSERS, WE DROP THEM.
YIPE!
CLICK
SHNNK!

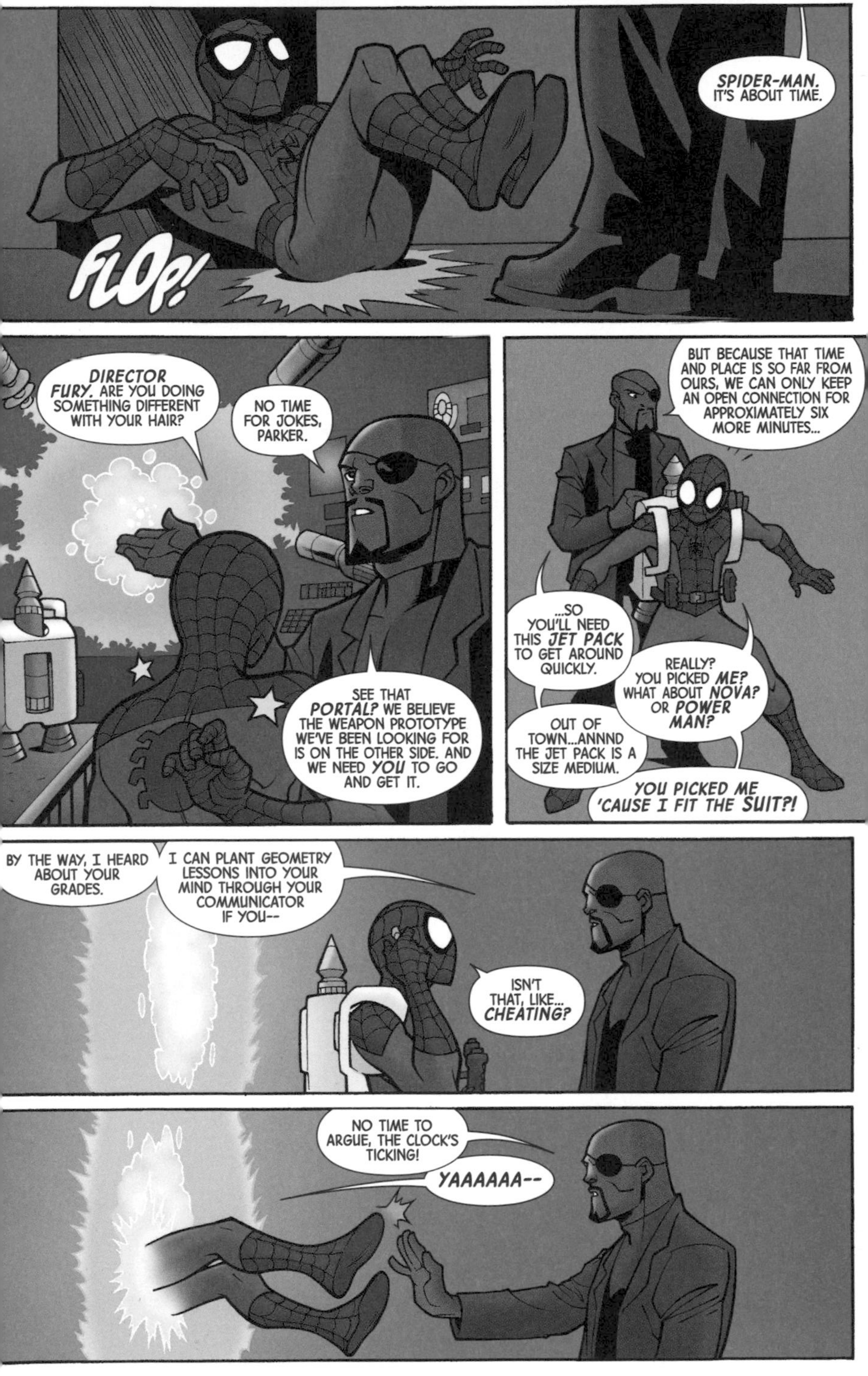
FLOP!
SPIDER-MAN. IT'S ABOUT TIME.
DIRECTOR FURY. ARE YOU DOING SOMETHING DIFFERENT WITH YOUR HAIR?
NO TIME FOR JOKES, PARKER.
SEE THAT PORTAL? WE BELIEVE THE WEAPON PROTOTYPE WE'VE BEEN LOOKING FOR IS ON THE OTHER SIDE. AND WE NEED YOU TO GO AND GET IT.
BUT BECAUSE THAT TIME AND PLACE IS SO FAR FROM OURS, WE CAN ONLY KEEP AN OPEN CONNECTION FOR APPROXIMATELY SIX MORE MINUTES...
...SO YOU'LL NEED THIS JET PACK TO GET AROUND QUICKLY.
REALLY? YOU PICKED ME? WHAT ABOUT NOVA? OR POWER MAN?
OUT OF TOWN...ANNND THE JET PACK IS A SIZE MEDIUM.
YOU PICKED ME 'CAUSE I FIT THE SUIT?!
BY THE WAY, I HEARD ABOUT YOUR GRADES.
I CAN PLANT GEOMETRY LESSONS INTO YOUR MIND THROUGH YOUR COMMUNICATOR IF YOU--
ISN'T THAT, LIKE... CHEATING?
NO TIME TO ARGUE, THE CLOCK'S TICKING!
YAAAAAA--

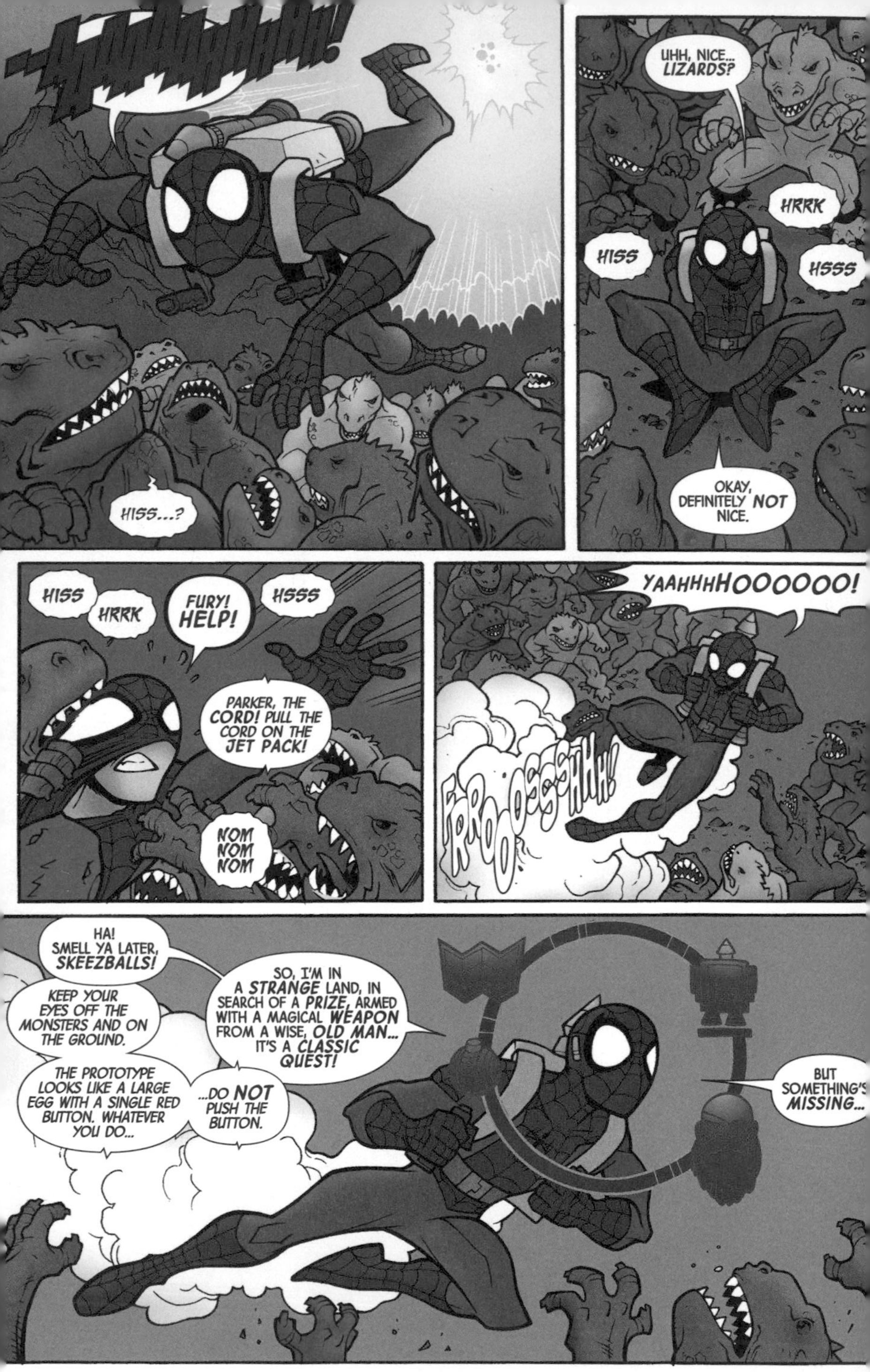
UHH, NICE... LIZARDS?
HISS...?
HISS
HRRK
HSSS
OKAY, DEFINITELY NOT NICE.
HISS
HRRK
FURY! HELP!
HSSS
PARKER, THE CORD! PULL THE CORD ON THE JET PACK!
NOM NOM NOM
YAAHHHHOOOOOOO!
FRROOOSSSHHH!
HA! SMELL YA LATER, SKEEZBALLS!
KEEP YOUR EYES OFF THE MONSTERS AND ON THE GROUND.
THE PROTOTYPE LOOKS LIKE A LARGE EGG WITH A SINGLE RED BUTTON. WHATEVER YOU DO...
...DO NOT PUSH THE BUTTON.
SO, I'M IN A STRANGE LAND, IN SEARCH OF A PRIZE, ARMED WITH A MAGICAL WEAPON FROM A WISE, OLD MAN... IT'S A CLASSIC QUEST!
BUT SOMETHING'S MISSING...

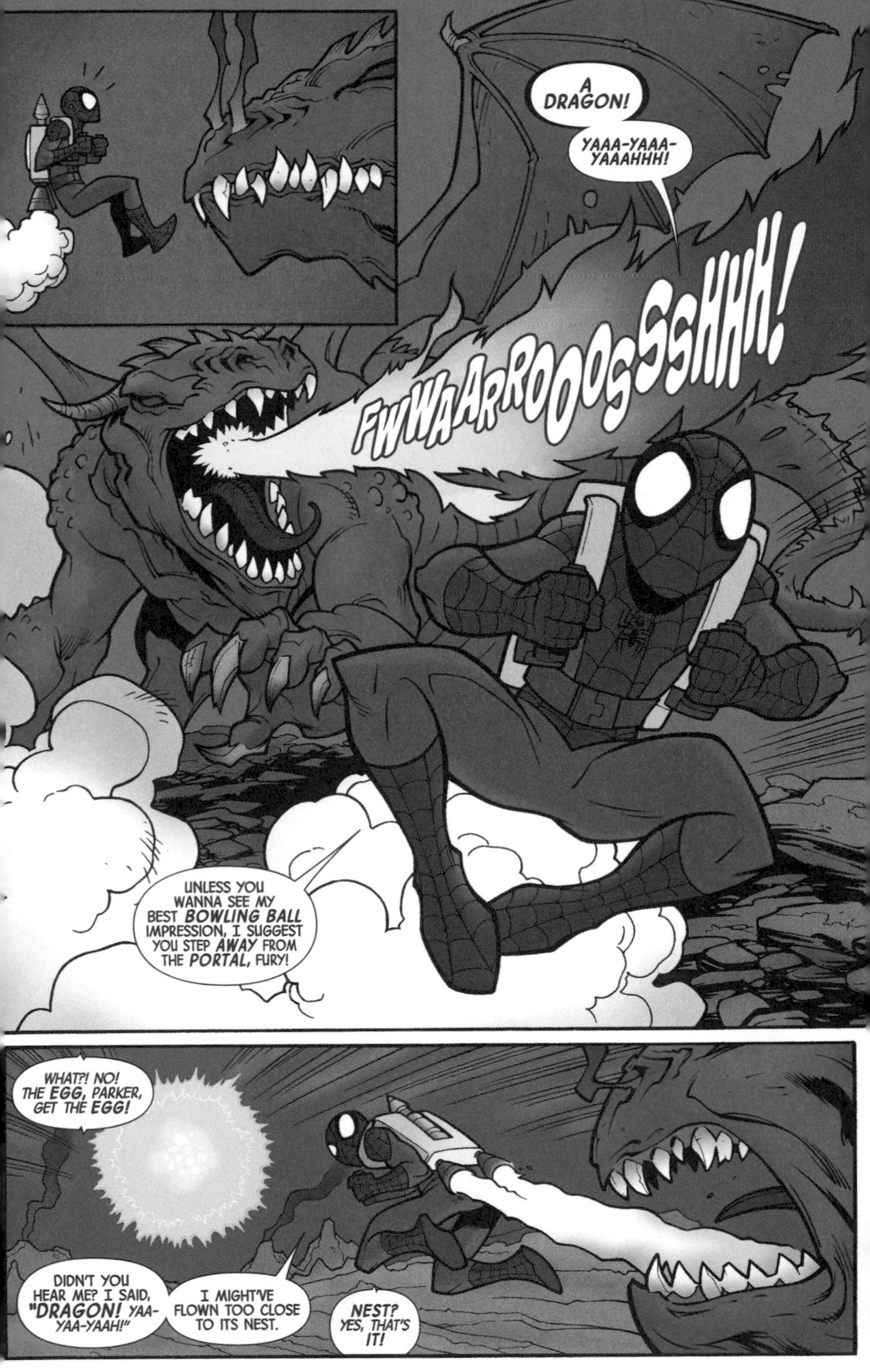
A DRAGON!
YAAA-YAAA-YAAAHHH!
FWWAARROOOSSHHH!
UNLESS YOU WANNA SEE MY BEST BOWLING BALL IMPRESSION, I SUGGEST YOU STEP AWAY FROM THE PORTAL, FURY!
WHAT?! NO! THE EGG, PARKER, GET THE EGG!
DIDN'T YOU HEAR ME? I SAID, "DRAGON! YAA-YAA-YAAH!"
I MIGHT'VE FLOWN TOO CLOSE TO ITS NEST.
NEST? YES, THAT'S IT!

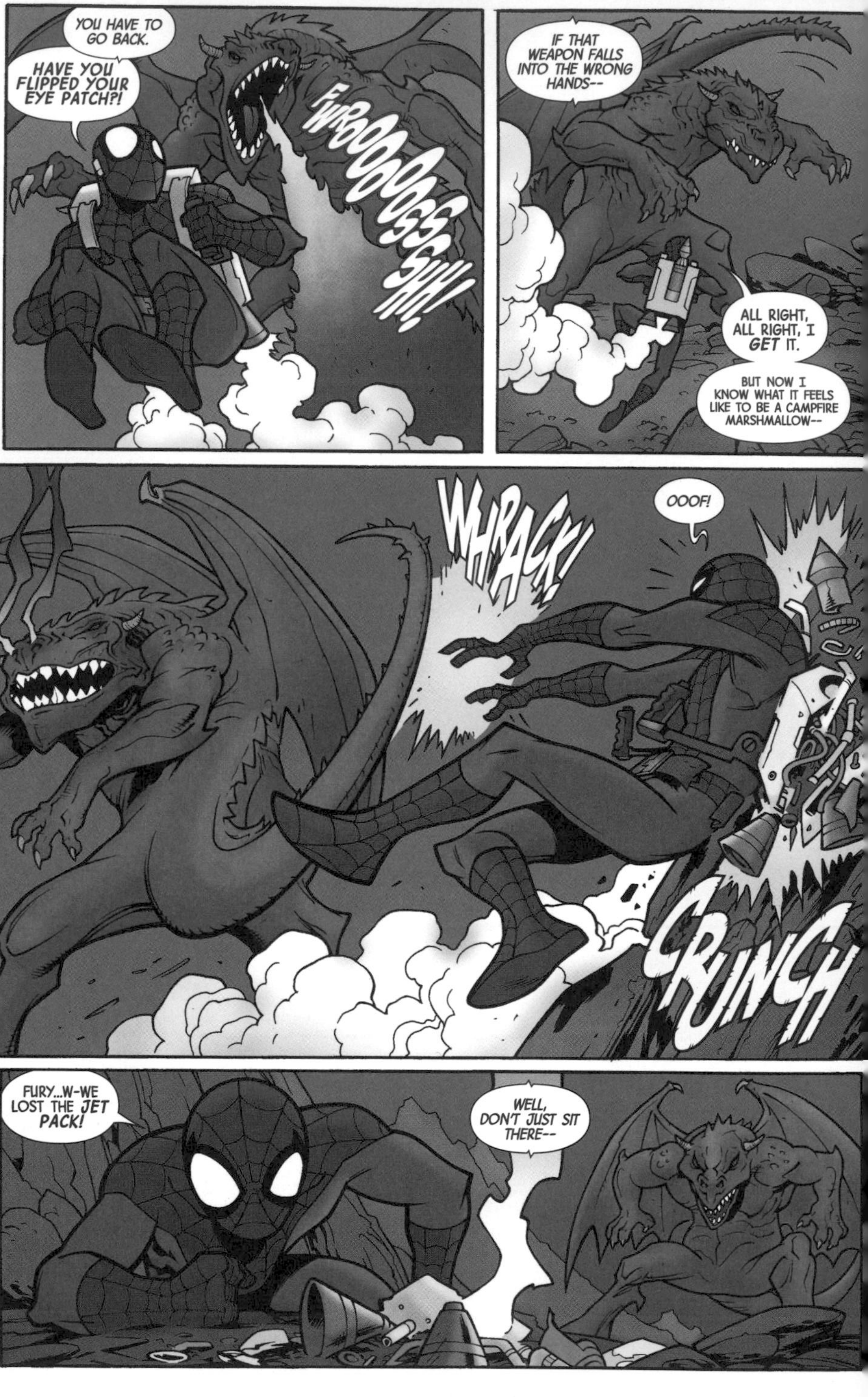
YOU HAVE TO GO BACK.
HAVE YOU FLIPPED YOUR EYE PATCH?!
FWROOOOOOSSSHH!
IF THAT WEAPON FALLS INTO THE WRONG HANDS--
ALL RIGHT, ALL RIGHT, I GET IT.
BUT NOW I KNOW WHAT IT FEELS LIKE TO BE A CAMPFIRE MARSHMALLOW--
WHRACK!
OOOF!
CRUNCH
FURY...W-WE LOST THE JET PACK!
WELL, DON'T JUST SIT THERE--

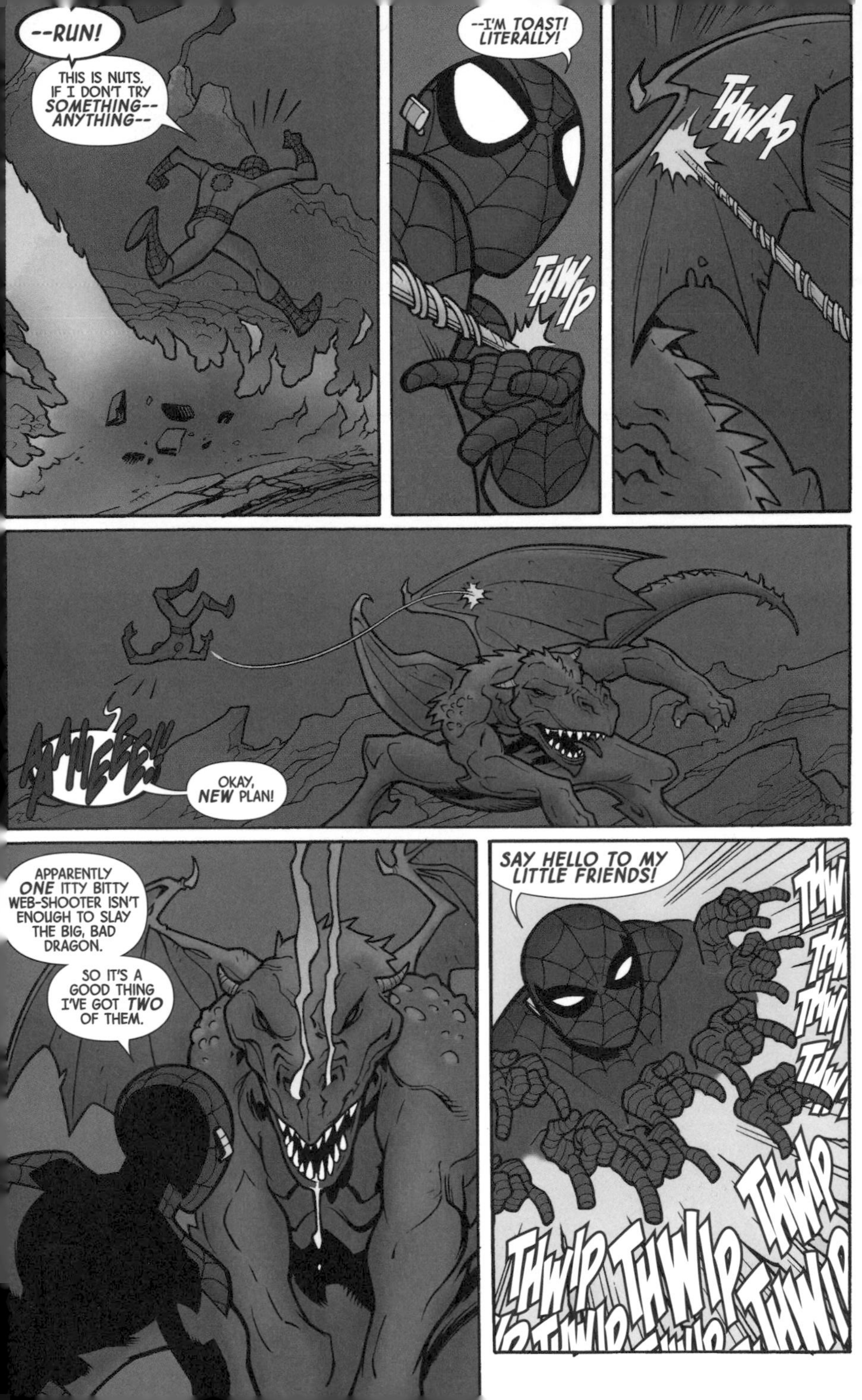
--RUN!
THIS IS NUTS. IF I DON'T TRY SOMETHING-- ANYTHING--
--I'M TOAST! LITERALLY!
THWIP
THWAP
AAAHEEEE!!
OKAY, NEW PLAN!
APPARENTLY ONE ITTY BITTY WEB-SHOOTER ISN'T ENOUGH TO SLAY THE BIG, BAD DRAGON.
SO IT'S A GOOD THING I'VE GOT TWO OF THEM.
SAY HELLO TO MY LITTLE FRIENDS!
THWIP THWIP THWIP THWIP

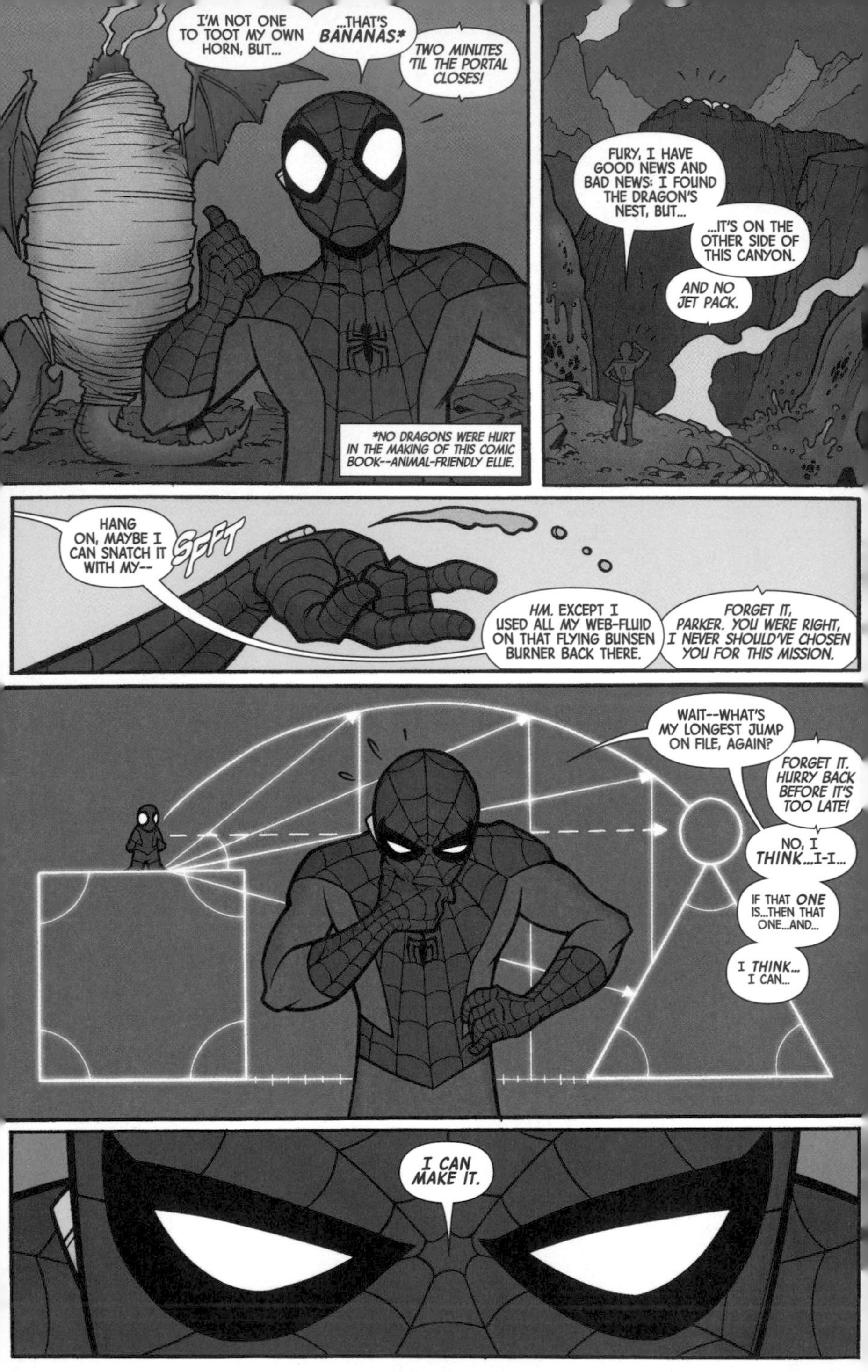
I'M NOT ONE TO TOOT MY OWN HORN, BUT...
...THAT'S BANANAS!*
TWO MINUTES 'TIL THE PORTAL CLOSES!
*NO DRAGONS WERE HURT IN THE MAKING OF THIS COMIC BOOK--ANIMAL-FRIENDLY ELLIE.
FURY, I HAVE GOOD NEWS AND BAD NEWS: I FOUND THE DRAGON'S NEST, BUT...
...IT'S ON THE OTHER SIDE OF THIS CANYON.
AND NO JET PACK.
HANG ON, MAYBE I CAN SNATCH IT WITH MY--
SFFT
HM. EXCEPT I USED ALL MY WEB-FLUID ON THAT FLYING BUNSEN BURNER BACK THERE.
FORGET IT, PARKER. YOU WERE RIGHT, I NEVER SHOULD'VE CHOSEN YOU FOR THIS MISSION.
WAIT--WHAT'S MY LONGEST JUMP ON FILE, AGAIN?
FORGET IT. HURRY BACK BEFORE IT'S TOO LATE!
NO, I THINK...I-I...
IF THAT ONE IS...THEN THAT ONE...AND...
I THINK... I CAN...
I CAN MAKE IT.

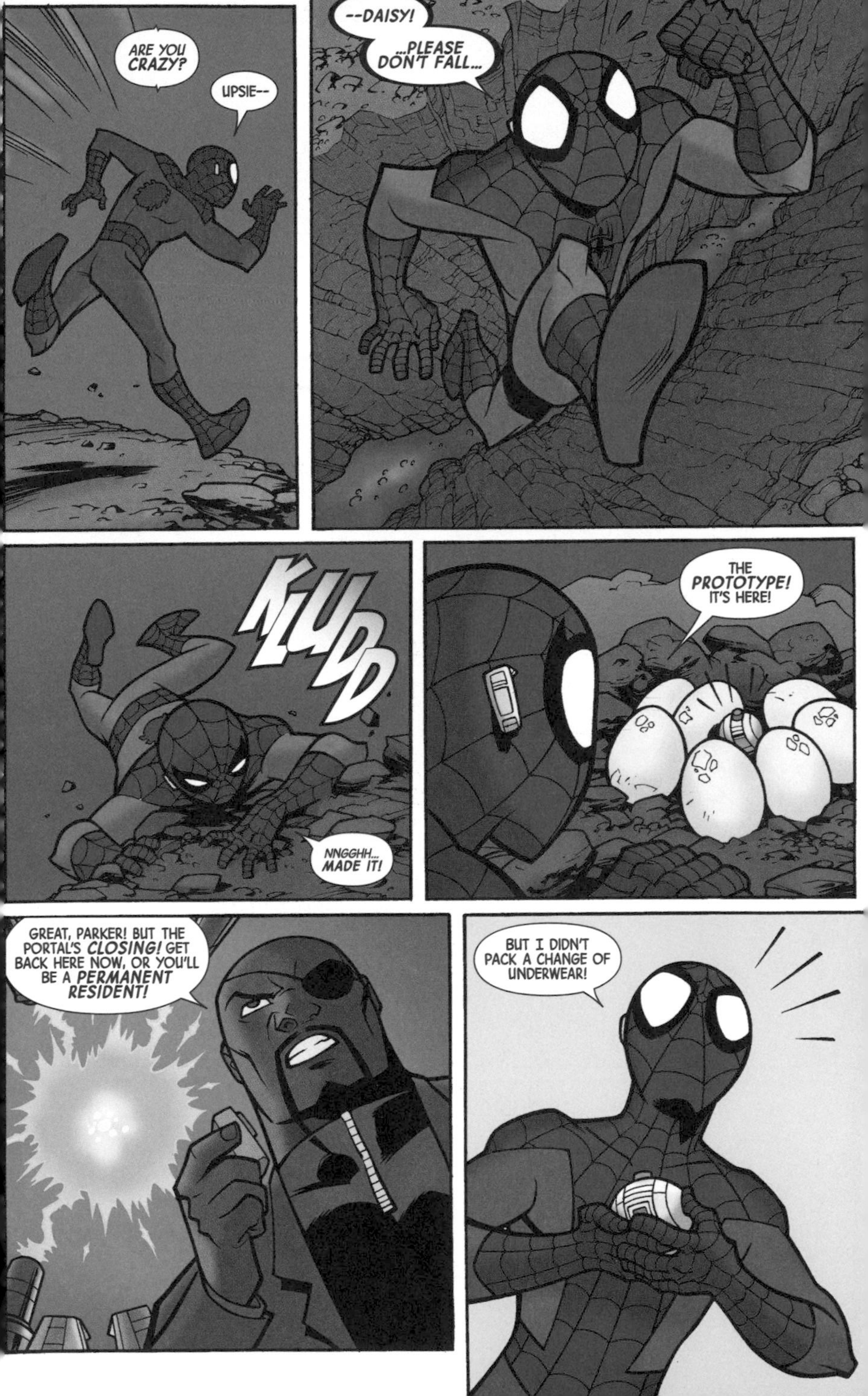
ARE YOU CRAZY?
UPSIE--
--DAISY!
...PLEASE DON'T FALL...
KLUDD
NNGGHH... MADE IT!
THE PROTOTYPE! IT'S HERE!
GREAT, PARKER! BUT THE PORTAL'S CLOSING! GET BACK HERE NOW, OR YOU'LL BE A PERMANENT RESIDENT!
BUT I DIDN'T PACK A CHANGE OF UNDERWEAR!

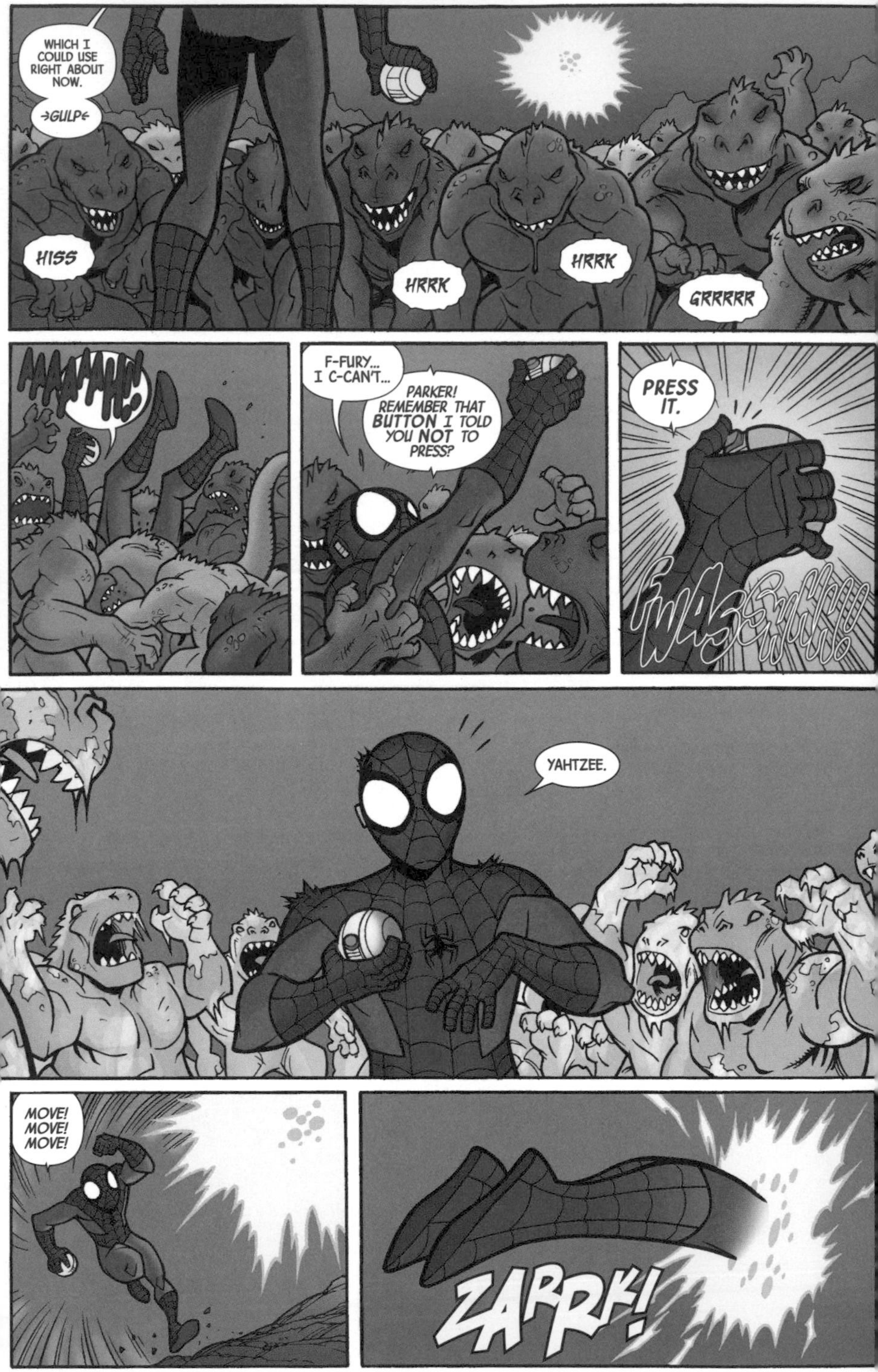
WHICH I COULD USE RIGHT ABOUT NOW.
→GULP←
HISS
HRRK
HRRK
GRRRRR
F-FURY... I C-CAN'T...
PARKER! REMEMBER THAT BUTTON I TOLD YOU NOT TO PRESS?
PRESS IT.
YAHTZEE.
MOVE! MOVE! MOVE!
ZARRK!

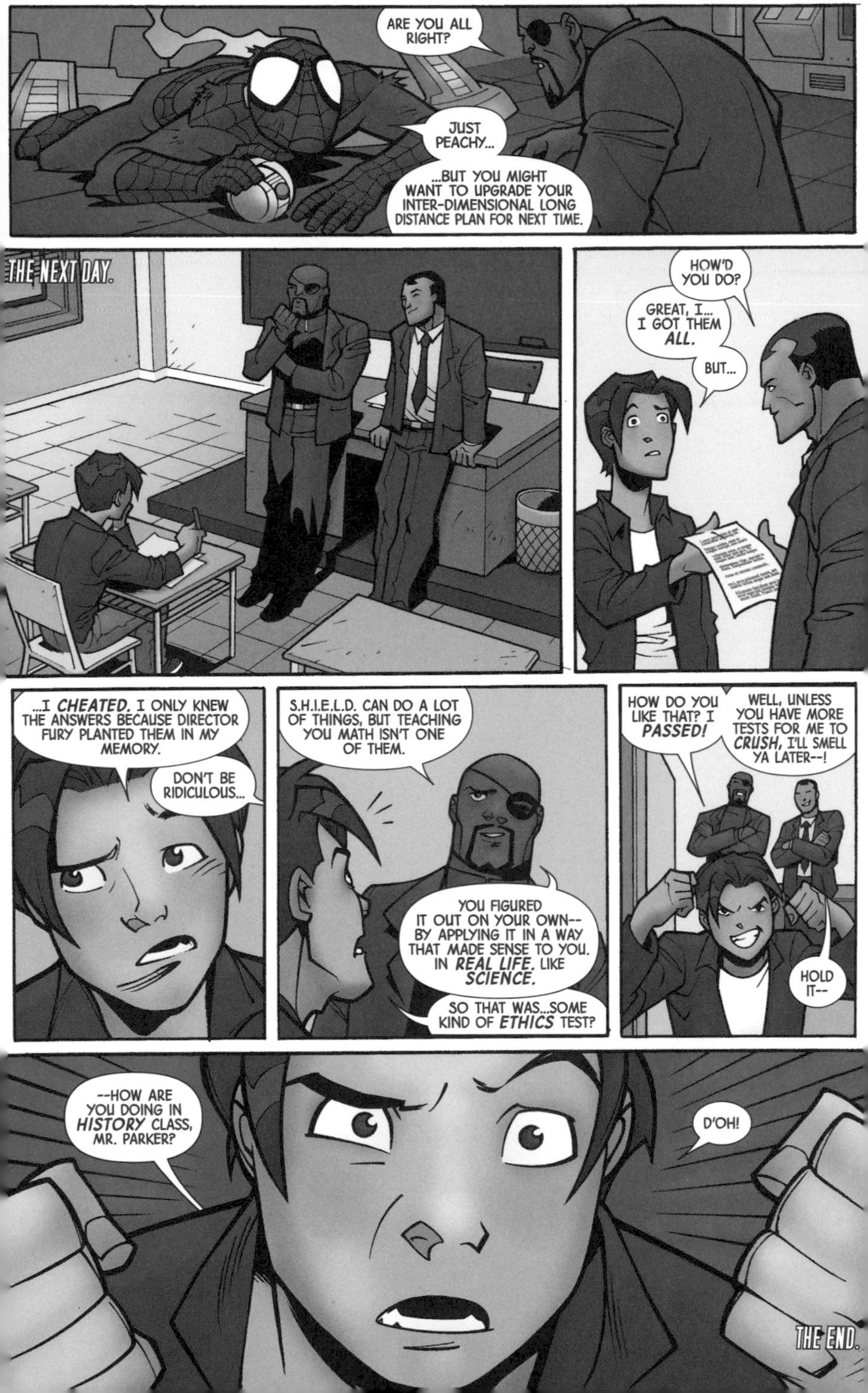
ARE YOU ALL RIGHT?
JUST PEACHY...
...BUT YOU MIGHT WANT TO UPGRADE YOUR INTER-DIMENSIONAL LONG DISTANCE PLAN FOR NEXT TIME.
THE NEXT DAY.
HOW'D YOU DO?
GREAT, I... I GOT THEM ALL.
BUT...
...I CHEATED. I ONLY KNEW THE ANSWERS BECAUSE DIRECTOR FURY PLANTED THEM IN MY MEMORY.
DON'T BE RIDICULOUS...
S.H.I.E.L.D. CAN DO A LOT OF THINGS, BUT TEACHING YOU MATH ISN'T ONE OF THEM.
YOU FIGURED IT OUT ON YOUR OWN-- BY APPLYING IT IN A WAY THAT MADE SENSE TO YOU. IN REAL LIFE. LIKE SCIENCE.
SO THAT WAS...SOME KIND OF ETHICS TEST?
HOW DO YOU LIKE THAT? I PASSED!
WELL, UNLESS YOU HAVE MORE TESTS FOR ME TO CRUSH, I'LL SMELL YA LATER--!
HOLD IT--
--HOW ARE YOU DOING IN HISTORY CLASS, MR. PARKER?
D'OH!
THE END.

AND NOW... THE FOUR SEASONS!

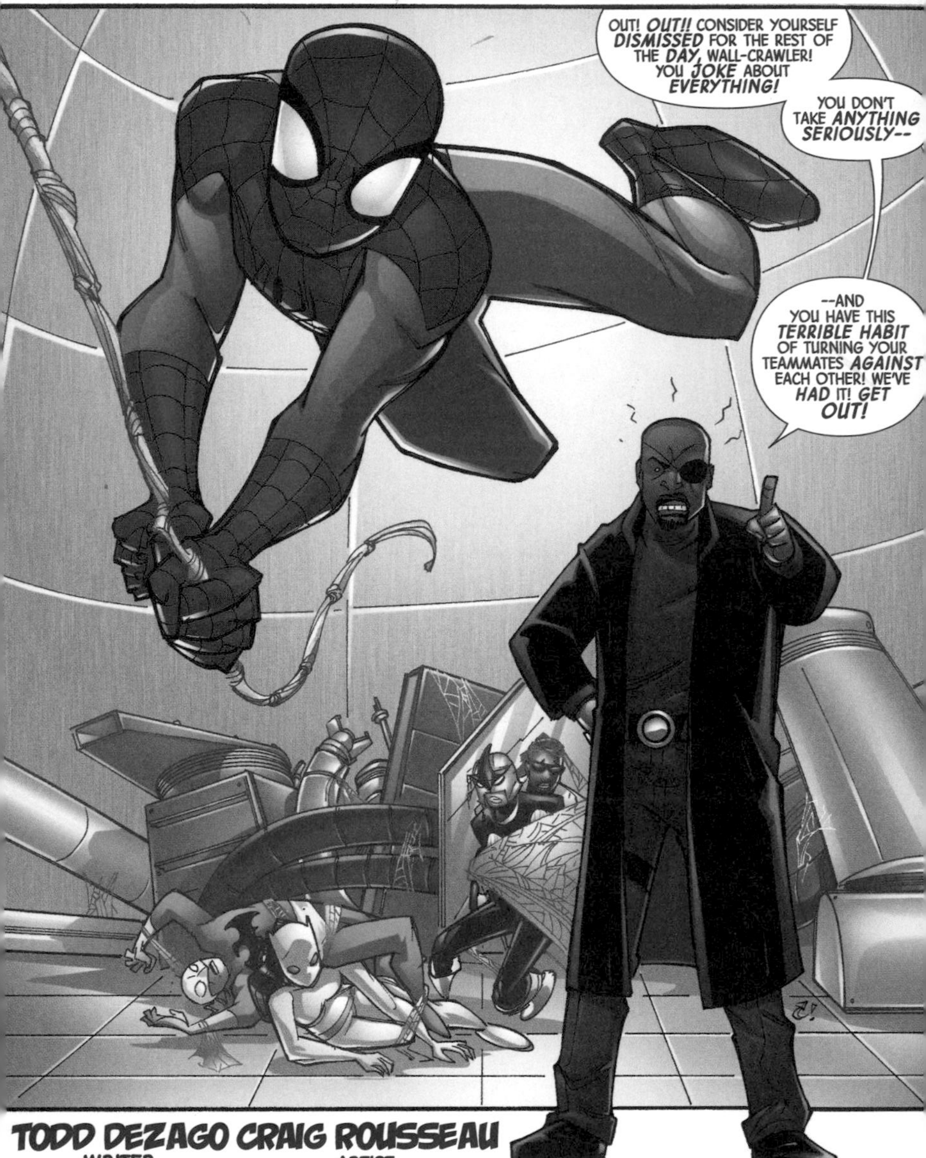

OUT! OUT!! CONSIDER YOURSELF DISMISSED FOR THE REST OF THE DAY, WALL-CRAWLER! YOU JOKE ABOUT EVERYTHING!
YOU DON'T TAKE ANYTHING SERIOUSLY--
--AND YOU HAVE THIS TERRIBLE HABIT OF TURNING YOUR TEAMMATES AGAINST EACH OTHER! WE'VE HAD IT! GET OUT!

TODD DEZAGO WRITER
CRAIG ROUSSEAU ARTIST
PETE PANTAZIS COLOR ARTIST
VC'S CLAYTON COWLES LETTERER
ELLIE PYLE & TOM BRENNAN EDITORS
STEPHEN WACKER SENIOR EDITOR
AXEL ALONSO EDITOR IN CHIEF
JOE QUESADA CHIEF CREATIVE OFFICER
DAN BUCKLEY PUBLISHER
ALAN FINE EXEC. PRODUCER

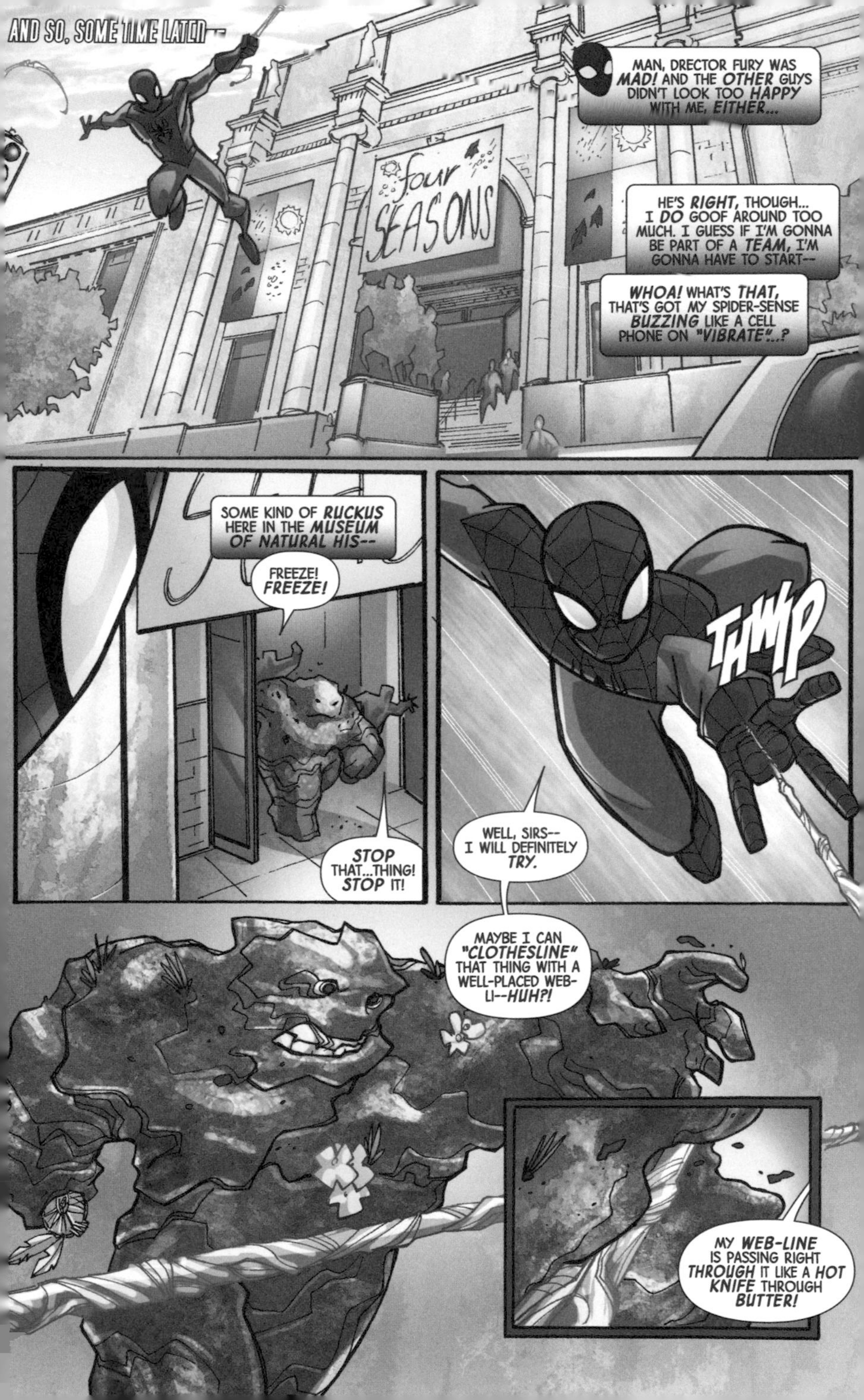
AND SO, SOME TIME LATER--
MAN, DRECTOR FURY WAS MAD! AND THE OTHER GUYS DIDN'T LOOK TOO HAPPY WITH ME, EITHER...
four SEASONS
HE'S RIGHT, THOUGH... I DO GOOF AROUND TOO MUCH. I GUESS IF I'M GONNA BE PART OF A TEAM, I'M GONNA HAVE TO START--
WHOA! WHAT'S THAT, THAT'S GOT MY SPIDER-SENSE BUZZING LIKE A CELL PHONE ON "VIBRATE"...?
SOME KIND OF RUCKUS HERE IN THE MUSEUM OF NATURAL HIS--
FREEZE! FREEZE!
STOP THAT...THING! STOP IT!
THWIP
WELL, SIRS-- I WILL DEFINITELY TRY.
MAYBE I CAN "CLOTHESLINE" THAT THING WITH A WELL-PLACED WEB-LI--HUH?!
MY WEB-LINE IS PASSING RIGHT THROUGH IT LIKE A HOT KNIFE THROUGH BUTTER!

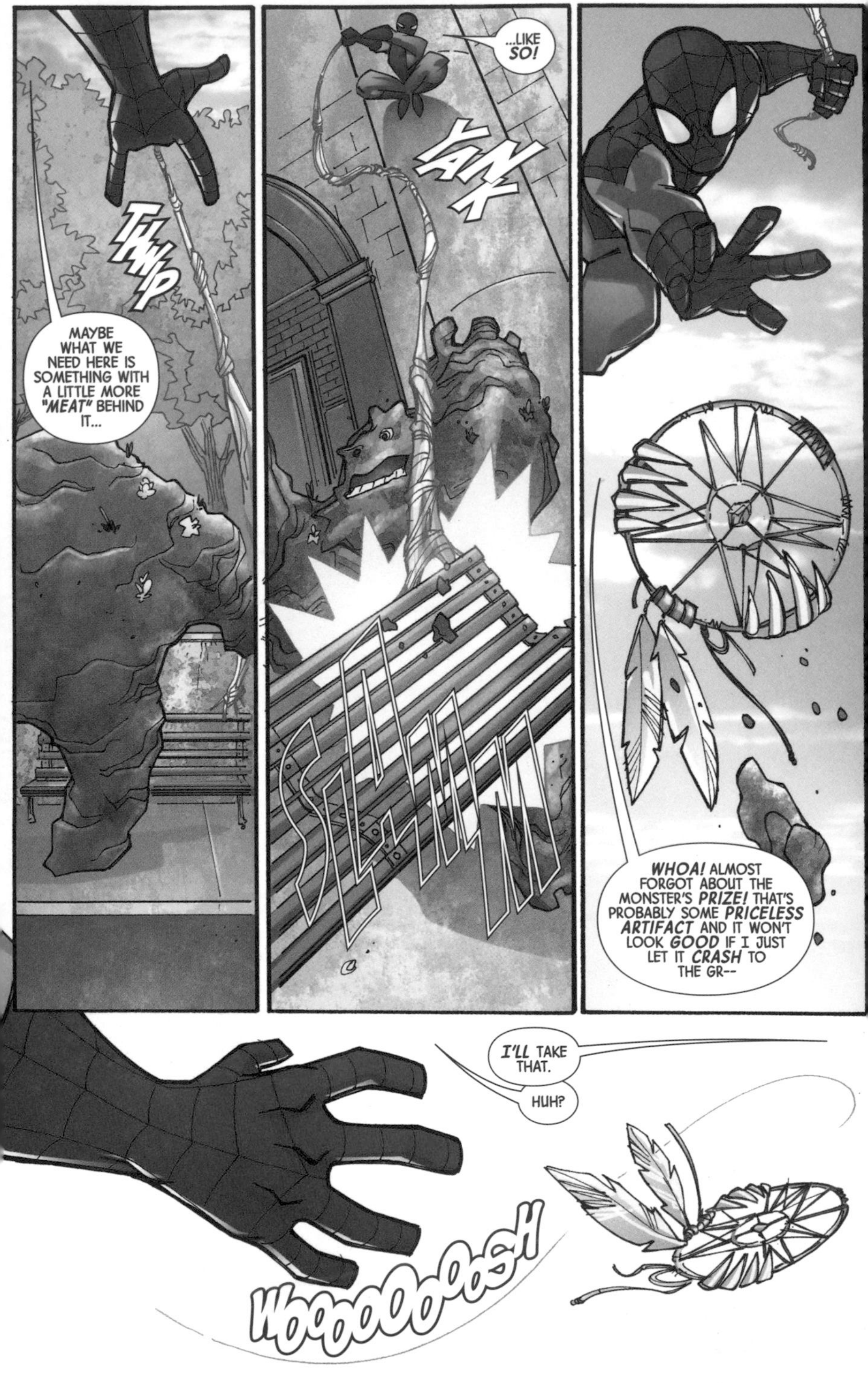
THWIP
MAYBE WHAT WE NEED HERE IS SOMETHING WITH A LITTLE MORE "MEAT" BEHIND IT...
...LIKE SO!
YANK
WHOA! ALMOST FORGOT ABOUT THE MONSTER'S PRIZE! THAT'S PROBABLY SOME PRICELESS ARTIFACT AND IT WON'T LOOK GOOD IF I JUST LET IT CRASH TO THE GR--
I'LL TAKE THAT.
HUH?

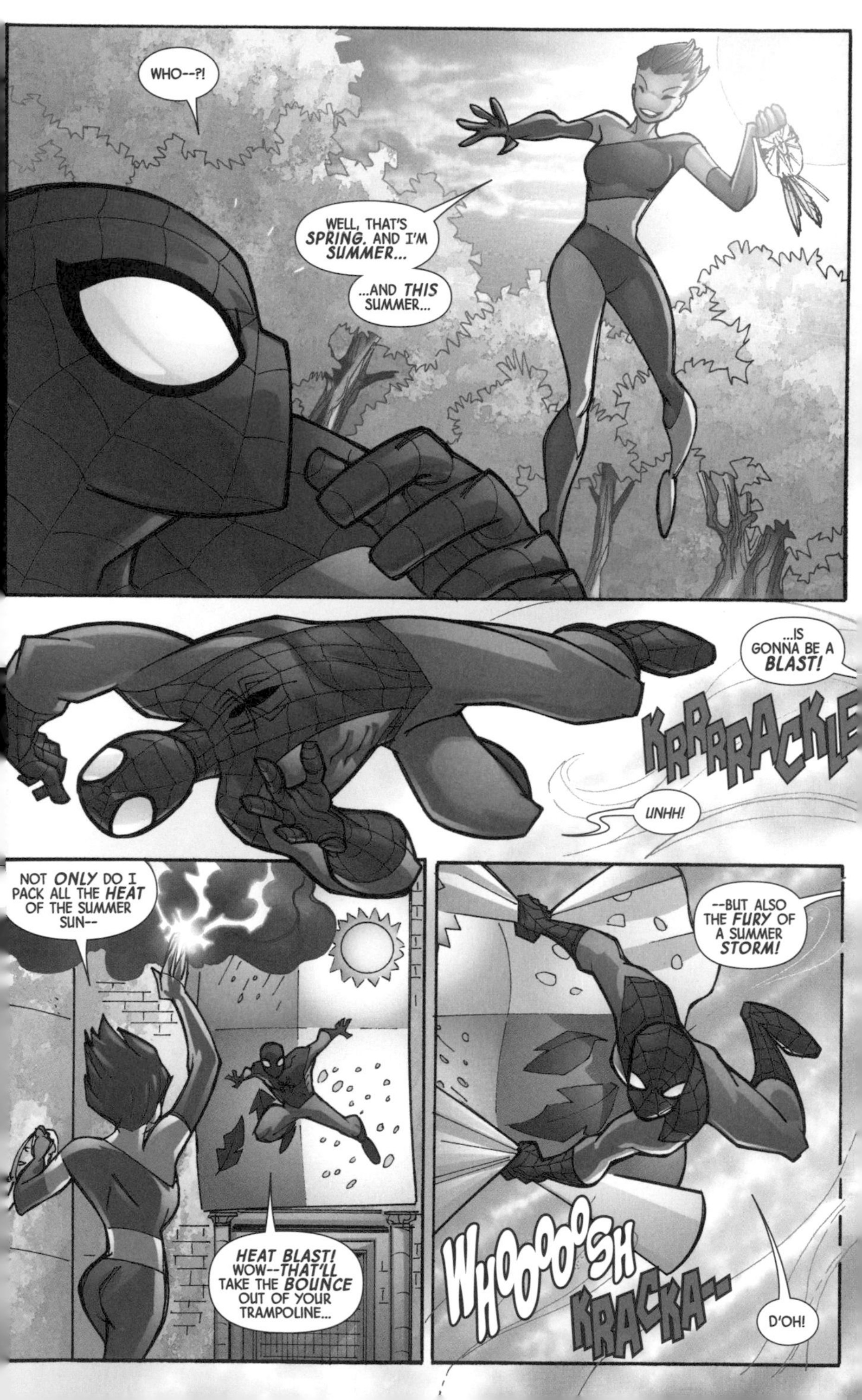
WHO--?!
WELL, THAT'S SPRING. AND I'M SUMMER...
...AND THIS SUMMER...
...IS GONNA BE A BLAST!
KRRRRACKLE
UNHH!
NOT ONLY DO I PACK ALL THE HEAT OF THE SUMMER SUN--
HEAT BLAST! WOW--THAT'LL TAKE THE BOUNCE OUT OF YOUR TRAMPOLINE...
--BUT ALSO THE FURY OF A SUMMER STORM!
WHOOOOOSH
KRACKA--
D'OH!

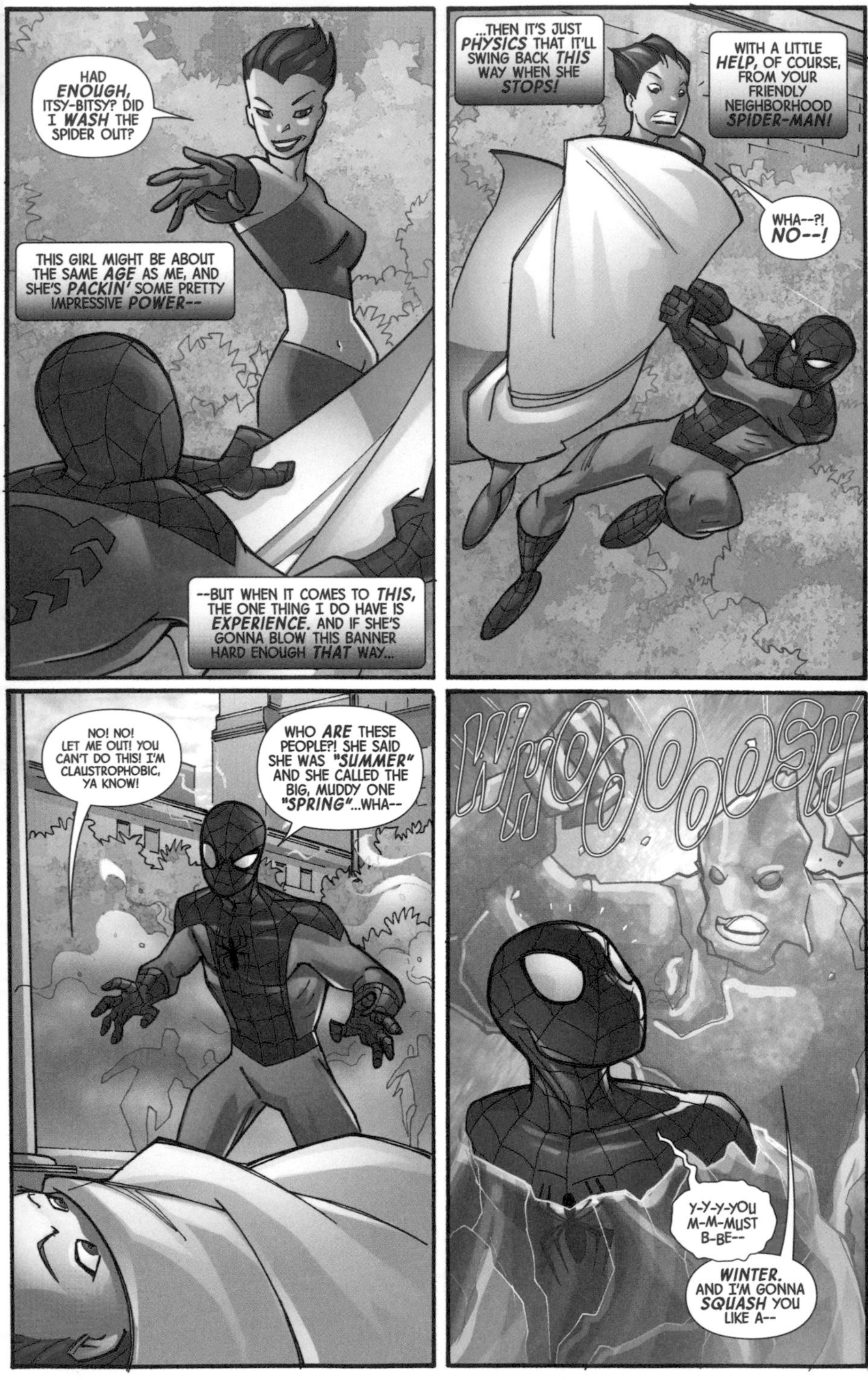
HAD ENOUGH, ITSY-BITSY? DID I WASH THE SPIDER OUT?
THIS GIRL MIGHT BE ABOUT THE SAME AGE AS ME, AND SHE'S PACKIN' SOME PRETTY IMPRESSIVE POWER--
--BUT WHEN IT COMES TO THIS, THE ONE THING I DO HAVE IS EXPERIENCE. AND IF SHE'S GONNA BLOW THIS BANNER HARD ENOUGH THAT WAY...
...THEN IT'S JUST PHYSICS THAT IT'LL SWING BACK THIS WAY WHEN SHE STOPS!
WITH A LITTLE HELP, OF COURSE, FROM YOUR FRIENDLY NEIGHBORHOOD SPIDER-MAN!
WHA--?! NO--!
NO! NO! LET ME OUT! YOU CAN'T DO THIS! I'M CLAUSTROPHOBIC, YA KNOW!
WHO ARE THESE PEOPLE?! SHE SAID SHE WAS "SUMMER" AND SHE CALLED THE BIG, MUDDY ONE "SPRING"...WHA--
WHOOOOOOSH
Y-Y-Y-YOU M-M-MUST B-BE--
WINTER. AND I'M GONNA SQUASH YOU LIKE A--

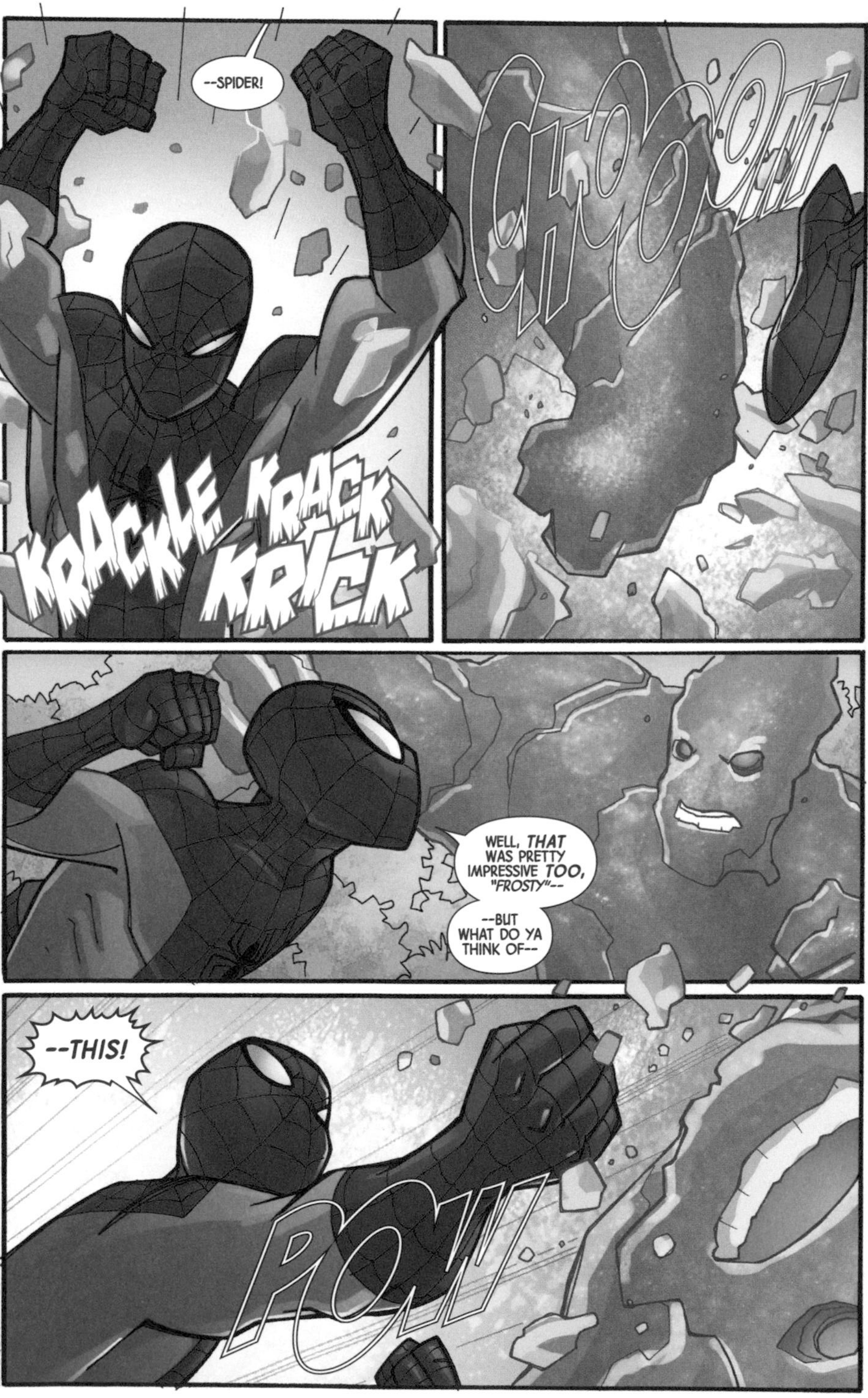
--SPIDER!
KRACKLE KRACK KRICK
CHOOOOM
WELL, THAT WAS PRETTY IMPRESSIVE TOO, "FROSTY"--
--BUT WHAT DO YA THINK OF--
--THIS!
POW

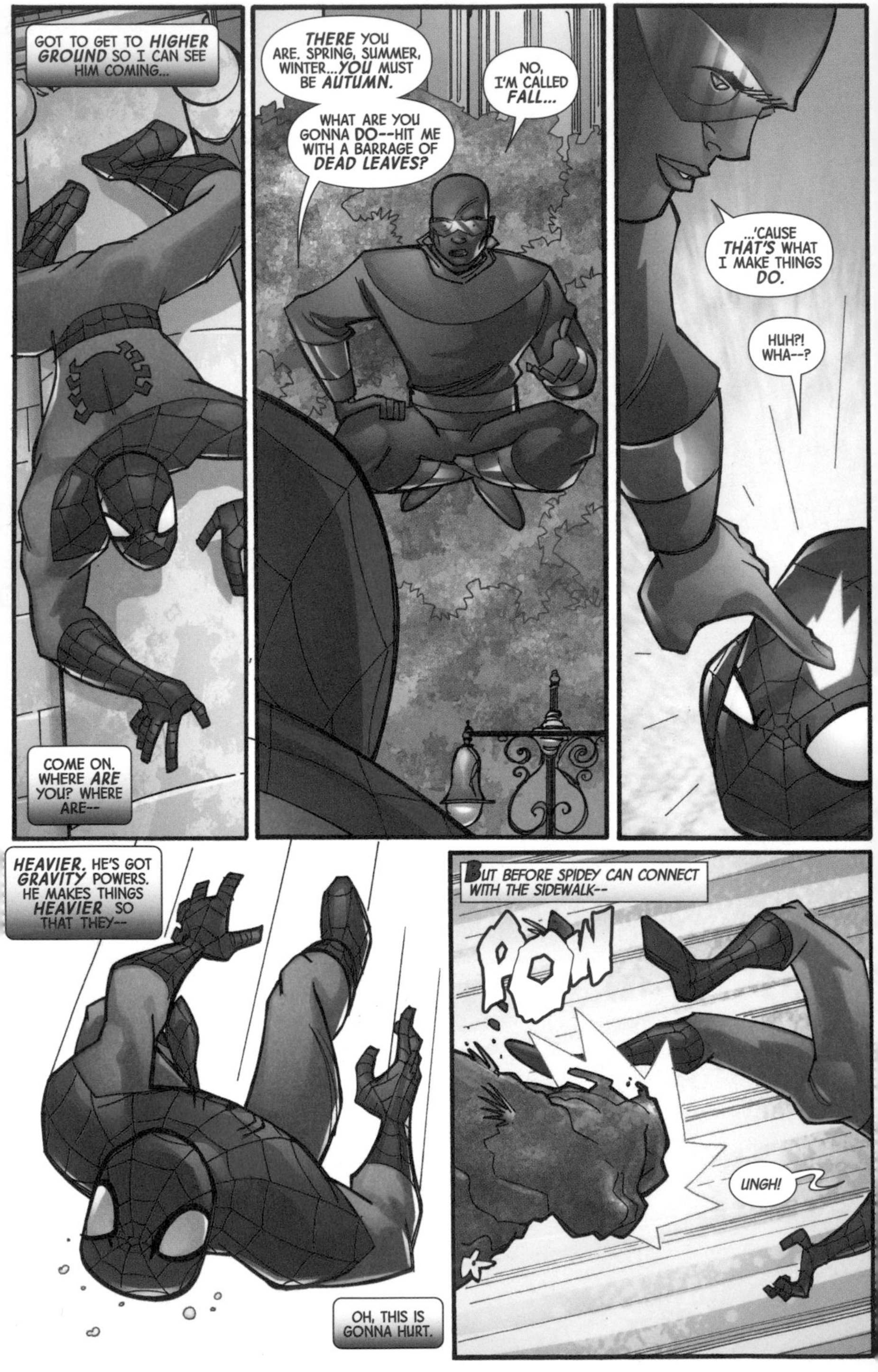

GOT TO GET TO HIGHER GROUND SO I CAN SEE HIM COMING...
COME ON. WHERE ARE YOU? WHERE ARE--
THERE YOU ARE. SPRING, SUMMER, WINTER...YOU MUST BE AUTUMN.
WHAT ARE YOU GONNA DO--HIT ME WITH A BARRAGE OF DEAD LEAVES?
NO, I'M CALLED FALL...
...'CAUSE THAT'S WHAT I MAKE THINGS DO.
HUH?! WHA--?
HEAVIER. HE'S GOT GRAVITY POWERS. HE MAKES THINGS HEAVIER SO THAT THEY--
OH, THIS IS GONNA HURT.
BUT BEFORE SPIDEY CAN CONNECT WITH THE SIDEWALK--
POW
UNGH!

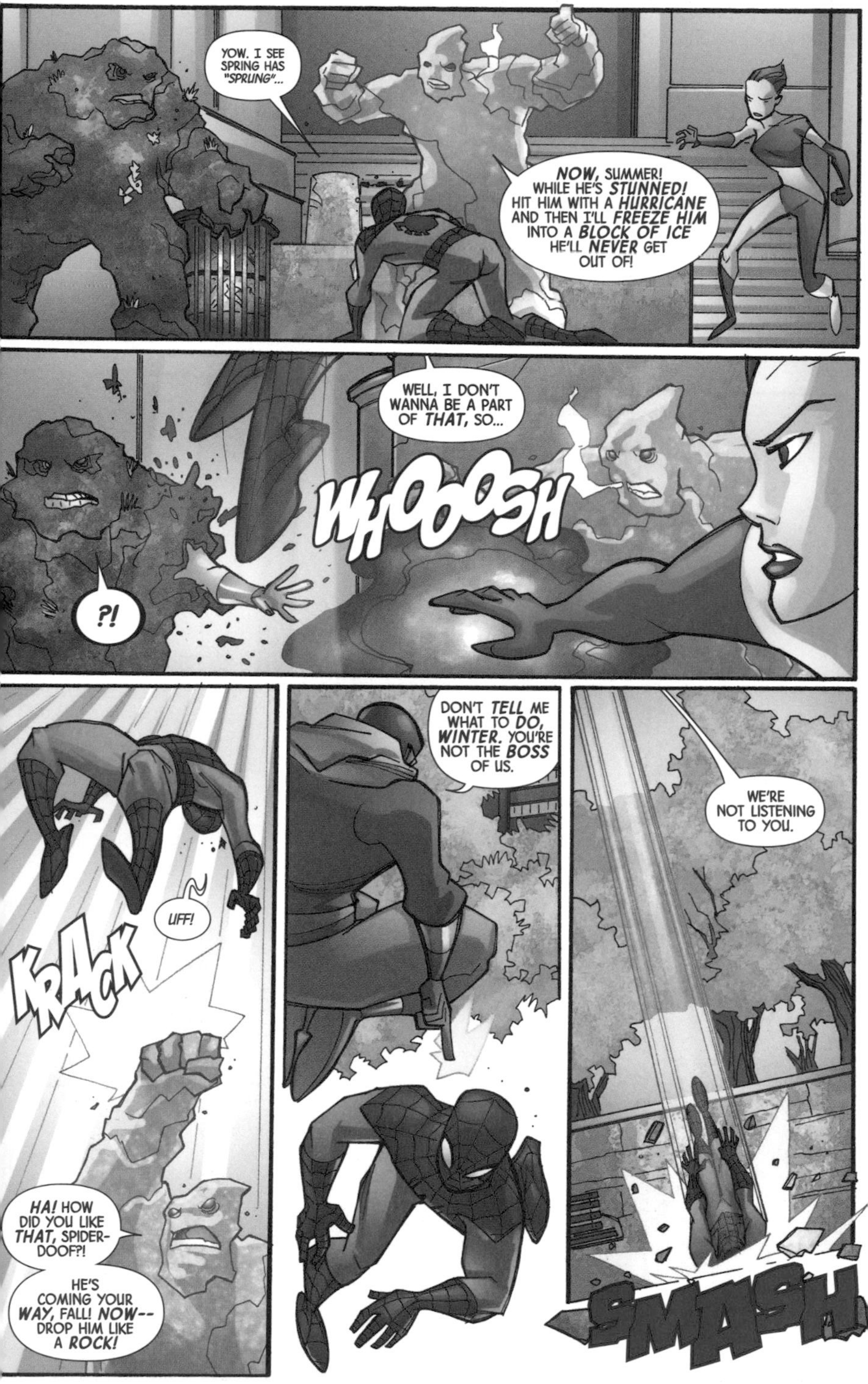
YOW. I SEE SPRING HAS "SPRUNG"...
NOW, SUMMER! WHILE HE'S STUNNED! HIT HIM WITH A HURRICANE AND THEN I'LL FREEZE HIM INTO A BLOCK OF ICE HE'LL NEVER GET OUT OF!
WELL, I DON'T WANNA BE A PART OF THAT, SO...
WHOOOOSH
?!
UFF!
KRACK
HA! HOW DID YOU LIKE THAT, SPIDER-DOOF?!
HE'S COMING YOUR WAY, FALL! NOW-- DROP HIM LIKE A ROCK!
DON'T TELL ME WHAT TO DO, WINTER. YOU'RE NOT THE BOSS OF US.
WE'RE NOT LISTENING TO YOU.
SMASH

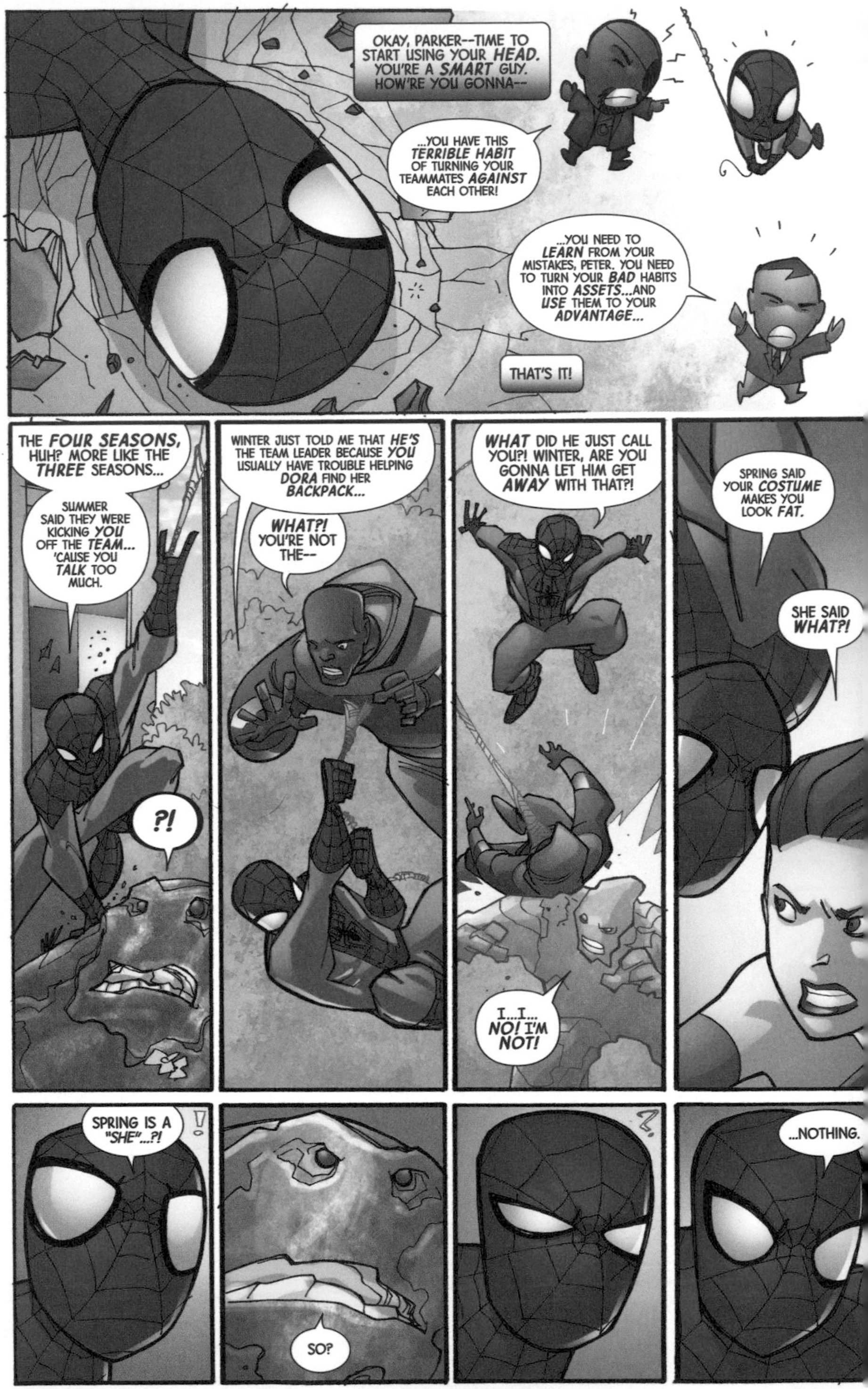

OKAY, PARKER--TIME TO START USING YOUR HEAD. YOU'RE A SMART GUY. HOW'RE YOU GONNA--
...YOU HAVE THIS TERRIBLE HABIT OF TURNING YOUR TEAMMATES AGAINST EACH OTHER!
...YOU NEED TO LEARN FROM YOUR MISTAKES, PETER. YOU NEED TO TURN YOUR BAD HABITS INTO ASSETS...AND USE THEM TO YOUR ADVANTAGE...
THAT'S IT!
THE FOUR SEASONS, HUH? MORE LIKE THE THREE SEASONS...
SUMMER SAID THEY WERE KICKING YOU OFF THE TEAM... 'CAUSE YOU TALK TOO MUCH.
?!
WINTER JUST TOLD ME THAT HE'S THE TEAM LEADER BECAUSE YOU USUALLY HAVE TROUBLE HELPING DORA FIND HER BACKPACK...
WHAT?! YOU'RE NOT THE--
WHAT DID HE JUST CALL YOU?! WINTER, ARE YOU GONNA LET HIM GET AWAY WITH THAT?!
I...I... NO! I'M NOT!
SPRING SAID YOUR COSTUME MAKES YOU LOOK FAT.
SHE SAID WHAT?!
SPRING IS A "SHE"...?!
SO?
...NOTHING.

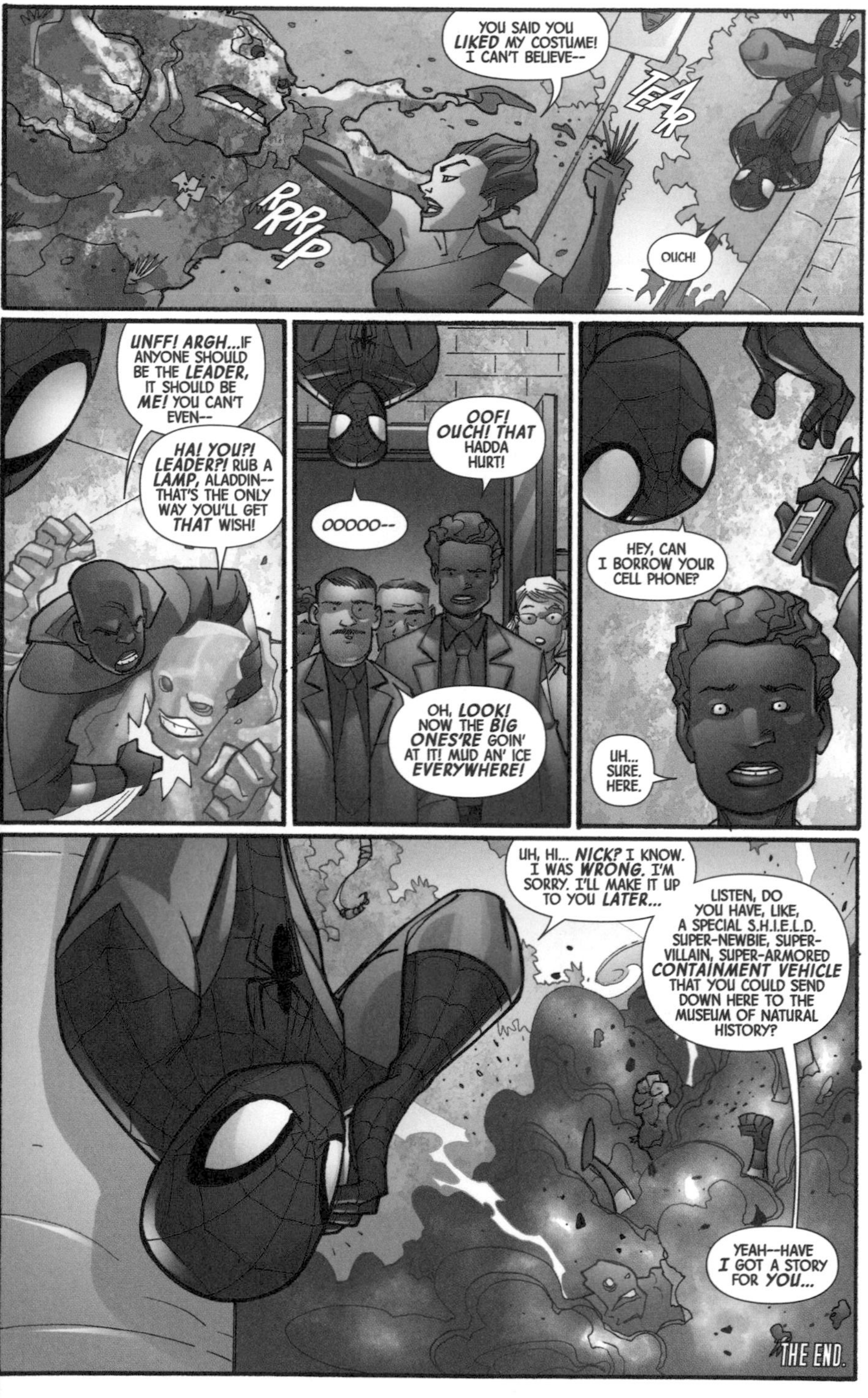
YOU SAID YOU LIKED MY COSTUME! I CAN'T BELIEVE--
TEAR
RRRIP
OUCH!
UNFF! ARGH...IF ANYONE SHOULD BE THE LEADER, IT SHOULD BE ME! YOU CAN'T EVEN--
HA! YOU?! LEADER?! RUB A LAMP, ALADDIN-- THAT'S THE ONLY WAY YOU'LL GET THAT WISH!
OOF! OUCH! THAT HADDA HURT!
OOOOO--
OH, LOOK! NOW THE BIG ONES'RE GOIN' AT IT! MUD AN' ICE EVERYWHERE!
HEY, CAN I BORROW YOUR CELL PHONE?
UH... SURE. HERE.
UH, HI... NICK? I KNOW. I WAS WRONG. I'M SORRY. I'LL MAKE IT UP TO YOU LATER...
LISTEN, DO YOU HAVE, LIKE, A SPECIAL S.H.I.E.L.D. SUPER-NEWBIE, SUPER-VILLAIN, SUPER-ARMORED CONTAINMENT VEHICLE THAT YOU COULD SEND DOWN HERE TO THE MUSEUM OF NATURAL HISTORY?
YEAH--HAVE I GOT A STORY FOR YOU...
THE END.

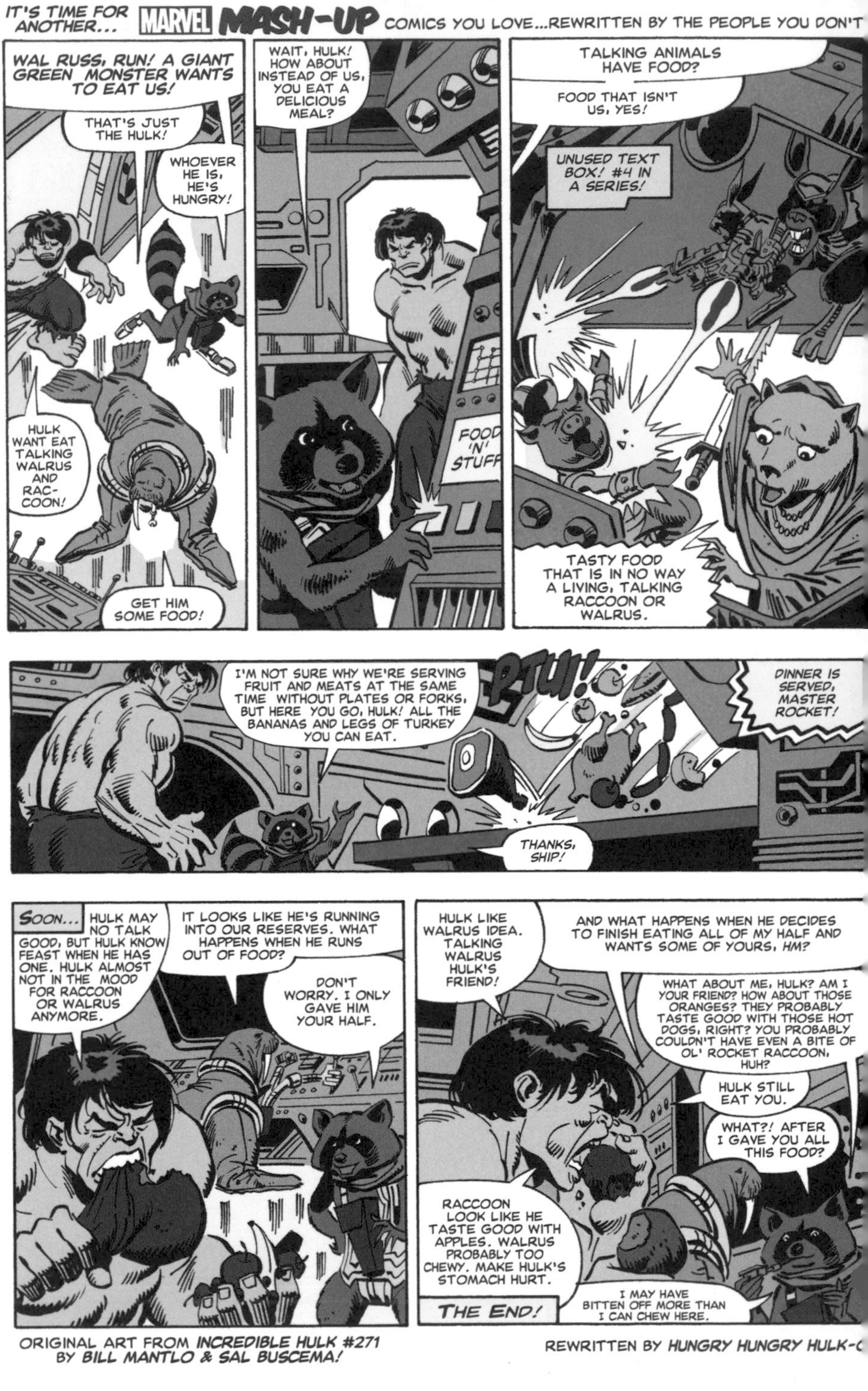
IT'S TIME FOR ANOTHER... MARVEL MASH-UP COMICS YOU LOVE...REWRITTEN BY THE PEOPLE YOU DON'T
WAL RUSS, RUN! A GIANT GREEN MONSTER WANTS TO EAT US!
THAT'S JUST THE HULK!
WHOEVER HE IS, HE'S HUNGRY!
HULK WANT EAT TALKING WALRUS AND RAC-COON!
GET HIM SOME FOOD!
WAIT, HULK! HOW ABOUT INSTEAD OF US, YOU EAT A DELICIOUS MEAL?
FOOD 'N' STUFF
TALKING ANIMALS HAVE FOOD?
FOOD THAT ISN'T US, YES!
UNUSED TEXT BOX! #4 IN A SERIES!
TASTY FOOD THAT IS IN NO WAY A LIVING, TALKING RACCOON OR WALRUS.
I'M NOT SURE WHY WE'RE SERVING FRUIT AND MEATS AT THE SAME TIME WITHOUT PLATES OR FORKS, BUT HERE YOU GO, HULK! ALL THE BANANAS AND LEGS OF TURKEY YOU CAN EAT.
PTUI!
DINNER IS SERVED, MASTER ROCKET!
THANKS, SHIP!
SOON... HULK MAY NO TALK GOOD, BUT HULK KNOW FEAST WHEN HE HAS ONE. HULK ALMOST NOT IN THE MOOD FOR RACCOON OR WALRUS ANYMORE.
IT LOOKS LIKE HE'S RUNNING INTO OUR RESERVES. WHAT HAPPENS WHEN HE RUNS OUT OF FOOD?
DON'T WORRY. I ONLY GAVE HIM YOUR HALF.
HULK LIKE WALRUS IDEA. TALKING WALRUS HULK'S FRIEND!
AND WHAT HAPPENS WHEN HE DECIDES TO FINISH EATING ALL OF MY HALF AND WANTS SOME OF YOURS, HM?
WHAT ABOUT ME, HULK? AM I YOUR FRIEND? HOW ABOUT THOSE ORANGES? THEY PROBABLY TASTE GOOD WITH THOSE HOT DOGS, RIGHT? YOU PROBABLY COULDN'T HAVE EVEN A BITE OF OL' ROCKET RACCOON, HUH?
HULK STILL EAT YOU.
WHAT?! AFTER I GAVE YOU ALL THIS FOOD?
RACCOON LOOK LIKE HE TASTE GOOD WITH APPLES. WALRUS PROBABLY TOO CHEWY. MAKE HULK'S STOMACH HURT.
I MAY HAVE BITTEN OFF MORE THAN I CAN CHEW HERE.
THE END!
ORIGINAL ART FROM INCREDIBLE HULK #271 BY BILL MANTLO & SAL BUSCEMA!
REWRITTEN BY HUNGRY HUNGRY HULK-C

T'S TIME FOR ANOTHER... MARVEL MASH-UP COMICS YOU LOVE...REWRITTEN BY THE PEOPLE YOU DON'T!

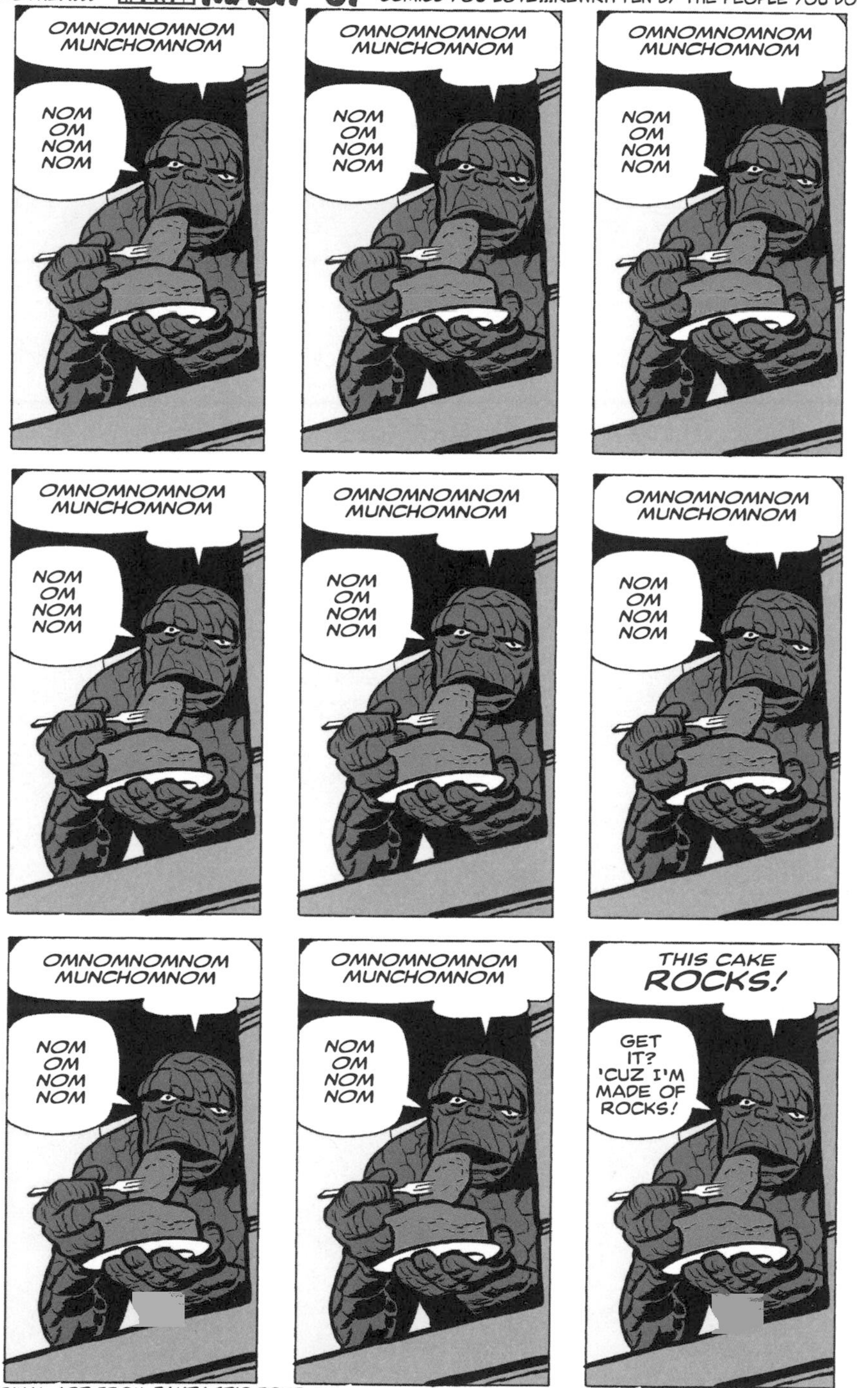
OMNOMNOMNOM MUNCHOMNOM
NOM OM NOM NOM
OMNOMNOMNOM MUNCHOMNOM
NOM OM NOM NOM
OMNOMNOMNOM MUNCHOMNOM
NOM OM NOM NOM
OMNOMNOMNOM MUNCHOMNOM
NOM OM NOM NOM
OMNOMNOMNOM MUNCHOMNOM
NOM OM NOM NOM
OMNOMNOMNOM MUNCHOMNOM
NOM OM NOM NOM
OMNOMNOMNOM MUNCHOMNOM
NOM OM NOM NOM
OMNOMNOMNOM MUNCHOMNOM
NOM OM NOM NOM
THIS CAKE ROCKS!
GET IT? 'CUZ I'M MADE OF ROCKS!

RIGINAL ART FROM *FANTASTIC FOUR #11* BY *STAN LEE & JACK KIRBY!*

REWRITTEN BY *MMMMM! CAKE!*

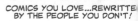

LIVE! ON PAPER! IT'S TIME AGAIN FOR... MARVEL MASH-UP

COMICS YOU LOVE...REWRITTE
BY THE PEOPLE YOU DON'T!

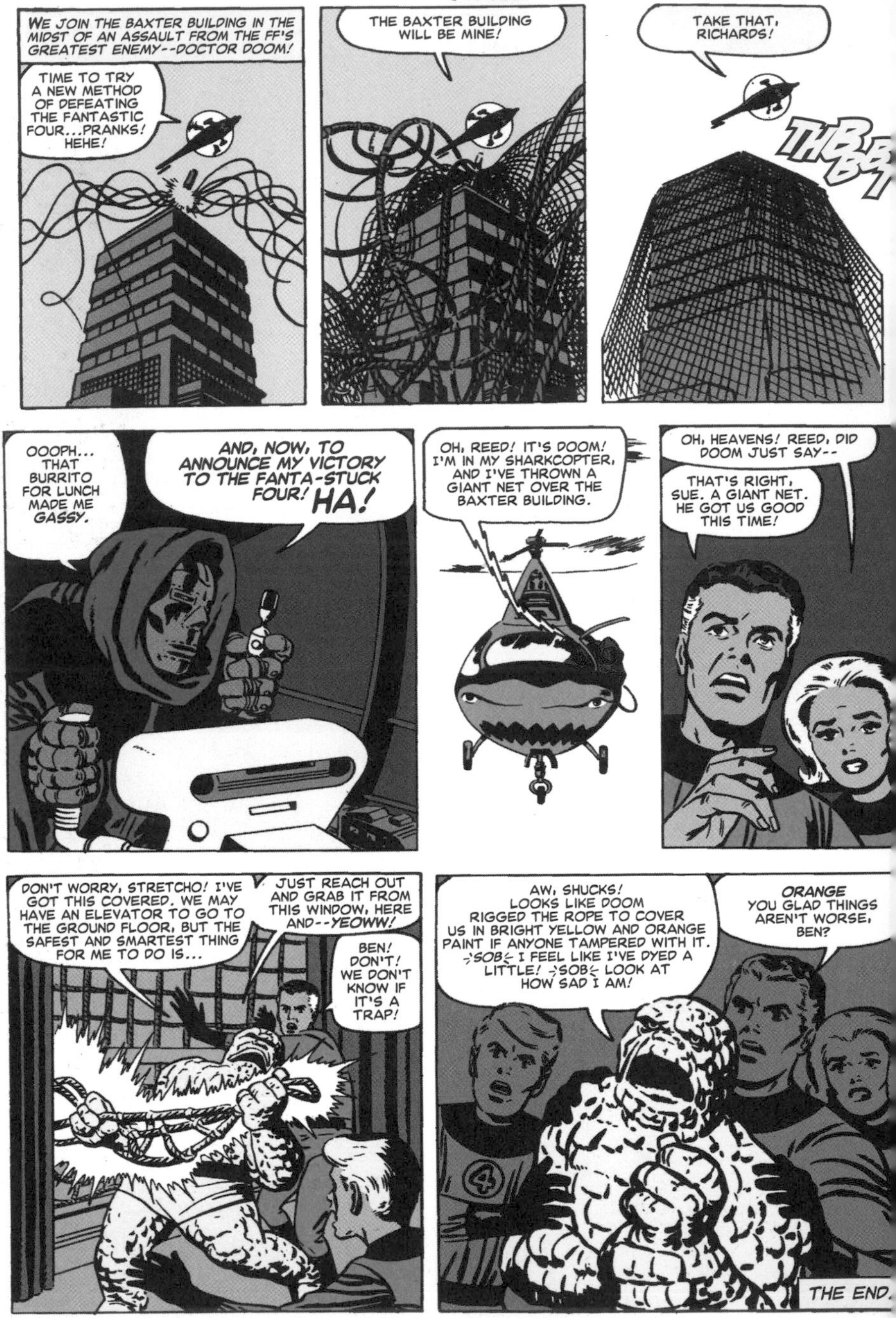

WE JOIN THE BAXTER BUILDING IN THE MIDST OF AN ASSAULT FROM THE FF'S GREATEST ENEMY--DOCTOR DOOM!
TIME TO TRY A NEW METHOD OF DEFEATING THE FANTASTIC FOUR...PRANKS! HEHE!
THE BAXTER BUILDING WILL BE MINE!
TAKE THAT, RICHARDS!
THBBBT
OOOPH... THAT BURRITO FOR LUNCH MADE ME GASSY.
AND, NOW, TO ANNOUNCE MY VICTORY TO THE FANTA-STUCK FOUR! HA!
OH, REED! IT'S DOOM! I'M IN MY SHARKCOPTER, AND I'VE THROWN A GIANT NET OVER THE BAXTER BUILDING.
OH, HEAVENS! REED, DID DOOM JUST SAY--
THAT'S RIGHT, SUE. A GIANT NET. HE GOT US GOOD THIS TIME!
DON'T WORRY, STRETCHO! I'VE GOT THIS COVERED. WE MAY HAVE AN ELEVATOR TO GO TO THE GROUND FLOOR, BUT THE SAFEST AND SMARTEST THING FOR ME TO DO IS...
JUST REACH OUT AND GRAB IT FROM THIS WINDOW, HERE AND--YEOWW!
BEN! DON'T! WE DON'T KNOW IF IT'S A TRAP!
AW, SHUCKS! LOOKS LIKE DOOM RIGGED THE ROPE TO COVER US IN BRIGHT YELLOW AND ORANGE PAINT IF ANYONE TAMPERED WITH IT. SOB I FEEL LIKE I'VE DYED A LITTLE! SOB LOOK AT HOW SAD I AM!
ORANGE YOU GLAD THINGS AREN'T WORSE, BEN?
THE END.

ORIGINAL ARTWORK FROM FANTASTIC FOUR #5
STAN LEE & JACK KIRBY

RE-WRITTEN BY
MELLOW YELLOW

LETTERED BY
VC'S JOE SABI